T0369587

Religion as Resistance

Religion as Resistance

Negotiating Authority in Italian Libya

EILEEN RYAN

OXFORD
UNIVERSITY PRESS

Oxford University Press is a department of the University of Oxford. It furthers
the University's objective of excellence in research, scholarship, and education
by publishing worldwide. Oxford is a registered trade mark of Oxford University
Press in the UK and certain other countries.

Published in the United States of America by Oxford University Press
198 Madison Avenue, New York, NY 10016, United States of America.

Library of Congress Cataloging-in-Publication Data
Names: Ryan, Eileen, 1978- author.
Title: Religion as resistance : negotiating authority in Italian Libya / Eileen Ryan.
Description: New York, NY : Oxford University Press, [2018] |
Includes bibliographical references (pages 227-239) and index.
Identifiers: LCCN 2017032534 (print) | ISBN 9780190673796 (hardcover : alk. paper) |
9780190673819 (epub) | 9780197532683 (pbk.)
Subjects: LCSH: Libya--History—1912–1951—Religious aspects. | Libya—Colonization—
Religious aspects.
Classification: LCC DT235 .R93 2018 | DDC 961.2/03
LC record available at https://lccn.loc.gov/2017032534

To my parents

Contents

List of Maps

List of Figures

Acknowledgments

IT IS IMPOSSIBLE to thank everyone who contributed to this book, but I will try. Thanks to Alexandra Dauler at Oxford University Press for her untiring work. I should thank Bruce Lincoln for telling me to become a historian and Martin Reisebrodt for suggesting Columbia University as the best fit for my interests. So many people helped me along the way at Columbia. Victoria De Grazia offered constant inspiration and pushed me in new directions. Lisa Anderson, Rashid Khalidi, Gregory Mann, and Mark Mazower provided invaluable mentorship and support. Thanks also to Nicola Labanca and Mauro Canali for assistance in the archives of Rome and to Luigi Goglia and Alessandro Volterra for sharing the incredible collection of photographs at the Università degli Studi Roma Tre. And I extend a special thanks to Mia Fuller for taking me with her into the desert.

I thank my fellow graduate students in the history department at Columbia for their camaraderie. Claire Edington, Aimee Genell, Isabel Gabel, James Chappel, Adam Bronson, Giuliana Chamedes, Claudia Gazzini, and Hitomi Yoshio all contributed to my intellectual growth and sometimes to my travel plans. Thank you to Mostafa Minawi for answering my questions about Ottoman Libya, and for Montreal.

The past few years at Temple University have been a whirlwind of activity. I want to thank my colleagues for their support in this new adventure. Rita Krueger, Travis Glasson, Peter Lavelle, and Jessica Roney especially provided valuable feedback on portions of the book. Richard Immerman has been an incredibly supportive mentor. I also thank my students at Temple for their energy and curiosity.

The research for this book would not have been possible without generous funding. The American Institute for Maghreb Studies and the Council for European Studies helped me take my first research trips to Tripoli and

Rome. I could not have completed the research without the generous support of the American Academy in Rome. I also thank the Columbia Institute for Religion and Public Culture, the Cesare Barbieri Endowment for Italian Culture, and the Foreign Language and Area Studies Program for funding language training and research trips, and Sciences Po for supporting my final dissertation year.

The research for this book also would not have been possible without the help of many archivists and librarians. In Tripoli, I thank Muhammad Jerary and the staff at the Markaz al-Jihad for their tireless work. I wish you all the best in these uncertain times. Too many archivists and librarians in Rome contributed to the completion of this book for me to list them all, but I would like to make special note of Stefana Ruggeri and the staff in the Archivio Storico Diplomatico del Ministero degli Affari Esteri.

My heart overflows with gratitude for the many friends and family members who helped me through this long process. Special thanks are due to Venessa Mendenhall for housing me so many times between research stints. Your constant presence throughout this intellectual and personal journey has been a joy. Thanks also to Annie Schlecter, Russell Maret, Annie Labatt, Caroline Renfroe, Emma and Pelle, Olivia and Sofia, Margaret and Joe, and David Suisman.

Note on Transliteration

ITALIAN IMPERIALISTS USED a range of methods for transliterating Arabic names. Except for rare instances when maintaining the Italian style provides clarity, I have followed the transliteration standards of the *International Journal of Middle East Studies*.

EAST AFRICA CA. 1900

ITALY
Rome

Istanbul

OTTOMAN

EMPIRE

Tunis

TUNISIA

Mediterranean Sea

Tripoli

Benghazi

Cairo — Suez Canal

EGYPT

Red Sea

FEZZAN

ERITREA
Dogali ✕ Massawa

FRENCH
SOMALILAND

✕
Adwa Assab

BRITISH
SOMALILAND

Addis Ababa

ETHIOPIAN
EMPIRE

SOMALIA
• Mogadishu

INDIAN
OCEAN

0 km 350   700

0 miles   350   700

MAP 1 East Africa ca. 1900

ITALIAN LIBYA, CA. 1911

Mediterranean Sea

TUNISIA

Tripoli

Khoms

Misrata

Benghazi

Al-Bayda

Derna

Tobruk

Jabal al-Akhdar

Jabal Nafusa

T R I P O L I T A N I A

Ghadames

Antelat

Ajdabiya

Jalu

EGYPT

F E Z Z A N

C Y R E N A I C A

Kufra

ALGERIA

NIGER

CHAD

0 km 100 200

0 miles 100 200

MAP 2 Italian Libya, ca. 1911

Religion as Resistance

Introduction

WHEN LIBYAN LEADER Muammar Qadhafi landed in Rome for his first official visit to Italy in June 2009, he wore a photograph of ʿUmar al-Mukhtar
pinned to his lapel. The iconic image showed the charismatic leader of
anti-Italian armed resistance shackled in chains and surrounded by Italian
officials after his arrest in 1931. The relentless pursuit of ʿUmar al-Mukhtar
during the military campaign that the fascist government referred to as
the "reconquest" of the Libyan interior in the 1920s made this "Lion of the
Desert" a potent symbol of the violence of European imperialism in North
Africa and the Middle East.[1] Qadhafi wore the photograph to remind the
world of Italy's colonial crimes even as he celebrated the possibility of
new economic and political ties across the Mediterranean. In the context
of postcolonial Libya, Qadhafi's use of the image laid claim to a legacy of
anti-imperial, anti-Italian, and antifascist armed resistance as a source of
political legitimacy.[2]

The deployment of ʿUmar al-Mukhtar's image as a symbol of Italian
imperial transgressions, however, obscured a more complex relationship
between resistance and collaboration in Libya's colonial past. ʿUmar al-
Mukhtar emerged as a leader of anti-imperial armed resistance in the
1920s from his position as a prominent member of the *ṭarīqa* (pl. *ṭuruq*) of
the Sanusiyya.[3] A Sufi religious movement featuring a Salafist message of
returning to the days of the Prophet Muhammad, the Sanusiyya developed
in the interior of the eastern Libyan administrative district of Cyrenaica
(al-Barqa in Arabic) in the mid-nineteenth century.[4] Early leaders of the
Sufi *ṭarīqa* found fertile ground for proselytization. By the time Italian
troops landed on the Libyan shores in October 1911, the Sanusiyya had
grown into an extensive organization that provided many of the functions
associated with a modern state, including education and armed defense.

For authorities in European capitals from London to Istanbul, the leading figures of the Sanusiyya seemed ideal intermediaries for extending state control in a region considered tantalizingly inaccessible. As the Sanusiyya expanded its reach, Ottoman and European explorers, officials, and intellectuals created a body of literature purporting to explain the nature of this religious movement and the potential for Sanusi elites to act as local intermediaries. Their debates fueled an interimperial competition for influence in North Africa. Italian imperialists entered fully into this competition in their occupation of the Libyan territories.[5]

During more than thirty years of Italian occupation from 1911 to 1943, official attitudes toward the Sanusiyya ranged from hopeful expectations of close collaboration to wary distrust and downright hostility. The relationship between the Italian colonial administration and the Sanusi elites can be divided into four phases. First, from approximately 1904 until the Ottoman Empire conceded sovereignty over the region in 1912 Italian imperialists anticipated friendly relations. A belief that elites of the Sanusiyya opposed Ottoman control in the Sahara informed predictions in Rome that Italian troops would face little resistance from local populations, or that they might even be greeted as liberators. From 1912 until 1916 a sense of disillusionment and doubt among Italian imperialists about the possibilities of an alliance with the Sanusi elite defined the second phase. Rather than acquiescence or acceptance, Italian troops met the full weight of combined Sanusi-Ottoman opposition. These forces deterred Italian expansion into the interior of the region.[6] The desperation of World War I led to a third phase of Italo-Sanusi relations from 1916 until 1923, during which Italian representatives (with British assistance) negotiated a series of treaties with a grandson of the founder of the Sufi *ṭarīqa*, Idris al-Sanusi. These agreements led to the establishment of a semiautonomous Sanusi emirate in the Cyrenaican interior. The era of accords ended in 1923 with the departure of Idris for exile in Egypt and the emergence of a fascist government in Rome that embraced a message of aggressive imperial expansion. This fourth phase featured brutal warfare between Italian troops and resistance forces, with civilian populations caught in the crossfire. The violent military campaign involved the internment of tens of thousands of civilians in state-run camps that were meant to isolate resistance forces. The campaign culminated in the capture of ʿUmar al-Mukhtar in 1931, when Mussolini declared the entire Libyan interior pacified and ready for Italian settlement.

In all of these phases the nature of the Sanusi religious and political authority was a hotly debated topic among Italian imperialists. It seemed that anyone with a stake in the prospect of Italian expansion had something to say on the matter. Diplomatic officials and secret agents operating in the Ottoman Empire wrote reports on the reputation and influence of the Sanusiyya throughout the Arab-Muslim world. Academics translated French, German, and English studies of the Sanusiyya, analyzing their significance for an Italian audience. Colonial societies brought professional scholars together with hobby orientalists, merchants, and bankers. They founded libraries in grand palazzos in Italy's major cities, where they collected books on the subject, and they funded explorations and scientific studies of Libya's resources that inevitably included musings on the people, their culture, and their customs. After the initial invasion in October 1911 military commanders offered their own interpretations of the Sanusiyya as potential enemies or allies. Journalists communicated a composite of these impressions of the Sanusiyya to a broader public.

This broad array of Italian imperialists based their analyses of the possibility or desirability of an alliance with Sanusi elites on what they understood to be the connection between the religious and political authority of the Sufi *ṭarīqa*. A malleable image in the Italian imperial imagination, the Sanusiyya appeared variously as a force of opposition to state centralization or a force of stability; a group of strict ascetics or astute merchants; a collection of Muslim fanatics or amenable moderates. These characterizations of the Sanusiyya exposed the limitations of the reductive categories Europeans assigned to the social and political structures in Muslim North Africa in an era when regional identities and opposition to imperialism were increasingly expressed in relation to Islam.

But imagining the Sanusiyya was primarily a self-reflexive process. When an Italian explorer celebrated the possibility of appealing to the commercial interests of Sanusi elites to facilitate trade, or when a military official warned about the dangers of a Sanusi-led pan-Islamic revolt, their arguments expressed competing understandings of Italian identity in the process of national expansion. The Sanusiyya served as that "surrogate and sometimes underground self" that according to Edward Said strengthened European identities in the era of high imperialism.[7] Debates over the nature of the Sanusiyya offered space for experimentation with the confines of the religious and the political in Italian nationalism.

Catholic Identity and a Pro-Islamic Approach

When Italy gained international recognition of its rights over the Libyan territories in the autumn of 1912, Italian nationalists celebrated the opportunity to heal the wounds left by the wars of Italian unification. The Italian Risorgimento—or rebirth, as the movement leading to the establishment of the Kingdom of Italy in 1861 came to be known—had exposed deep divisions in Italian society. The occupation of the Papal States during the wars of unification stripped the Holy See of temporal authority, and in the early twentieth century the Catholic Church remained fiercely opposed to the national government and the liberal politicians who dominated it. As unification became the new normal and the Italian state moved to widen enfranchisement in the early twentieth century, however, the need to fully incorporate church elites and the general Catholic population into national politics became apparent to many on both sides of the divide. The occupation of the Libyan territories did much to further that goal. Enthusiasm for colonial expansion helped forge an alliance between Catholic and liberal interests in mutual opposition to a socialist platform that stood against Italian imperialism. The Catholic press applauded the opportunity to spread a Catholic version of *italianitá*—or Italian civilization—in Muslim North Africa. At the same time, state officials in Rome and an array of nonstate imperialists welcomed Catholic involvement. Church leaders served as champions of a national cause, while missionaries worked on the ground to facilitate an expansion of Italian cultural influence. Over the long term the connection between church interests and imperialism also contributed to the development of a conservative Catholic variety of Italian nationalism, one that would inform facets of the fascist movement.

A wide variety of types of people—some formally associated with the church, others not—favored the idea of imbuing Italian imperialism with a strong Catholic identity. But they did not always agree on what that might mean for Italian relations with Muslim populations. Broadly speaking, we can divide pro-Catholic imperialists into two camps with starkly different visions of Italy as an imperial power. First were those who favored an approach to colonial rule based on accommodation with local Muslim elites. Some within this camp saw Italian Catholicism as a potential source of strength in that it could establish common ground based on a shared sense of religious traditionalism. Second were those who were more interested in pursuing direct control as a means of bolstering national prestige, to whom asserting a Catholic identity in the Libyan territories meant celebrating Italian cultural superiority. The divisions between these two camps intersected with different understandings of Sanusi elites as either interested in conciliation (and therefore useful as a tool for state control) or diametrically opposed to Christian Europe. Both camps, however, were in conflict with those Italian imperialists who saw Catholic identity as a detriment to either approach to colonial rule, either because they feared it would offend Muslim elites or because they saw it as evidence of Italy's relative lack of a colonial culture. These tensions found expression in disagreements over the best approach to colonial rule over a Muslim population as Italians asked themselves to what extent—and to what end—they should use a Catholic identity in selling Italian expansion domestically and within the colonial space.

These tensions resonated in a series of proclamations issued in Arabic and Italian by the commanding officer of the Italian Occupying Forces, General Carlo Caneva, when Italian troops landed on the shores of the Ottoman provinces in October 1911. Dropped from airplanes in populated areas along the coast, Caneva's leaflets were meant to convince local populations to welcome the occupation as liberation from Ottoman rule. The troops under his command, Caneva claimed, were there "not to subdue and enslave the populations of Tripolitania, Cyrenaica, and other countries of the interior, now under the bondage of the Turks, but to restore to them their rights, punish the despots, make them free and in control of themselves, and to protect them against those very despots—the Turks—and against any others who try to enslave them."[8] Caneva's proclamation targeted the economic and political elites of the region, who seemed uneasy with the new political order in Istanbul after the Young Turk Revolution of 1908. To win them over, Caneva promised them a political voice, economic security—and respect for religious tradition in the transition to Italian rule.

The leaflets followed the model Napoleon had established in his proclamation to the Egyptians in 1798, in which he promised to uphold Islam. But Caneva's proclamations also hinted at a sense of Italian exceptionalism in the field of interimperial competition by emphasizing a Catholic identity. "We have the book," the leaflets claimed. "We are religious and honest."[9] This was an attempt to establish common ground in a shared recognition of the importance of religious belief, as a foundation for improved Italo-Muslim relations. The appeal to religious traditionalism reflected a particular strain of thought in an Italian imperial movement. Rather than seeing Italy's status as a latecomer to European expansionism and the least of the European powers as a weakness, some within

the Italian procolonial lobby believed it gave them an advantage in gaining the support of populations in North Africa jaded by the failures of
the Ottoman, British, and French governments to fulfill the promises
of nineteenth-century liberalism. Caneva's proclamation suggested that
the advantage would derive from Rome's unique position at the spiritual
center of the Catholic world. Calling on Italy's Catholicism as a potential benefit did not necessarily signify support for the proselytizing mission of the church. All European imperial powers shared a fear of mass
revolt through an appeal to pan-Islamic unity in the late nineteenth and
early twentieth centuries. That fear, along with a tradition of anticlericalism among the military commanders of post-Risorgimento Italy, led most
colonial officers to see the presence of missionaries as more of a burden
than a benefit. Rather than declaring support for proselytization, Caneva's
leaflets favored a general sense of religiosity as a basis for collaboration
with Muslim elites like the Sanusi family.

The anodyne appeal to cultural understanding in Caneva's leaflets
belied a deeper struggle over where Italy would land on the ever-shifting
continuum of coercion and conciliation that defined European imperialism. Even during the heightened aggression of fascist rule—after Idris
al-Sanusi fled the region in 1923 and the fascist administration began an
unremitting pursuit of territorial gains—debates over the desirability of
forging a relationship with Sanusi elites continued. Could an appeal to a
shared sense of religious traditionalism be a foundation for negotiations?
Or did too close an association with a Catholic identity pose a threat to
stability? Would an emphasis on republican ideals of secularism in the
Italian colonial administration better assure a Muslim population of the
state's intention to protect cultural and religious identities from the influence of the Catholic Church? In both the liberal and the fascist eras, disagreements over the best approach to negotiating with the Sanusi elites
can tell us more about uncertainty over religious identity in Italian nationalism than about the social or political history of the Sanusiyya.

The Sanusiyya

The Sanusiyya, of course, was not an empty set, waiting to be filled by
European interlocutors. Romantic strains of orientalist literature depicted
the Sanusiyya as a group of isolated ascetics, carving out lives of devo-
tion and faith in the desert expanse. Given the distinctly rural landscape
where the Sufi *ṭarīqa* first developed, one can easily see why this became

a trope; eastern Libya is a region perhaps most amenable to those who "value silence" and wide-open spaces.[10] But the Sanusiyya was far from isolated. From its very inception the Sanusi *ṭarīqa* was connected to networks that extended far beyond eastern Libya. The life of the man credited with founding the Sanusiyya, Muhammad ibn ʿAli al-Sanusi (ca. 1787–1857),[11] conformed to a certain pattern of regional mobility common to Islamic intellectuals of North Africa. Born in Algeria, al-Sanusi studied in Mecca under Ahmad ibn Idris, a scholar in the Salafist tradition who advocated an Islamic revival through a return to the practices of the Prophet Muhammad.[12] Al-Sanusi was just one of a number of his students who went on to establish Sufi *ṭuruq* in various places after their teacher's death in 1837, thus linking the Sanusiyya with a network of beliefs and practices.[13] The Sanusi *ṭarīqa* also served as a conduit for communications in North Africa through the construction of a network of *zawāyā*, clusters of buildings that functioned as places of worship, education, and community centers. Sanusi adherents often built *zawāyā* at strategic crossroads and near wells, making them valuable resting points along caravan routes.[14] Letters, merchandise, and people passed through, connecting Sanusi *zawāyā* to markets south of the Sahara and north to the Mediterranean.

Nor was the Sanusi *ṭarīqa* defined solely—or even primarily—by resistance to European expansion. Sanusi elites were fully engaged in the complex negotiations of local, regional, and international politics in the era of high imperialism. This was the case well before the Italian invasion of the Libyan coast. The delusional expectations among Italians for a swift victory in the initial occupation stemmed in part from a belief that the Sanusiyya opposed Ottoman political control and favored isolation in the Cyrenaican interior. Italians found evidence for this attitude in the transfer of Sanusi *zawāyā* to the south in the late nineteenth century, away from the coastal administrative centers. The reality was more complex. Sanusi elites were in regular contact with Ottoman officials as the Sufi *ṭarīqa* spread in the nineteenth century. Although there were moments of tension, the relationship that evolved was primarily collaborative; Sanusi expansion corresponded to Ottoman efforts at state centralization and reform in the Libyan interior.[15] As European powers vied with Istanbul for influence in the region, Sanusi elites often made bold and savvy choices in their alliances.

The Sanusi *ṭarīqa* was never a monolithic organization. European imperialists focused their attention on descendants of Muhammad ibn ʿAli al-Sanusi, often attributing to individuals in the Sanusi family vast power among the people of North Africa. Just as Italian imperialists differed in their views of the best approach to negotiating authority with Muslim interlocutors, however, Sanusi adherents differed in their views on what sorts of relationships the Sufi *ṭarīqa* should form with central authorities in Istanbul and Rome. The authority of the Sanusi family depended on its ability to defend the interests of a variety of tribes allied with the Sanusi *ṭarīqa*. Failure to do so left the leadership and the very meaning of the Sanusiyya open to contestation. Pressure from the Sanusi base informed shifts in alliances between Sanusi elites and imperial powers in the colonial era in ways that escaped the understanding of colonial officials at the time and have remained largely misunderstood by historians since Libyan independence.

Investigating the intersections between religious and political authority during the Italian occupation raises contentious reminders of collaboration and resistance that are seldom far below the surface of national politics in postcolonial Libya. In Italy, the legacies of this relationship are less accessible, hidden behind a collective will to either forget the imperial experiment or bracket it off as an unfortunate side effect of fascism with little bearing on Italy's national history. But these legacies are no less important in the trajectory of post-imperial Italy than in postcolonial Libya.[16] This has become abundantly clear given Italy's position in recent years as a gateway to the European Union for predominantly Muslim migrants. Competing approaches to imperial rule in Italian North Africa point to a longer history of Italian involvement in the religious politics of the Mediterranean. Debates over religious authority in an Italian approach to colonial rule challenge assumptions of a neat division between a secular Europe and a religious North Africa.

1

Italian Imperialism and Sanusi Authority at the Turn of the Century

THE ITALIAN OCCUPATION of Libya in 1911 symbolized the culmination of decades-long colonial ambitions. Imperialism was meant to solve some of the most acute social ills confronting Italy after national unification. Many Italians hoped armed struggle in the service of imperial aggrandizement would contribute to a missing sense of national solidarity or at the very least provide access to land to quell dissent among southern agricultural workers chaffing under a system that favored large-scale estates. Initial attempts at imperial expansion in the 1880s and 1890s, focused along the Red Sea in Eritrea, Somalia, and Ethiopia, failed to fulfill those objectives. A series of military disasters detracted from the popularity of imperial expansion as a source of unification. The more successful approach of establishing and expanding overseas trading posts fell short of the expectations of Italian imperialists to provide agricultural opportunities or to promote an image of Italian strength on an international stage. The lack of extensive territorial control also meant that Italian expansion in East Africa before the occupation of the Libyan territories offered little in the way of experience to inform the subsequent development of a colonial administration. Nevertheless, the early decades of Italian imperialism contributed to debates over the best approach for Italian imperial rule in relationship to the Sanusiyya, if only in generating a sense of frustration at the slow rate of Italian imperial expansion.

When Italian imperialists began to consider the possibility of Libya as an overseas colony, they discovered a robust literature about the Sanusiyya.

European and Ottoman officials and adventurers had begun writing about the existence of the Sanusiyya as it first developed in the mid-nineteenth century. Italian imperialists looked to that body of literature to inform debates over the possibility of creating a power-sharing relationship. More often than not, Italians contributing to this literature disagreed with the images of the Sanusiyya inherited from this interimperial circuit of information. Even when they did adopt some of the same images of the Sanusiyya, Italian imperialists drew their own conclusions about what those images meant for an Italian approach to appealing to Sanusi elites. In so doing, Italian imperialists asserted the possession of a unique advantage in the contest for influence in the region, and their perceptions of the Sanusiyya often emphasized those aspects that seemed most promising for a distinctively Italian approach to colonial rule. Examining the early literature on the Sanusiyya thus helps to understand how Italian imperialists defined themselves in contrast to other European imperial powers.

Tracing the image of the Sanusiyya that Italian imperialists inherited also denaturalizes dominant narratives in the historiography of modern Libya and the emergence of the Sanusi *ṭarīqa*. Perceptions of the Sanusiyya from Paris to Istanbul fit the orientalist model of an interreferential system; definitions of the Sanusiyya from Euro-Ottoman scholars and officials revealed more about their own mentalities than about the social, political, or religious realities of the Cyrenaican interior. But we should not perceive the historical actors who produced these views of the Sanusiyya as being hermetically sealed off from the Sufi *ṭarīqa* as an object of study. Sanusi elites took full advantage of the space for political action created by orientalist images of their authority. Representations of the Sanusiyya in an array of travel literature and official reports became malleable forms. They could be molded to fit the objectives and interests of European imperialists, but they were also adopted by Sanusi elites as a means of engaging directly with the power struggles of interimperial conflict.

Italian Imperialism before Libya

When Italian troops invaded the Libyan coast in October 1911, Italian imperialists celebrated a new phase in national expansion. Italian unification had only recently preceded the beginning of a new era of European imperialism, and many Italian nationalists proved eager to catch up with other European powers. For some, overseas imperialism even seemed a natural progression of the Risorgimento, itself the product of territorial

expansion on the part of the Kingdom of Piedmont-Sardinia.[1] In the first
three decades after the formal establishment of the Kingdom of Italy in
1861, however, interest in imperialism was confined to a small cohort of
elites in a merchant and political class. The general public was focused
more on domestic issues of nation building and consolidation of power,
particularly in the restive south.[2] The moment that might be identified as
the beginning of Italian imperial expansion occurred after the opening of
the Suez Canal in 1869, when a shipping magnate, Raffaele Rubattino,
formally purchased a concession to the Bay of Assab on the Red Sea.
Though Rubattino received logistical support from the Italian state in his
endeavors, there was little public or political interest in using the acquisi-
tion as a toehold for imperial aggrandizement; when put to a vote in 1871,
the Italian parliament rejected a proposal to transform the port into an
official colony. For the remainder of the 1870s apathy about imperialism,
rather than outright opposition, dominated domestic politics. To the limited extent that the idea of expansion in Assab made its way into the forum
of public opinion, it generally provoked criticism as a weak substitute for a
more robust colonial policy.[3] Outright enthusiasm for adventures in Africa
remained confined to geographical societies (e.g., the Società Geografica
Italiana, founded in Florence in 1867, and the Società di Esplorazione
Commerciale in Africa, founded in Milan in 1878), among what Angelo
Del Boca has referred to as the "first vanguard" of a colonial movement.[4]

When the Italian parliament finally decided to claim direct control of
Assab in 1882, it inaugurated a new phase of direct state involvement in
overseas expansion. State involvement continued to escalate when Italian
forces took advantage of a decline in Egyptian control in the region to
seize the port of Massawa to the north of Assab in 1885. This increase
in state control in overseas territories did not reflect an increase in popular support for imperial adventures, despite efforts in the press to
sell the imperial agenda as an extension of the promises of the Italian
Risorgimento.[5] Expansion in East Africa fulfilled the ambitions of a political elite in Rome, who saw the occupation of Massawa as an opportunity to
assert Italian strength in foreign policy in the context of a wider European
land grab that seemed to be leaving Italy behind. The French occupation
of Tunisia in 1881, the British protectorate in Egypt in 1882, and Italy's
failure to acquire an equal footing at the Congress of Berlin in 1884–1885
informed a growing sense among Italy's governing class that action was
needed to prevent Great Britain and France from entirely edging Italy out
of the African adventures of the late nineteenth century.[6]

Neither the methods nor the location of Italian expansion in the 1880s promoted popular interest in imperialism. For one thing, the occupation of the Eritrean coast lacked the excitement of a colonial war. Italian troops, numbering fewer than one thousand, faced little opposition in what amounted to a mostly peaceful transfer of power over a territory only about four square miles in size.[7] International support rather than outright military strength allowed for Italy's claims to territory along the Eritrean coast. It was widely acknowledged that Italy would have had a more difficult time establishing its first colony if London had not considered Italian control of the region beneficial to British trade interests.[8] The lack of widespread popular interest also reflected a sense, even among the more enthusiastic representatives of the pro-imperial lobby, that Eritrea lacked the qualities necessary to enhance Italy's prestige on the global stage. Too small to serve as a destination for large-scale settlement, Eritrea also failed to fulfill the ambitions of many Italian imperialists for an increased presence in the Mediterranean. International media coverage of Italian imperialism reinforced the sense of inferiority. The Italian occupation of Massawa, for example, prompted derision from the *New York Times*, which claimed that "a more worthless possession than the Red Sea littoral could hardly be found, with the possible exception of the deserts of the interior into which ambitious Italy doubtless hopes to penetrate."[9]

If most Italians seemed to meet the idea of imperial expansion with general apathy, two groups expressed outright opposition to state expansionism: socialists and intransigent Catholics. Of the two, the Catholic voice of anti-imperialism proved more powerful during the early years of Italian expansion. It mirrored the defiance of the Holy See and circles of intransigent Catholic leadership against all aspects of liberal Italian politics. For Italians guided by the pope's *Non Expedit* (originally issued in 1868), which called on Catholics to abstain from national politics, the prospect of imperial expansion represented the strengthening of an enemy state on an international stage. Intransigent Catholic media outlets and organizations also opposed Italian imperialism on the grounds that it promoted the expansion of a secular culture in conflict with the evangelizing mission of the Catholic Church. Highlighting the violence and expense of colonial wars in contrast to the peaceful expansion of Catholic missionaries, this vein of Catholic opposition to imperialism mirrored socialist criticism of European expansionism as overly violent and costly. Unlike socialist criticism, however, Catholic opposition to Italian imperialism did not constitute a denunciation of imperialism in general; church leadership recognized the benefits of aligning their evangelist mission with the expansionist policies of friendly European powers. Rather, their critique targeted the specific imperial project of the Italian state.

News outlets closely linked to the Holy See, such as *L'Osservatore Cattolico*, portrayed Italian imperialism as having a particularly insidious nature, marked by a willingness to engage in unnecessary violence for the enrichment of a few.[10] The occupation of the port of Assab inspired *L'Osservatore Cattolico* to issue a series of articles critical of the nascent Italian imperial project. The paper was careful to note that it did not condemn colonialism in general: "Civilized nations have a duty to spread civilization, to whatever extent they can." But it objected to the methods of colonial expansion common to European governments in the late nineteenth century. All imperial powers were subject to criticism to the extent that "they carried themselves among the savages like assassins, with opium, with iron, with unheard of violence and tricks, destroying and stealing." The paper found two aspects of Italian imperialism particularly objectionable. The first, at least during the initial foray into the Red Sea, was the paltry scope of Italian imperial objectives. Britain and France might demonstrate "never-ending greed" in their imperial conquests, the paper noted, but at least it led to worthwhile colonial possessions. This aspect of *L'Osservatore Cattolico*'s disapproval reflected the paper's favorable perception of demographic colonialism as a potential boon to Italian peasants. The paper argued that Italy should be engaged in establishing agricultural colonies as an ideal form of a civilizing mission. Instead, expansion in East Africa involved, "a swarm of functionaries and speculators, more greedy and vicious than the barbarians themselves, protected by a government that does not recognize the natural rights of family and religion."[11] The second objection, predictably enough, was the lack of interest among Italian imperialists (whom *L'Osservatore Cattolico* depicted as a depraved band of Freemasons) in coordinating their efforts with the missionary objectives of the church. "The Italian government in this colonial war has not only renounced the peaceful mission that along with the Papacy they could have initiated and conducted with great success; but it also deprived itself of the grandiosity that surrounds the efforts of England, France, and Germany."[12] Far from condemning Italian expansionism, the Catholic press egged on the imperialist project and clamored for a seat at the table.

A military disaster in Eritrea, however, led the Catholic press to put aside its criticisms of Italy's imperial expansion. On January 26, 1887, Italian forces experienced an overwhelming defeat at the Battle of Dogali near Massawa. Italy lost five hundred troops in a battle against more than ten thousand troops under the leadership of Ras Alula, a provincial governor in the Ethiopian empire of Yohannes IV. Eager to restore national pride, Italy's parliament responded to the defeat with an influx of troops.[13] The loss generated a wave of support for imperialism, even within the Catholic Church. When the Holy See hosted a mass for the victims of the battle that included speeches from prominent intransigent leaders, it encouraged hope that the imperial project could spark reconciliation between the church and the liberal state. Such a reconciliation would prove elusive, taking many more years to develop. But the public outpouring of support for the new heroes from among Italy's colonial troops established a foundation for closer collaboration between the church's missionary activities and state expansionism.[14]

More immediately, widespread discontent with the human costs of imperial expansion after the defeat at Dogali contributed to the dissolution of the government of Prime Minister Agostino Depretis. The new government of Francesco Crispi, the Sicilian statesman and former lieutenant of the Risorgimento hero Giuseppe Garibaldi, adopted a new approach to expansion in Eritrea that promised to be at once more ambitious and less aggressive. Crispi's initial approach favored expansion through power-sharing strategies with local elites. His administration oversaw the successful expansion of Italian territory from Massawa inland to Asmara in 1889. From this position, Italian officials negotiated the highly controversial Treaty of Wichale in May 1889, under which Emperor Menelik II recognized Italy's claim to a formal colony in Eritrea. In exchange, Italy offered Menelik much-needed funds and arms to help him consolidate his authority as king of kings, a title he had recently wrested from opponents upon the death of Emperor Yohannes in March 1889.[15] Weakened by the simultaneous effects of cholera, cattle disease, and the absence of Ethiopian military support, the people of Eritrea could do little to resist the subsequent expansion of Italian occupation in 1889–1890. Taking advantage of the situation, Italian troops went well beyond the confines stipulated in the Treaty of Wichale. In a shortsighted attempt to prevent any subsequent development of an organized resistance—and in a dramatic reversal of Crispi's power-sharing strategies—the Italian military government executed more than one thousand Eritrean elites and their armed followers in 1890–1891 as Crispi declared Eritrea Italy's first colony, now open for Italian settlement.[16]

During the following five years Italian military commanders overestimated their own military strength and the willingness of local populations to submit to Italian rule. The Italian defeat at the Battle of Adwa in 1896 highlighted the fallacies in both assumptions. Citing discrepancies in the Amharic and Italian versions of the Treaty of Wichale, Emperor Menelik renounced the treaty in 1893 and began to amass an army. One article in particular became a point of contention. Italians claimed that the treaty defined Ethiopia as a protectorate of Italy, thereby obligating Menelik to operate through Italy in his international affairs. When Menelik's cousin Ras Makonnen visited Rome to seal the agreement and asked Umberto, king of Italy, for "the protection of [His] Majesty, so that peace and tranquility reign in Ethiopia and in the neighboring Italian possessions," that seemed to be public confirmation of the Italian interpretation of their relationship.[17] But just one year later, when British officials insisted on communicating with Menelik via Italian intermediaries, as befitting a territory under the official protection of another European power, Menelik expressed surprise at the arrangement and set a course of opposition against his onetime allies that would culminate in the decisive victory of Menelik's army over Italian forces in Adwa.

Menelik's ability to unite regional Ethiopian forces against Italian expansion, however, had more to do with a response to Italian colonization schemes than with the technical aspects of the Treaty of Wichale. The Battle of Adwa occurred after several years of escalating tensions in response to the displacement of Africans from prime farmland in the Eritrean and Ethiopian highlands. For Italian imperialists, the seizure of land promised to fulfill a vision of Italian expansion as a means of harnessing the power of Italian emigration. With thousands of Italian families flooding out of the Italian peninsula every year in search of economic opportunity, there were those among Del Boca's "early vanguard" of Italian imperialism who envisioned Italian colonies as communities of small-scale family farms. Mass emigration of Italians in the decades after unification, previously celebrated as a source of Italian influence abroad, became symbolic of the inability of the state to support its people. Colonial expansion offered a possible solution by providing land for agricultural workers while utilizing what many understood as a problem of excess population to the nation's advantage in the quest for imperial expansion.[18]

Crispi came to power championing this populist vision of imperial expansion. As the most prominent southern political figure during the course of national unification in Italy and the first Sicilian prime minister,

Crispi claimed a special interest in using imperial expansion as a solution to the problems of the south. Violent clashes in the Italian south between agricultural workers organized into the Fasci Siciliani and military forces sent to quell their protests added a sense of urgency to the problem. Political solutions proved elusive; Crispi's administration faced stiff opposition to legislation meant to reform Sicily's *latifondi* system of large-scale land ownership that kept Italian agricultural workers in a subordinate position. Instead, Crispi emphasized agricultural settlements in East Africa as a possible solution. A colonial war also promised to paper over domestic political tensions in Crispi's Italy by appealing to a growing chorus of nationalists calling for the ultimate unification of the Italian nation through a baptism of blood.[19] The link between emigration and territorial expansion made imperialism a potent political issue with an economic edge.

Crispi's increasing emphasis on agricultural settlement, however, also solidified Ethiopian unity in opposition to Italian expansion. The Italian state began a gradual program of subsidized settlement in the autumn of 1893 with the arrival of nine families. The program continued for the next two years despite a tepid response from the Italian public and outright opposition from military commanders in the colony, who saw agricultural settlement as a threat to stability. Under the leadership of Leopoldo Franchetti, a vocal proponent of settlement programs as a solution to the southern problem in the Chamber of Deputies, "some four hundred thousand hectares (nearly a million acres) of the finest farm and pastureland in the Eritrean highlands was set aside for settlers and ruled off-limits to the local African population."[20] As Italian intentions about settlement became clear, Menelik's political rivals in the Tigray region of Northern Ethiopia traveled to his seat of power in Addis Ababa in June 1894 to make a public display of their submission to the authority of the emperor, thus providing Menelik with the military means to oppose Italian expansion.[21] It was in this context that the commander of Italian forces, Oreste Baratieri, began a series of occupations in Northern Ethiopia in late 1894 and early 1895 that promised to answer the calls to seize colonial territory for agricultural settlement. Blinded by initial successes and unaware of the size and skill of the forces gathering around Menelik and his powerful consort Taytu as they made a slow march from Addis Ababa to the north, Baratieri set Italian forces on a path to defeat in Adwa in March 1936 that would haunt Italian imperialists in subsequent decades as the definitive rejoinder to Italy's attempts to join the club of European imperial powers.[22]

After Adwa: A Turn to Conciliation

The defeat of Italian troops in the Battle of Adwa led to the fall of Crispi's government and a subsequent swing of the pendulum away from policies of imperial aggression. Colonial wars and attempts at territorial aggrandizement fell into disfavor, and pro-imperial groups focused instead on spreading Italian cultural and financial influence through emigration and commerce.[23] The turn against colonial wars involved a willful forgetting of Adwa as imperialists sought to redefine the possibilities of Italian expansion; except for sporadic examples of public commemoration for fallen soldiers in the first years after 1896, the Battle of Adwa was largely absent from public memory until the fascist regime revived it as a nationalist cause in celebration of the invasion of Ethiopia in 1935–1936.[24]

Despite the turn away from imperial aggression, there was little interest in abandoning the colony of Eritrea. But the military loss in Adwa factored into shifting tactics in colonial rule. A new governor, Ferdinando Martini (r. 1897–1907), turned the focus away from Eritrea as a destination for Italian settlement to reimagine the colony as a source of raw materials and, eventually, of soldiers for later colonial ventures.[25] Given the unpopularity of colonial warfare after Adwa, Martini embraced collaboration with Eritrean elites as a means of expanding state control. Martini's policies laid the groundwork for an administrative system that would continue to develop under his successor, Giuseppe Salvago Raggi (r. 1908–1914) and that would later be echoed in the administration of the Libyan territories. Martini's approach was to establish a hierarchical administrative system with villages as the basic unit. The state assigned each village a chief from a list of those considered "traditionally entitled to the office"[26] according to tribal structures, with skeleton district offices overseeing local governance. As Tekeste Nagash has demonstrated, due to the availability of extra tax revenue and a fixed salary from the Italian state, Ertirean elites stood to benefit from this arrangement, both financially and in terms of solidifying their positions of authority.[27]

Religious leaders also played a role in the conciliatory period of Italian colonial rule in Eritrea, establishing important parallels for later policies in relation to the Sanusiyya in the Libyan territories. From the beginning of the occupation of Eritrea, the Italian state contributed financial resources to Islamic institutions by funding mosques and paying salaries to Muslim notables. Its purpose in doing so was twofold. First, this was part of an effort to extend influence among the population of the Eritrean lowlands, which at the time of the initial Italian occupation was about 60 percent Muslim. Outreach to the Muslim population offered the chance to bring into Italy's orbit strategically located allies who were defined as distinctive from the Christian populations of the Eritrean highlands and were therefore useful as a buffer. Muslim populations of the lowlands gained particular value as a symbol of opposition to the Christian identity of the Ethiopian Empire following a Christianization campaign of Emperor Yohannes IV in the 1870s. In an effort to unify the empire, Yohannes claimed to have baptized some fifty thousand Muslims by 1880; maintaining a Muslim identity seemed to imply resistance to his policies even after his death in 1889.[28]

Second, Italian officials hoped that by developing relationships with Muslim leaders, the latter would be more willing to prevent the potential influence of the Mahdist revolution from spreading into the region from the Sudan. Starting in 1881, the Mahdist state in the Sudan espoused a messianic Islamic message in opposition to Ottoman-Egyptian rule and increased British influence in the region. In the late 1880s the Mahdist state also counted Christian Ethiopia as an enemy. Tensions between the two states were the result less of religious identities than of the establishment of a military alliance between Yohannes IV and Britain that committed Ethiopian forces to fight against Mahdists on Ethiopian's western border after 1884. The ensuing conflicts had the potential to benefit Italian interests in the region, but no one was eager to encourage the Mahdist revolt. The anti-imperialist messianic message of the Sudanese Mahdists carried too much of a threat to European imperialism as a whole. In an attempt to manage the situation, Martini sought out relationships with Muslim notables who stood apart from Yohannes IV (and after his death in 1898, from Menelik) but also opposed the influence of the Mahdist state. By the time Salvago Raggi arrived in the colony in 1908, the Italians counted fifteen religious leaders—primarily Muslim—on their payroll.[29]

Italian officials developed their most significant relationship in the region with Hashim al-Mirghani, a leading figure of the Khatmiyya *ṭarīqa* (also known as the Mirghaniyya). As in the Libyan territories, Eritrea was host to Islamic revival movements in the form of Sufi *ṭuruq* in the nineteenth century. Founded by Mohammed 'Uthman al-Mirghani (1794–1852), another student of Ahmad ibn Idris (of whom Mohammed ibn Ali al-Sanusi was also a follower), the Khatmiyya *ṭarīqa* was among the most active in the region.[30] At the time of the Italian occupation of Massawa in 1885, members of the Khatmiyya were divided over how they should understand their relationship to the Mahdist movement in the Sudan. Hoping to shore up a defense against a broader anti-imperial movement, Italian officials identified Hashim al-Mirghani as a prominent figure opposed to Mahdist influence and therefore useful for preventing widespread revolt. Starting in 1885, the Italian state paid Hashim al-Mirghani to establish a permanent presence in the region as a force of stability and an informant about pro-Mahdist activities. Hashim al-Mirghani's relationship to Italian officials was rocky at best, but it created a precedent for Italian systems of accommodation in imperial expansion. After his death in 1901 Italian officials had better luck with his nephew's son, Ja'far bin Bakri bin Ja'far bin Muhammad 'Uthman al-Mirghani (1871–1943). From that point on, the Khatmiyya *ṭarīqa* played a crucial role in expanding Italian authority in Eritrea. In exchange, members of the al-Mirghani family often gained appointments to prominent positions in the Italian colonial administration.[31] Italian efforts were effective in creating a sense of loyalty with a goal of mutual benefit. Consider, for example, the way in which Hashim al-Mirghani's daughter, 'Alawiyya, challenged Ja'far's position as leader of the *ṭarīqa*. To undermine Ja'far's leadership, 'Alawiyya attracted followers of her own, but she never questioned his ties to the Italian state and advocated in favor of Italian colonial rule.[32] 'Alawiyya even wrote an open letter to her cousin in December 1911 to protest his public suggestion that the Italian occupation in the Libyan territories would somehow threaten Islam. Her pro-Italian rhetoric echoed that of some imperialists by extolling Italians for what she perceived as a national characteristic of religiosity: "The Italians observe their religion as we observe ours."[33]

The experience of establishing a system of accommodation with the *ṭarīqa* of the Khatmiyya in Eritrea set a precedent for efforts to reach out to elite members of the Sanusi *ṭarīqa* in the Libyan territories, although the kinds of relationships they established differed in important aspects. For one thing, notables of the al-Mirghani family worked directly for the Italian colonial administration, unlike the Sanusi elites, who established a semi-independent government in Cyrenaica during an era of negotiations with the Italian state. As part of the initial phase of Italian imperial expansion, furthermore, the Italo-Khatmiyya relationship developed absent a comprehensive Italian approach to governing Muslim populations. After the occupation of the Libyan territories in 1912, the newly formed Ministry of Colonies provided at least the illusion of a coherent structure and systematic planning to Italian native policy as the colonial administration attempted to negotiate relationships with Sanusi notables. In the occupation of Eritrea, on the other hand, accommodation with the Khatmiyya represented a reaction to defeat in Adwa rather than a programmatic strategy.

It was in this context of a turn away from military aggrandizement after Adwa that the Libyan territories beckoned as the object of formal imperial ambitions. Italian interests in Libya emerged in the 1880s following the French occupation of Tunisia in 1881 and the British occupation of Egypt in 1882. International agreements, first secured in 1887, recognized Italy's claims to the Libyan territories in the event that the Ottoman Empire lost control of the region. For many Italian imperialists, the prospect of territorial expansion in North Africa eclipsed the colonies on the Red Sea; the entire adventure in Eritrea seemed like an unprofitable distraction from the ultimate goal of using Libya to create an Italian empire in the Mediterranean.[34] Italian explorers and regional experts began writing about the potential for Italian commercial expansion in the Libyan territories at the end of the nineteenth century. In 1896, for example, the Società Geografica Italiana published a study on the economic promise of the Libyan territories by Luigi Robecchi Brichetti, an engineer and explorer famous for making an earlier journey through Somalia. In *Il commercio di Tripoli*, Robecchi Brichetti detailed the products available for export and the potential for developing markets in North Africa, with Tripolitania and Cyrenaica to serve as "the emporiums of all of the commerce of the orient and the west, and Italy, bridge across the Mediterranean, would become its great throughway."[35] Envisioning a purely commercial endeavor, Robecchi Brichetti's incredibly optimistic analysis of the economic possibilities of the region suggested little engagement with the inhabitants, beyond noting the potential for Italian banks to appeal to a local base of customers with little competition for their services.

Separate from the book, however, Robecchi Bricchetti also sent reports to the Italian Ministry of Foreign Affairs that betrayed an awareness of the importance of the Sanusi elite for Italian designs in the region. Concerned that the Mahdist revolt in the Sudan might spill over into the Libyan territories in a unified wave of anti-European sentiment, Robecchi Bricchetti tracked the activities of the Sanusiyya to determine their attitude toward the Mahdist state. His reports relayed uncertainty based on conflicting rumors and interpretations of Sanusi intentions. By turning a spotlight on the notables of the Sufi *ṭarīqa*, however, Robecchi Brichetti's reports fed a consensus among Italian imperialists that the best possibility for the expansion of Italian interests in the Libyan territories depended on a successful appeal to the Sanusi elites as allies.[36] The idea of gaining the support of the Sanusiyya for an Italian occupation came to have such force that even when the nominal head of the Sufi *ṭarīqa*, Ahmad al-Sharif, made clear his decision to join forces with the Ottoman opposition to the Italian occupation in 1911–1912, few within the Italian administration relinquished the hope of establishing some kind of understanding with the Sanusi family.

The Sanusiyya on the Eve of Italian Occupation

When Italian imperialists began to consider the possibility of expansion in Ottoman Libya, there seemed to be little choice but to take into consideration the possible reactions of the Sanusiyya. The Sanusiyya emerged as a religious movement in the mid- to late nineteenth century, a period defined by the second Ottoman occupation of North Africa in 1835 and the French occupation of the Lake Chad region in 1901–1902. The development of the Sanusi *ṭarīqa* occurred gradually. The first *zāwiya* was constructed in al-Bayda in 1843, but Muhammad ibn 'Ali al-Sanusi did not settle permanently in the region until 1853, when, after a period of traveling back and forth between Mecca and Cyrenaica, he established his home base in the oasis town of Jaghbub near the current Egyptian border.[37] Muhammad ibn 'Ali al-Sanusi never explicitly declared his intention to establish a Sufi *ṭarīqa* or used the term "Sanusiyya"; his son Muhammad al-Mahdi al-Sanusi began to refer to the family's collection of *zawāyā* as part of the Sufi *ṭarīqa* of the Sanusiyya after his father's death in 1859.[38] Muhammad al-Mahdi also initiated a period of rapid expansion of *zawāyā* associated with the Sanusiyya into the southern reaches of Fezzan in the Libyan interior. By the end of the nineteenth century the name of the Sanusiyya was attached to *zawāyā* stretching from Benghazi south toward Lake Chad and Darfur.[39]

In a pattern common to the development of Sufi *ṭuruq* throughout North Africa, the Sanusi *zawāyā* served multiple functions. They were centers for education and prayer, resting points along caravan trade routes, and even agricultural settlements in a mostly nomadic society. With Muhammad al-Mahdi al-Sanusi in a leadership position known as "The Grand Senusso" (al-Senusso al-Akbar), the Sanusiyya became an irresistible force in North Africa. With the Sanusi *ikhwān*—or brothers—spreading a message calling for a return to the ways of the Prophet Muhammad among Bedouin communities of the Northern Sahara, state officials in the imperial centers of Europe and Istanbul eyed the expansion of the Sanusi *ṭarīqa* with suspicion as they tried to determine whether it signaled a threat to state authority or a possible ally in promoting stability in a strategic region.[40]

In their attempts to establish a beneficial relationship with Sanusi elites, Italian imperialists entered into an international field of competition; all of the imperial powers involved in North Africa in the late nineteenth century actively sought out a relationship with the Sanusiyya. Nineteenth-century accounts of the Sanusiyya by European explorers and orientalists helped to fuel this competition by depicting the Sanusi *ṭarīqa* as a religious organization with the potential for all-encompassing power among Bedouin tribes. It was a perception of the Sanusiyya that conformed to a general understanding of Islam in North Africa as a potent force that inherently combined religious and political authority, an understanding bolstered by the efforts of Sultan Abdulhamid II (r. 1876–1909) to encourage a sense of shared Muslim identity in the shrinking territories of the Ottoman Empire. Not all accounts of the Sanusiyya from the late nineteenth century, however, agreed on whether the combined religious and political authority of the Sanusiyya represented a threat or a useful tool for imperial expansion in the region. Conflicting images of the Sanusiyya alternated between a virulent sect of religious fundamentalists opposed to any state presence on the one hand and a rationalist intermediary necessary for efforts to impose central state control in Cyrenaica on the other.

The confusion bleeds into the historiography of the Sanusiyya in modern Libya. Tracing the early history of the Sanusiyya thus involves linked historical and historiographical problems. Much of the historiography of modern Libya reflects an interest in identifying the Sanusiyya as a precolonial power structure to bolster the legitimacy of the postindependence kingdom of Idris al-Sanusi. This objective informed an emphasis on identifying a moment of transition in the nineteenth century when the Sufi *ṭarīqa* changed from a religious organization spreading a Salafist message of a return to the ways of the Prophet Muhammad into a political structure. The study of the Sanusiyya that most heavily influences the historiography of modern Libya, E. E. Evans-Pritchard's *The Sanusi of Cyrenaica*, laid the groundwork for this emphasis. Evans-Pritchard wrote his study as evidence of the viability and desirability of Idris's leadership in the Kingdom of Libya after 1951. Working as an official in the British military administration of postwar Libya, Evans-Pritchard had a vested interest in portraying the Sanusiyya as a political movement that would promote regional stability; the British were eager to have their Sanusi ally in power across Egypt's western border. To that end, Evans-Pritchard made an effort to distance the Sanusiyya from any hint of religious zeal by depicting it as a movement that had transitioned into a political structure soon after it was founded. The development of the Sanusiyya, he suggested, had favored "its political, to the detriment of its religious, functions."[41] The Bedouin tribes that made up the core of Sanusi adherents, he argued, looked to Sanusi elites for their personal and political leadership, not for messages of religious faith. Evans-Pritchard's account of the Sanusiyya identified the *ṭarīqa* as a proto-nationalist entity in nineteenth-century North Africa that offered the best foundation for the establishment of a unity government after independence: one that would appeal to Western allies for its moderation and openness to rational market forces. Sanusi philosophy generally preached a renunciation of worldly wealth, but Evans-Pritchard characterized Sanusi adherents as "far from extreme ascetics," "even using scent" and being "amiable and merry companions."[42]

The focus on identifying the moment of transition from religious to political authority commits the mistake of imposing a teleological drive toward a Eurocentric vision of nation-state formation. In the deeply politicized historiography of modern Libya, it also runs the risk of reading proto-nationalist intentions onto a religious movement in a region and a time period that by all accounts were devoid of a clear commitment to ethnic or national identity. To be sure, the Sanusi *zawāyā* performed many statelike functions, particularly in education. But ascribing a sense of proto-nationalism as an inherent characteristic of the Sufi *ṭarīqa* from its very beginnings ignores the ways in which the Sanusiyya transformed in the context of interimperial competition. Many of the state functions of the Sanusiyya emerged later and as a consequence of relationships with central authorities in imperial centers.

There was an unmistakable link between the early expansion of Sanusi *zawāyā* and the economic activities of regional trade routes. In a pattern similar to other Sufi orders in North Africa, Sanusi *zawāyā* provided resting points and communication centers for trans-Saharan traders. The oasis of Kufra—the site of a significant Sanusi *zāwiya* that alternated with Jaghbub as a central hub for the Sanusi family in the late nineteenth century—sat in the middle of a particularly difficult stretch of a trade route between Tekro in Borkou and the Cyrenaican oasis of Jalu, and caravans typically rested in Kufra for up to ten days before heading north to Benghazi.[43] The details of economic ties within the Sanusiyya are difficult to ascertain in historical records. But assuming a pattern of development similar to that of the Sufi *ṭarīqa* of the Nasiriyya in Morocco, for merchants, adherence to the Sanusiyya carried with it the benefit of access to scarce resources along their trade routes, a benefit that would have only increased as the Sufi *ṭarīqa* grew during the nineteenth century.[44] An interest in collecting libraries in the *zawāyā* indicates a further role for Sanusi adherents as educators and communicators along the trans-Saharan trade routes. A class of educated elites, Sanusi *ikhwan* provided necessary services in communication and organization on trade routes in collaboration with the Bedouin tribes who acted as guides and merchants. This position of the Sanusiyya followed a pattern that could be seen throughout the Sahara in the nineteenth century.[45]

Territorial politics linked to tribal identities also shaped the development of the Sanusi *ṭarīqa*. The adherence of members of the powerful Awlad Sulayman tribes, along with the Maghārba and the Zuwaya—all tribes that dominated trans-Saharan trading patterns because of their access to camels and water sources in the nineteenth century—eased the Sanusiyya expansion into the Libyan interior and northern Chad.[46] According to the accounts of Europeans traveling in the region in the nineteenth century, the original introduction of the Sanusiyya into the oases of Kufra correlated to Zuwaya migration south from eastern Sirte. Drought conditions in the 1840s drove a combined Zuwaya-Maghārba force to invade Kufra and claim control of its rich palm groves. The move to Kufra allowed the Zuwaya to establish control over the portion of the trans-Saharan trade route from Wadai to Kufra. By maintaining ties to Maghārba merchants in eastern Sirte, they were able to extend a trading network.[47] Their migration, however, displaced Tibbu tribes. Some Tibbu continued to work the land and pay tribute to Zuwaya, but the arrangement fostered intertribal tensions. Zuwaya notables subsequently invited Muhammad al-Mahdi al-Sanusi to move from Jaghbub to Kufra in 1895 to mediate a truce and end a conflict that threatened their control of the oasis and connected trade routes.[48] A mutually beneficial relationship flourished; Sanusi religious authority lent legitimacy to the Zuwaya dominance over the Tibbu population in Kufra, and the alliance with the Zuwaya facilitated expansion of the Sufi *ṭarīqa* to the south.

Shifting alliances during the Italian colonial era offer further evidence that Sanusi authority—both religious and political—depended on the support of tribal figures with ties to trans-Saharan trade. As we will see in a later chapter, it was the loss of that support that put an end to Idris al-Sanusi's position as an intermediary power between the Italian colonial state and regional tribal powers in Cyrenaica in 1923. There are two conclusions to draw from this discussion of the contingent nature of Sanusi authority in Cyrenaica. First, tracing a link between Sanusi expansion and trade networks in the region from the early development of the Sufi *ṭarīqa* belies the insistent efforts in the historiography of modern Libya to identify a point of transition from a religious to a political organization; in their reliance on tribal support for Sanusi expansion, moral authority and the influence that came with access to scarce resources were deeply intertwined. Second, we should avoid any hint of understanding the Sanusiyya as a static organization. Far too often, characterizations of the Sanusi *ṭarīqa* fail to offer adequate historical context in a negligent repetition of imperial perspectives, especially in defining the Sanusiyya as a force of resistance to state centralization. The position of the Sufi *ṭarīqa* in the region's social and political structures and in relation to central state authority shifted dramatically from the early emergence of the Sanusi *zawāyā* to the establishment of the Sanusi kingdom at independence.

Imperial Circuits of Knowledge: Sanusiyya and Central Authorities

The very act of writing the sources that continue to inform our understanding of the development of the Sanusiyya in the nineteenth century worked to transform the position of the Sufi *ṭarīqa*. European observers created a mythology around the Sanusiyya that fueled international competition for influence among Sanusi elites and shaped the possibilities for Sanusi political activity in relationship to European imperial centers. French explorers wrote some of the earliest studies of the Sanusiyya between 1855 and 1870; based on travel narratives of journeys across the Sahara that involved only marginal direct contact with Sanusi adherents, these early accounts exaggerated the potential for Sanusi elites to pose a threat to French interests.

In his detailed, two-volume study of the subject, Jean-Louis Triaud identified Henri Duveyrier, the vice president of the Société Géographique de France, as the author responsible for drawing public attention in France to the Sanusiyya. Duveyrier's distinctive upbringing informed his approach to writing about the inhabitants of North Africa. Henri Duveyrier was raised in Paris in a household that followed a sect of Saint-Simonism under the leadership of Prosper Enfantin, who sought a future of unity between Europe and Africa. Duveyrier's relationship with Enfantin and Saint-Simonians was not always harmonious. But Enfantin provided the funds for Duveyrier's first journey to North Africa, and the utopian ideals of Saint-Simonism informed his objectives during the trip. Duveyrier traveled to North Africa in search of allies in what he imagined would be a coupling of France and Africa leading to the birth of a utopian future. He seemed to identify those allies in the book that would catapult him to fame in France, *Explorations of the Sahara: The Tuareg of the North* (*Exploration du Sahara: Les Touâreg du nord*, 1864). Duveyrier's Tuareg's were noble savages, characterized by matriarchal social structures that made them ideal intermediaries for French expansion. According to Duveyrier, the feminine hierarchy made the Tuareg particularly receptive to penetration by France and immune to the insidious influence of Islam.[49]

The Sanusiyya served as a foil to Duveyrier's romanticized vision of the Tuareg. He wrote about the Sanusiyya both in *Les Touâreg du nord* and in a later book on the Sanusiyya specifically, *Le Confrérie musulmane de Sidi Mohammed Ben 'Ali Es-Senousi et son domaine géographique* (1884). Duveyrier presented the Sanusiyya as religious fanatics who posed an overwhelming danger to French interests in North Africa. His assessment reflected what he understood to be the combined effects of religious and political aspirations in a highly centralized hierarchical organization. The head of the Sanusiyya he depicted as a strict ascetic with the capacity to mobilize massive numbers of fanatically dedicated followers, who were forced to keep their involvement in the *ṭarīqa* secret. The goal of the Sanusiyya, according to Duveyrier, was to establish Muslim dominance over the Christian world in a religious empire. To emphasize the danger, he compared the Sanusiyya to Jesuits and Freemasons, both of which carried negative values in French public opinion at the time as secret religious societies with political goals.[50]

The dissemination of Duveyrier's characterization of the Sanusiyya led to a shift in what had been positive French attitudes toward Sufi *ṭuruq* throughout North Africa. At the beginning of French interest in the Sahara in the 1840s, prevailing opinion held that the French should adopt policies similar to what they understood was the approach of the Ottoman Empire toward the Sanusiyya: treat them like friendly religious organizations and allow them limited influence over local administrative decisions.[51] But following Duveyrier's negative portrayal of the Sanusiyya, the French began to watch all Sufi *ṭuruq* with deepening suspicion. Starting in the 1870s, French intelligence officers established surveillance on the Sanusiyya and

followed communications between Sanusi elites and other regional leaders in an attempt to determine the capacity of the Sanusiyya to influence
the political climate. French preoccupation with the Sanusiyya bordered
on obsession with what was referred to in the French literature as *"le légend
noire"*: the black legend of the Sahara. At the height of the French hysteria
over the supposed threat of the Sanusiyya to imperial interests in North
Africa, Duveyrier claimed that the Sanusiyya had the ability to assimilate
other Sufi orders to create a vast network that would place 2.5 to 3 million
followers under the supreme command of the "Grand Senusso," ready to
take up arms against European imperialists.[52]

The French *legénde noire* became something of a self-fulfilling proph-
ecy. Based on this idea of a highly centralized Sanusi authority figure,
European and Ottoman officials began to send gifts of arms and supplies
to gain favor, thus contributing to the militarization of the region and the
dominance of the Sanusiyya as a political, social, and economic force. The
depictions of the Sanusiyya as a centralized power in the French literature
also shaped subsequent understandings of the Sanusiyya among imperial
officials as the effective political leaders in the Cyrenaican interior, spur-
ring competition among British, Italian, German, and Ottoman authorities for an alliance with the Sanusi elite as a means of securing influence
in North Africa. Thus a symbiotic relationship developed between the
literature about the Sanusiyya and the involvement of Sanusi elites in
the politics of interimperial competition; the more European orientalists wrote about the religious and political authority of the Sanusiyya, the
more imperial authorities contributed to the authority of the Sanusi elite
as part of an effort to gain influence in the region.

The focus on the Sanusiyya in French literature about North Africa
might even have influenced Ottoman attitudes toward the expansion of
Sanusi *zawāyā*. When French and later Italian imperialists explained the
potential value of an alliance with the Sanusiyya (or the danger of Sanusi
enmity) to the central authorities, they would often sell the idea as a simple adoption of Ottoman practices in the region. But the exact nature of
the relationship between the Ottoman central authorities and Sanusi elites
during the early decades of the development of the Sufi *ṭarīqa* is far from
clear. There is some evidence to suggest that the relationship between
Istanbul and the Sanusi elites in the early years of the *ṭarīqa's* existence
was defined by a sense of antagonistic mistrust.[53] In his 1949 study of the
Sanusiyya, however, Evans-Pritchard identified a rapid shift toward a more
conciliatory relationship. He cited an illusory Ottoman *firman* from 1856

that exempted the Sanusi properties from taxes in exchange for security among Bedouin tribes of the interior as evidence of limited cooperation. At the very least, Evans-Pritchard reckoned that the tax-free status guaranteed Sanusi preference for Ottoman rule over the potential expansion of Christian European powers in the region.[54] An often-cited apocryphal story about the conversion of the Ottoman governor general in Tripoli, Ali ʿAshqar Pasha, to the Sanusi cause after meeting Mohammed ibn Ali al-Sanusi during the latter's first foray into Cyrenaica implied a warm relationship during the initial period of Sanusi expansion, at least on a local level.[55] But confirmation of the story has proven difficult, and there are few concrete details to paint a clear picture of the Sanusi-Ottoman relationship in the first decades of the development of the *ṭarīqa*.

In the last quarter of the nineteenth century Ottoman attitudes toward the Sanusi elites came into sharper focus. As the Sanusi *zawāyā* spread into the Libyan interior, Ottoman officials proved eager to reach out to Sanusi elites as local intermediaries. This can be explained in part by the increasing importance of North Africa to Istanbul. After insurrections against Ottoman rule in the Balkans in 1875–1876, the French invasion of Tunisia in 1881, and the British occupation of Egypt in 1882, Tripolitania and Cyrenaica gained symbolic value as the last remaining Ottoman territories in North Africa. Calling on Islamic unity to shore up support among Muslims in the remaining Ottoman provinces, Sultan Abdulhamid II (r. 1876–1909) engaged in tactics similar to those of European imperialists in the competition for the hearts and minds of North Africa, though with the advantage of being able to emphasize the sultan's position as caliph. Abdulhamid hoped to increase imperial influence by bringing regional notables to Istanbul and appointing them to high positions in the central government "so that they could act in enlisting and preserving the loyalties of their people to the state and the Sultan Caliph."[56] His attempt to incorporate Muslim notables from North Africa included extending an invitation to Muhammad al-Mahdi al-Sanusi to visit Istanbul.

In a highly politicized debate, some historians argue that the Sanusi family rejected Ottoman overtures. Michel Le Gall, for example, has portrayed the Ottoman-Sanusi relationship as acrimonious. He claims that Muhammad al-Mahdi al-Sanusi chose to move the headquarters of the Sanusi *ṭarīqa* from Jaghbub on the Egyptian border to the oasis of Kufra deep in the southern reaches of Cyrenaica to distance the Sanusiyya from Ottoman administrative centers and increasingly aggressive efforts to extend centralized taxation among Sanusi-affiliated tribes.[57] In a more recent example, Salim Husayn Kabti suggests that Muhammad al-Mahdi al-Sanusi maintained friendly relations with Ottoman authorities, but that he also taught the men of the *tarīqa* to "steer clear" of Ottoman officials. Focusing on tensions between Istanbul and Sanusi elites in this way serves to highlight the Sanusiyya as an independent, proto-nationalist movement rather than a mere proxy for Ottoman state power, contributing to a sense of political legitimacy for Sanusi leadership in postindependence Libya.[58]

A more compelling understanding of Ottoman-Sanusi relations, how-ever, rests on evidence of extensive collaboration to achieve common objectives of centralization and reform. Mostafa Minawi, for example, argues that Sanusi and Ottoman "work on the ground was complemen-tary, cooperative, and at times even synergetic."[59] The pivotal issue in this debate is the reading of a document from a visit by Sanusi representatives to Istanbul in 1895. Some have argued that the visit resulted in an exten-sion of the earlier *firman* established between the Ottoman sultan and the Sanusiyya that amounted to direct orders to Ottoman administrators in Tripoli and Benghazi to recognize the Sanusiyya as a tax-exempt religious order.[60] This collaborative relationship becomes clear when considering how the Sanusiyya fit into broader Ottoman goals in the era of high impe-rialism. The sultan wanted a relationship with Sanusi elites to take advan-tage of new international norms for imperial expansion. The General Act of the Conference of Berlin in 1885 (of which the Ottoman Empire was a signatory power) established new legal parameters to allow for European expansion in overseas territories. As Minawi has expertly demonstrated, Istanbul used the new language codified in the international agreement to reinforce Ottoman claims to sovereignty in the Libyan territories. In par-ticular, the Ottoman sultan pointed to the concept of "effective occupation" in article 35 of the General Act to assert territorial control. Deliberately vague, the concept of effective occupation was meant to allow for a variety of methods to demonstrate the sustained presence of an imperial power in a particular region as evidence of that power's claims to sovereignty. In the case of Cyrenaica and the Libyan Desert, a friendly relationship with Sanusi elites—as well as an unrealized plan to construct telegraph lines—served as evidence for what Minawi refers to as "occupation by proxy," allowing Istanbul to claim Sanusi *zawāyā* as "signifiers of its rule."[61]

Leaving aside any possible reservations the Sanusi elites might have felt about the extension of Ottoman authority in the Libyan interior, the fact that Abdulhamid sought out an alliance with the Sanusiyya placed the Ottoman central government firmly in the context of the European "scramble for Africa" of the late nineteenth and early twentieth centuries.[62] In an approach Selim Deringal has termed "borrowed colonialism," Abdulhamid extended increased funding for education, mosques, and other religious sites in an effort to win the loyalty of imperial subjects in an era of heightened interimperial competition.[63] Definitive signs that the Ottoman sultan succeeded in extending state authority into the oases of Kufra—via Sanusi intermediaries—by 1910 suggest that the Ottoman authorities had an advantage in that competition, even if it is difficult to date the beginning of Ottoman-Sanusi collaboration.[64]

The evidence of a positive Ottoman-Sanusi relationship in the late nineteenth century is also suggestive of a pattern among Sanusi elites of working in tandem with imperial authorities from the early decades of the *ṭarīqa*'s development. The idea that the Sanusiyya expanded in collaboration with central imperial authorities runs counter to characterizations of the Sufi *ṭarīqa* as an anti-imperial force, fiercely defending its independence. It also has the potential to recast our understanding of the decisions Sanusi elites made during the Italian occupation. The central choice for Sanusi elites in the early twentieth century was not one of resistance or collaboration; rather, it was a matter of choosing an alliance with whichever imperial power seemed best positioned to serve the interests of the *ṭarīqa* and its affiliates. During the initial Italian occupation, most Sanusi adherents hewed close to the Ottoman alliance, but the tumultuous era of World War I forced a reconsideration of that principle among various factions of the Sanusi elites.

Armaments and Regional Alliances

The effects of the positive Ottoman-Sanusi relationship can be seen most clearly in traces of an increased supply of Ottoman arms in Sanusi *zawāyā* in the late nineteenth century. Istanbul began to send arms and ammunition to the region after the Triple Alliance recognized in 1887 Italy's right to claim Ottoman Libya as a "sphere of influence" in the event of a loss of Ottoman control. Facing a variety of threats to Ottoman sovereignty in Central Africa—from the anti-Ottoman Mahdist movement in the Sudan to Italian and French ambitions in the Sahara—Istanbul increased deliveries of weapons in the last decade of the nineteenth century.[65] The movement of arms was centered in Sanusi *zawāyā* and associated trade routes, leading one British officer in the region to assert by 1905 "that practically every Senussiite [*sic*] is in possession of some sort of fire-arm and ammunition."[66] The influx of arms represented a dramatic shift in the Sanusiyya and in the relationship between the Ottoman Empire and Sanusi authority. It was a shift, Mostafa Minawi has suggested, that represented a transition from a "growing political relationship to a secret unified military front."[67]

Reports of the trend alarmed French officials in particular, convincing some that the Sanusi elite planned to establish a vast Islamic empire as a form of direct resistance against European expansion in the region. Indeed, the militarization of Sanusi *zawāyā* suggested a heightened level of collaboration between Ottoman officials and Sanusi elites in staving off the incursions of competing imperial powers. Direct contact with European forces accelerated the armament process. In November 1901 a battle at Bir Alali—the southernmost *zāwiya* of the Sanusiyya—initiated a decade of direct conflict between Sanusi and French forces in Chad, Algeria, and Niger.[68] Sanusi-affiliated tribes, reinforced by the recent arrival of Tuareg exiles pushed out from southern Algeria and Niger by French invaders, managed to repel the attack on the Sanusi *zāwiya*, but French troops finally took control in January 1902.[69] Coming just months before the death of Muhammad al-Mahdi and the subsequent recognition of his nephew, Ahmad al-Sharif (1875–1933), as the leader and spiritual guide of the Sanusiyya, the struggles between French and Sanusi forces in 1901 and 1902 established an enduring cycle of conflict between Sanusi forces and French officials. In later attempts by French officials to negotiate a truce, al-Sharif depicted the Sanusi *ikhwān* as persecuted by a relentless French war that went beyond a targeting of caches of weapons to the confiscation and destruction of books, potent symbols of Sanusi wealth, power, and educational mission in the region.[70]

The conflicts with French forces increased the importance of Sanusi ties to trade routes in an era of restricted access to goods. In the decade following the French invasion of Bir Alali, European military, political, and economic presence led regional leaders to seek out relationships with Sanusi elites as a conduit for arms and other scarce supplies. In particular, French military action in the region strengthened relationships between Ahmad al-Sharif (as the new head of the Sanusi *ṭarīqa*) and the sultans of Darfur and Wadai. Among the few indications of the direct involvement of the Sanusiyya in the nineteenth- and early twentieth-century caravan trade, a collection of letters in the National Record Office of Sudan in Khartoum that British officers took from the palace of Sultan ʿAli Dinar when they invaded the area in 1916 documents the development of a favorable relationship with Sanusi elites during the period of Sanusi expansion in the late nineteenth century. Their relationship only improved following the initiation of expansionist measures by French troops in Borkou and the Lake Chad region.[71] The letters from Khartoum demonstrate the development of an interdependent trade relationship between the Sanusi elites (acting on behalf of the Zuwaya trading interests) and ʿAli Dinar. Sanusi *zawāyā* relied on these ties for basic supplies, and ʿAli Dinar in turn depended on the Sanusi networks for arms and ammunition. The position of the Sanusi elite within regional trade networks increased the influence of the Sufi *ṭarīqa* as constraints on traditional trade routes caused by the pressures of French aggression and regional politics made political and military leaders dependent on the Sanusiyya.[72]

French expansion deepened the less well-documented relationship between the Sanusiyya and the sultan of Wadai as well. A series of conflicts and a subsequent civil war in Wadai prevented the establishment of Sanusi *zawāyā* or a strong level of cooperation between Sanusi *ikhwān* and merchant-traders in that region in the mid- to late nineteenth century. However, after the French invasion of Bir Alali, the proclamation of the new sultan Dudmurrah in 1902 initiated an era of heightened communication between the sultan and a Sanusi shaykh in Borkou as they recognized a shared interest in circumventing the restrictions on trade in the Central Sudan caused by the French presence. By the time tensions with French troops in the region reached their height in 1910, British intelligence reported that a combination of Zuwaya and Maghārba forces connected to the Sanusiyya had attacked French forces alongside Dudmurrah, the former sultan of Wadai. British and French officials painted the defensive strategies as a sign of Sanusi intentions to organize a vast Islamic empire in resistance to European imperialism.[73] The longer trajectory of regional ties to Sanusi elites, however, suggests the inverse. While the Sanusi *zawāyā* provided access to arms and ammunition, the survival of the Sanusi *ṭarīqa* depended on maintaining its utility to regional political and economic leaders.

Conclusion

The death of Muhammad al-Mahdi al-Sanusi and the subsequent recognition of his nephew, Ahmad al-Sharif, as the nominal head of the Sanusiyya in 1902 occurred in a moment of heightened tensions when Sanusi *ikhwān* responded to the threat that the French military presence posed to the security of the Sanusi *zawāyā* and access to trade routes. It was precisely during this time that Italian imperialists began to focus renewed attention on the prospect of annexing the Libyan territories. In preparation, a variety of state agents, exploratory and commercial societies, and social science institutions—the standard assortment of people that constituted pro-imperial lobbies in Europe in the era of high imperialism—began to collect any information that could be of value in facilitating an occupation of the Libyan territories. Due to Italy's relatively late entry into the field of interimperial competition, many of these early initiatives focused on collecting and translating literature from other European sources. And even after the initial occupation of the Libyan territories, Italian colonial officials continued to look abroad for to information and analyses of the Sanusiyya. Italian imperialists inherited an ambiguous image of the Sanusiyya as religious and political authorities in North Africa.

Increasingly in the years leading up to and following Italy's initial occupation in 1911–1912, these accounts expressed new uncertainty about the status of the Sanusiyya as a source of religious and political authority in the Libyan territories. Some French reports hinted at doubts over Duveyrier's portrayal of the Sanusiyya as a serious threat to any state authority in North Africa. Conflicting opinions on the extent of Sanusi authority demonstrate the extent to which the fear of what the French referred to as the *légende noire* represented a malleable image in the fantasy of imperial powers. It was a fantasy that provided colonial authorities with a means of ignoring widespread opposition to European presence by fixating on the Sanusiyya as a singular source of anti-European sentiment. When confronted with the strength of resistance in Wadai, for example, authorities in Paris latched onto the presence of Sanusi forces as a clear enemy responsible for organizing that resistance. Reports circulated in the French Ministry of Foreign Affairs that warned of Sanusi elites in Cyrenaica preaching a "holy war" to defend Wadai, contributing to the accumulation of a sizable force from the north while "from Kufra and Borkou fighters descended by the thousands."[74]

However, reports from French officers on the ground in the region contradicted the impression that the Sanusiyya could call on such sizable forces, especially south of Kufra. When instructions came from Paris to attempt to establish friendly relations with Sanusi leaders in the region to calm tensions and neutralize the potential threat of a pan-Islamic uprising, the French commander of the military territory of Chad, Colonel Largeau, dismissed the suggestion as attributing too much power to the

Sanusiyya in Wadai. In his account, the Sufi *ṭarīqa* were outsiders in the region who lacked true political or even moral authority. While he extolled the spirituality of the Sanusi family, the few Sanusi adherents in the Wadai he characterized as "pirates," interested only in gaining a "handful of well-chosen black boys they would make into pages and black concubines to charm their leisure time."[75]

British reports in the years leading up to the Italian occupation of 1911 confirmed the reservations of Largeau, greatly attenuating the general French alarm over the potential threat of the Sanusi *ṭarīqa*. British intelligence did identify a shift in the Sanusiyya from a religious to a political organization under the leadership of al-Mahdi, who "gradually acquired the authority of a temporal power in the entire territory of Darfur, Wadai, and Bornu to the north of the coast of Tripoli." Under the leadership of Ahmad al-Sharif, British intelligence officers claimed, this political shift "translated into a species of nationalism in all of North Africa, the development of which was aided by the Young Turk revolution and the Italian campaign." But British intelligence questioned the threat the Sanusiyya posed to European imperial stability in North Africa. "The stories of the Sanusiyya as a global danger are an exaggeration of the real state of things," British intelligence reports surmised. "Their adherents, though spread through distant districts, are too dispersed to constitute more than a temporary, local danger."[76]

With mounting evidence to support the idea that the Sanusiyya might not represent the pan-Islamic terror earlier accounts had made it out to be, French diplomatic agents and military officers began actively seeking the support of Ahmad al-Sharif after 1910–1911. In part this was in recognition of the ability of al-Sharif to control regional trade routes based on evidence that Sanusi *ikhwān* had blocked the movement of essential goods into the region to protest the French presence and the seizure of Sanusi properties. Yet the tone of subsequent discussions with the Sanusi figurehead revealed a sense of uncertainty concerning the true extent of his authority and the nature of his intentions. When French diplomatic services in Cairo sent representatives in July 1911 to negotiate a settlement, al-Sharif agreed to resume normal trade in the region only if the French recognized his regional authority by limiting their direct communications with local Sanusi shaykhs. He demanded that French officials communicate through him as an intermediary. The French administration refused his request and began to express doubts concerning the extent of al-Sharif's authority based on the sense that his demand betrayed a desire to shore up weak control over the network of Sanusi *zawāyā*.[77] Still, the logic of an interimperial competition for influence in the region seemed to require an alliance with the Sanusiyya, even if that ran the risk of overestimating the value of al-Sharif's authority. Despite these uncertainties, Colonel Largeau agreed to resume communication with the Sanusi leader, with the caveat that doing so might lead al-Sharif to believe, "that the French government is disposed to treat him as one power to another; it could, in effect, exaggerate the importance of what is, in our view, his very relative authority."[78]

Disagreements over the nature of the Sanusi presence in the region among French colonial officers and central officials in the Ministry of Colonies highlights the slippery quality of Sanusi influence in the shifting context of the scramble for Africa. The ambiguities surrounding the nature of the Sanusiyya amplified among Italian imperialists. Engaging in the interimperial circuits of knowledge about the Sanusiyya in the years leading up to and after the initial occupation, doubts about the Sufi *tarīqa* in Italian literature reflected a diversity of opinions about the best course of action for establishing Italian hegemony in the Libyan territories. The dominant opinion in public debates and among politicians in Rome expressed an expectation that Italy would enjoy a relatively easy relationship with Sanusi elites, though prescriptions for achieving that relationship differed depending on the perspective of various commentators on the nature of the religious and political authority of the Sanusi *tarīqa*. Even among those opposed to the annexation of the Libyan territories, the Sanusiyya featured as a potential ally or enemy. It represented an enigmatic force against which Italian imperialists would define the religious politics of colonial expansion.

2

Crafting an Italian Approach to Colonial Rule

IN THE YEARS leading up to the invasion of the Libyan territories, it seemed like anyone with even a modicum of interest in Italy's prospects in North Africa had something to write about the Sanusiyya. Most of these accounts are by those who fall under the category of what Barbara Sòrgoni has referred to as "accidental ethnographers"—"travelers, military officers, and colonial civil servants"—who wrote about Cyrenaica and the Sanusiyya out of a mixture of personal interest and preoccupation with the prospect of imperial expansion.[1] What all of these works had in common was the belief that the successful occupation of the Libyan territories required the support of the Sanusi elite. In the years leading up to the Italian invasion in 1911, these "accidental ethnographies" presented a counternarrative to earlier accounts that had painted the Sanusiyya as virulent, anti-Christian, religious fanatics. The tendency among Italian imperialists instead was to present Sanusi elites as friendly allies.[2]

Italian studies of the Sanusiyya, however, could not agree on how to secure an alliance. One of the methods advocated by proponents of an Italo-Sanusi power-sharing relationship was an appeal to a shared sense of religiosity. Casting Italy as a force for a conservative religious agenda— even a Muslim conservative religious agenda—had the potential added benefit of affirming the importance of a Catholic identity in expansionist policies. After decades of tensions following the fall of the Papal States, the popularity of colonial expansion generated a new level of enthusiasm for Italian national politics among Catholic interest groups. As we have seen, the Catholic Church led resistance to early Italian imperial ambitions primarily out of broader opposition to the secular Italian state. But in the years leading up to the occupation of the Libyan territories, state officials and church leadership built on initial signs of reconciliation that developed in the aftermath of Italian military losses at Dogali and Adwa. The Catholic Church and the Catholic press sold the idea of the imperial project in the Libyan territories as an opportunity to spread Italian culture and commercial interests in conjunction with the missionary objectives of the Holy See, and preexisting missionary and financial networks of the Catholic Church in North Africa facilitated the initial expansion of the Italian state presence in the region.

The idea of projecting a Catholic identity in overseas expansion, however, did not meet with universal approval among Italian imperialists. Some feared that a pro-Catholic attitude might give the impression that an Italian occupation would coincide with mass conversions or threaten to upend Islamic cultural norms. Others opposed increased involvement of the Catholic Church in a nationalist enterprise. Conflicting views of the proper role of religious identity in imperialism laid bare tensions over church involvement in national politics. These tensions were expressed in debates over the nature of political and religious authority in the Sanusi *ṭarīqa*. As an unknown entity, the Sanusiyya were a convenient foil in the writings of these "accidental ethnographers" against which they would define an Italian approach to colonial rule.

Insabato and the "Pro-Islamic" Approach

One of the more colorful figures to promote the idea of collaborating with Sanusi elites in Italian expansionism was Enrico Insabato (1878–1963). Trained as a doctor, Insabato first traveled to Cairo in December 1902 to attend an international medical conference. He remained in North Africa as an agent of the Italian state police and with the direct support of the minister of the interior and later prime minister, Giovanni Giolitti. Tasked with laying the groundwork for an Italian invasion of the Libyan coast, Insabato connected with an assortment of people in the Egyptian capital who shared a distaste for British dominance in the region. As part of a public relations campaign to promote Italian influence in North Africa as an alternative to British liberalism, Insabato advocated active outreach to Sufi *ṭuruq* and Muslim elites, adopting an approach its detractors referred to as "pro-Islamic."

A controversial figure at the time, Insabato's direct influence on policy decisions involved in the expansion of Italian presence in the Libyan territories remains a matter of some debate.[3] If Enrico Insabato was a marginal figure in the history of Italian expansionism, it was in part because he operated in the shadows of official diplomatic circles in Cairo. Politically, Insabato was something of an enigma. He was known to frequent anarchist circles in his student years, but uncertainty over his loyalty to the cause—and perhaps suspicions that he was working as a spy—earned him the condemnation of the anarchist newspaper *Il Libertario* in October 1904.[4] He admitted to being a Freemason and would later prove a dedicated populist; after a period of being involved in Don Luigi Sturzo's Partito Popolare Italiana (PPI) after World War I, he served as a deputy for the province of Vicenza in the short-lived Party of Italian Peasants (Partito dei Contadini) in 1924–1925. In 1925 Insabato led a faction of this party that was in favor of fascism, and he joined the Partito Nazionale Fascista (PNF) when the Party of Italian Peasants was dissolved at the end of that year.[5] Insabato would even become an outspoken advocate for conservative Catholic politics after World War II; in 1956 he organized a much-publicized meeting of Catholic bishops and diplomatic representatives of Muslim countries to the Vatican to establish a "united front of Roman Catholics and Moslems to fight communism" around the world.[6] Insabato's role in organizing the meeting as the head of the Center for Italo-Arab Relations (Centro per le Relazione Italo-Arabe) indicates a lifelong commitment to the idea of alliances between Italy and the Muslim world through a shared sense of religious conservatism that began during his years in Cairo.

Suspicious of his anarchist associations, the Italian consulate began to follow his activities when he arrived in Cairo in 1902, but word that Insabato enjoyed the personal protection of Giovanni Giolitti put a quick end to the surveillance.[7] During his time in Cairo Insabato worked on developing intellectual, cultural, and economic exchange programs meant to improve the image of Italy in the Muslim world, especially in areas under Italian control in East Africa and the Libyan territories. At the same time he prepared a series of secret reports on his activities and the political atmosphere in North Africa for the head of the Italian national police. Insabato focused his initial efforts on generating goodwill for Italy among theological students at al-Azhar University. To that end, Insabato helped to establish a *ruwaq*, or dormitory, to house students from Italian Somalia and Eritrea, with the goal of expanding the *ruwaq* to include students from Cyrenaica and Tripolitania.[8] In further efforts to promote a pro-Islamic image abroad, Insabato called for the establishment of sharia law in

Italian-influenced territories, the construction of a mosque in Rome that would offer courses on Arabic instruction and knowledge of Islam, and active outreach to the leaders of Sufi *ṭuruq* in North Africa.[9] None of these ideas represented a particularly innovative approach to increasing Italian influence in the region; the idea of appealing to students studying at al-Azhar was a common tactic among imperial powers in North Africa.[10]

More unusual was the extent to which Insabato leveraged his marginal position to influence preparations for the Italian occupation of the Libyan territories in Italian official circles. As an agent of the minister of the interior, Insabato acted independently of the interests of the Ministry of Foreign Affairs. This arrangement caused considerable confusion and consternation at times in the Italian consulate in Cairo, but it provided Insabato with the flexibility to develop relationships that conflicted with Italian diplomatic interests for the purpose of pursuing an expansion of Italian influence in North Africa. Insabato was able to associate with an unconventional cross-section of anti-British activists, intellectuals, and radicals in Cairo, many of whom advocated particular interpretations of Islamic orthodoxy as a form of opposition to British and international liberalism.

Significant among Insabato's early contacts was Ivan Aguéli, a Swedish artist and author known for his involvement in anarchist and theosophist circles. Aguéli worked as an editor for two Italian-Arabic magazines that Insabato created in Cairo: *Il Commercio italiano* and *Il Convito* (issued under the title *al-Nadi* in Arabic).[11] Ostensibly, Insabato did not intend these publications to promote the idea of Italian occupation of the Libyan territories. The goal was rather to increase Italian economic activity, making Tripolitania "a major outlet for Italian commerce and emigration," but while maintaining an Ottoman administration. More important, Insabato's publication was intent on painting Italy as an alternative to other European powers vying for influence in North Africa. In one issue, *Il Convito/al-Nadi* called for the "salvation" of the region from French and British influence, bemoaning the possibility of the expansion of Italy's European competitors.[12]

Insabato and Aguéli promoted an image of Italy as a champion of conservative Muslim interests in contrast to an era of British-sponsored secularization and modernization. In the publication's first issue in 1904, Insabato introduced the magazine as a voice supporting Islamic orthodoxy. He argued for the necessity of such a voice in defense against widespread modernizing reform movements in the Muslim world that he claimed were directed by and for the benefit of British interests in the region. For many in the Ottoman Empire, Islamic reform and modernization seemed to offer a response to a growing sense of technological and economic disparity between the Muslim world and Christian Europe. But Insabato characterized modernizing reform movements instead as "a mongrel, restless, pretentious, and ridiculous world, composed of grotesque imitators of Europe. I have seen them conserve Islam in name only, trying to change it into a type of Protestantism in tarbush."[13] Through his publications, Insabato promoted the idea that what he considered to be orthodox Islam—and especially Sufism—played an essential civilizing role in the region. He identified Sufi *ṭuruq* as exemplary of "true" Islam and thus the best civilizing force in the Muslim world because of the mystical asceticism of Sufism, which Insabato saw as a concerted effort to resist modernization and liberalism.[14] Through *Il Convito/al-Nadi*, Insabato also sought to convince an Italian audience of the utility of conservative versions of Islam in expanding commercial opportunities for Italians in North Africa. Muslim editors for the publication called on Italians to support religious training in the region, arguing that "the more religious Muslims are, the more difficult it is to corrupt their . . . honor, and the easier it is to make them understand how much there is that is good and respectable in another country and within another population."[15] Insabato's declarations of support for religious conservatives in the public forum of *Il Convito/al-Nadi* mirrored the private reports he sent to the head of the Italian state police, Commander Vigliani. In a series of handwritten letters he sent to his superior during the Italo-Turkish War (1911–1912), Insabato noted his consistent warnings over the years against trusting in the kinds of urban elites, the "Europeanized people in that elegant world," with whom the Italian consulate preferred to deal: "The only element in the Islamic world with which it is possible to deal . . . securely and without fear of treachery is the religious element."[16]

Thanks to the influence of Aguéli, Insabato's endorsement of Sufism fit loosely with the sort of traditionalism that would come to characterize Rene Guènon's philosophy in the 1920s and 1930s. A philosopher located in Paris, Guènon developed a philosophy of traditionalism that looked for universal truths in all religions. He held Sufism in high regard for its mysticism, which he saw as offering a direct path to knowledge and a sharp rejoinder to modernity. It was Aguéli who introduced Guènon to Sufism, when he wrote for the latter's journal *La Gnose* in 1910–1912. The contributors to *La Gnose* explored a variety of non-Western religious traditions in search for esoteric truths as part of what Guènon considered a defense against "the parasitic vegetation" of the bourgeois values of the Western Enlightenment. Based on his experiences in Cairo, Aguéli served as the journal's expert on Sufi mysticism.[17] As Guènon would later do, Insabato favored Sufism above other forms of Islamic practice, for its mysticism. They both understood Sufism to avoid the corrupting influence of religious institutions in favor of direct experiences of the divine. There was an important difference in their attitudes toward religion, however. For Guènon, reverence for Sufism coincided with a rejection of the influence of the Catholic Church, but Insabato's attitudes toward the church—like his political affiliation—were more ambiguous. Considering Insabato's involvement in Catholic political activism in later years, he seemed less interested in renouncing Catholicism than in building bridges between Catholic Italy and Muslim North Africa.[18]

During his time in Cairo Insabato's interpretation of religious conservatism was designed primarily to frustrate British dominance. One of the key associations for Insabato in that effort was his relationship to ʿAbd al-Rahman ʿIlaysh, a prominent figure in the Sufi *ṭarīqa* al-Shadhiliyya in Egypt and a scholar at al-Azhar. Most likely it was Ivan Aguéli who brought ʿIlaysh into Insabato's orbit. Changing his name to ʿAbd al-Hadi, Aguéli converted to Islam as an adherent of the Shadhiliyya after his arrival in Cairo. ʿIlaysh subsequently became a regular contributor to *Il Convito/al-Nadi*, and the connection contributed to the anti-British tenor of Insabato's activities. ʿAbd al-Rahman ʿIlaysh was the son of Muhammad ʿIlaysh, a conservative Egyptian Maliki mufti who led opposition to Western reforms instituted by Khedive Ismaʿil (r. 1863–1879).[19] A key personality in the ʿUrabi revolt (1881–1882) against increasing British influence in Egypt and the predominantly Turkish control of the Ottoman army, Muhammad ʿIlaysh died in prison in 1882. Daniel Grange has suggested that ʿAbd al-Rahman ʿIlaysh may have seen his involvement with Italians in Cairo as a means of furthering the anti-British and antireformist activities of his father.[20] This was how many Italians understood his attitude at the time.

When ʿAbd al-Rahman ʿIlaysh demonstrated his goodwill toward Italians with the commemoration of a small mosque near al-Azhar University to the memory of Italy's deceased King Umberto I in 1906, the Italian media struck a self-congratulatory note, with an implied sense of superiority over European competitors. Both *L'Illustrazione Italiana* and *Corriere della Sera* reported that when asked "why he was so in love with Italy and Italians," ʿAbd al-Rahman ʿIlaysh replied: "Italy is the only power

that can come to agreement with us Muslims, because Italians are cor-
dial and loyal and treat us without pride, as brothers."[21] The construction
of the mosque seemed to point to Italy's relative strength in the realm of
interimperial competition for the hearts and minds of the Muslim world.
For Italians living in Egypt, the mosque offered language instruction, cultural exchange, and even a community center.[22]

Corriere della Sera also linked ʿAbd al-Rahman ʿIlaysh's grand gesture
to Insabato's growing influence in Cairo, noting that the commemoration of the mosque followed closely on the heels of ʿIlaysh's having used
Insabato as an intermediary to send gifts to King Vittorio Emanuele III.
While the newspaper lauded Insabato's activities and connections as a
sign of Italy's influence in Muslim North Africa, however, his increasingly public profile became a source of irritation to the Italian consulate. The Italian consul general in Cairo, Giuseppe Salvago Raggi, began
to take note of Insabato's activities in 1906. Judging him intelligent but
"maybe with a tendency to excessive excitement," Salvago Raggi's dis-
pleasure with Insabato's presence was palpable in messages to Rome.[23]
Salvago Raggi saw him as an individual engaged in activities in the name
of Italy, but seemingly on his own initiative, with unclear sources of
funding and no evident direction from central authorities. Salvago Raggi
began calling for the Ministry of Foreign Affairs to send Insabato elsewhere in the Muslim world, where he could continue to do the loose work
of cultural promotion he had initiated in Cairo, but far from the delicate
diplomatic issues in Egypt—and far from Salvago Raggi himself. Yemen
or Albania came to mind.[24]

Insabato's presence was more than a source of personal or professional
irritation; officials in the consulate also disapproved of his activities as
a potential threat to Italian relations with their Anglo-Egyptian hosts in
Cairo. The nature of Insabato's connections and his support for religious
traditionalism as a criticism of British liberalism had already garnered
negative attention in Cairo. On the surface, Insabato's attempts to build
consensus for Italian influence through cultural means in Cairo fit with
international expectations for Italian imperial expansion; the British in
particular rested their support for Italian claims to the Libyan territories
on an understanding that in the event of occupation, Rome would establish a protectorate while maintaining the official sovereignty of the sultan,
similar in spirit to the British presence in Egypt.[25] Insabato's efforts to
generate goodwill among Muslim notables through his publications and

contacts in al-Azhar seemed to provide the surest path to such an arrangement. But British support for Italian claims in the Libyan territories belied
a deeper strain between British and Italian intentions in North Africa, tensions Insabato's anti-British stance brought to the surface. Accusing him
of the crime of "conspiring against Islam," British officials requested that
the Italian diplomatic agency in Cairo eject Insabato from the region in
1907.[26] Anxious to avoid antagonizing Britain, the Italian minister of foreign affairs, Tommaso Tittoni, instructed the consulate in Cairo to comply
with the request (which they were more than happy to do), and Insabato
was forced to return to Italy in 1908.[27] The Ministry of the Interior would
send Insabato back to the region in 1910 in preparation for the occupation
of the Libyan coast, but his temporary ejection from North Africa underscored the volatility of international competition for influence in North
Africa in the first decade of the twentieth century.[28]

Muhammad ʿAli ʿAlawi and the Sanusi Connection

Despite his marginal position outside of the Ministry of Foreign Affairs,
Insabato's introduction to the Sanusiyya as a possible ally in Italian expansion occurred through his relationship with an interpreter for the Italian
consulate, Muhammad ʿAli ʿAlawi (see figure 2.1a and b). ʿAlawi was a
uniquely qualified intermediary for Italian interests in the region. Born in
Cairo in 1872, he studied in Italian schools in the city during his youth and
later returned to those schools to teach Arabic. He began working as an
interpreter for the Italian diplomatic agency in 1901. Almost immediately
the Italian consulate recognized his value as an informant; in April 1901
consulate officials forwarded a memorandum from ʿAlawi with detailed
information on the Sanusi *ṭarīqa*, citing family connections to followers of
the Sanusiyya in Cairo and Darfur as evidence of his authority on the subject.[29] His status as a valuable informant was confirmed when a contingent
of emissaries from the Sanusi family paid him a visit to ask him to write
a letter to Muhammad al-Mahdi al-Sanusi to relay the intentions of the
Italians in the Libyan territories—and to explain Italian attitudes toward
Islam.[30] ʿAlawi became more than a mere interpreter. As the Italian journalist Osea Felici described it, ʿAlawi became a private agent for Giovanni
Giolitti, who, like Insabato, reported directly to the commander of the state
police.[31] ʿAlawi also became an integral part of Insabato's efforts to portray

FIGURE 2.1 A AND B Photographs of Muhammad ʿAli ʿAlawi, dedicated to minister of colonies, Ferdinando Martini, "as a sign of admiration, loyalty, and respect," May 24, 1916.

Source: ASMAI II 137/4/26.

Italy as friendly to Islam in North Africa. As a close associate of ʿAbd al-Rahman ʿIlaysh, he was involved with the Arabic courses provided at the mosque of Umberto I, and he helped to manage the pro-Italian *ruwaq* at al-Azhar University. Italian diplomatic documents frequently cited the Egyptian interpreter as an important intermediary whose extensive social network might be leveraged to Italy's advantage.

When Muhammad al-Mahdi al-Sanusi died in 1902, officials in the Italian consulate in Cairo turned to ʿAlawi to establish contact with his twenty-five-year-old nephew and the presumed successor as the head of the Sanusi *ṭarīqa*, Ahmad al-Sharif. On March 31, 1903, ʿAlawi sent a packet of gifts on behalf of the Italian government via a regular supplier of the Sanusi family that included, among other items, two rapid-fire rifles engraved with al-Sharif's name.[32] In return, ʿAlawi received a favorable response along with a request for more gifts, and from early 1905 until after the Italian invasion of the Libyan coastline in the autumn of 1911, ʿAlawi served as a primary point of contact in what many in the Italian Ministry of Foreign Affairs came to understand as a positive relationship of mutual support with members of the Sanusi family. The exchanges between ʿAlawi and the Sanusi family seemed beneficial for all involved. For al-Sharif and his emissaries, they offered an opportunity to gain access to weapons and ammunition needed to hold off French troops in the Sahara; for Italian imperialists, the exchanges of gifts provided evidence of Sanusi support for increased Italian influence in the region—or even indications of the possibility of supplanting Istanbul in the ability to claim the Sanusi *ṭarīqa* as a proxy for Italian rule.

With a new line of communication established through the mediation of ʿAlawi after 1905–1906, Insabato became one of the most vocal proponents in Italian imperialist circles of the active pursuit of an alliance with Ahmad al-Sharif. Based primarily on information from the Egyptian interpreter, Insabato produced a report for Giolitti and the Ministry of Foreign Affairs in which he presented the Sanusiyya as a growing force in Islam that the Italians could use against other European powers. Insabato saw a relationship with the Sanusiyya, because of their dominant position in regional trade routes, as a means of facilitating Italian economic penetration in Cyrenaica and Tripolitania. To that end, he recommended measures to deepen ties with the Sanusi family that included a plan to send the sons of the previous spiritual leader of the Sufi *ṭarīqa*, Muhammad al-Mahdi, to universities in Italy.[33] For Insabato, the goal of developing an alliance between Italian interests and the Sanusi family in the Libyan territories necessitated a dual effort to reach out to a network of Sanusi elites while simultaneously working to convince Italian officials of the viability of a "pro-Islamic" approach. The concept had to counter powerful images of the Sanusi *ṭarīqa* as a group of anti-European Islamic fanatics, which stemmed not only from French portrayals of the Sanusiyya, but also from contemporary assessments of the danger of the Sufi *ṭarīqa* and its *zawāyā* from the Italian consulate in Benghazi.[34]

The idea of forming an alliance with the Sanusiyya gained support from more official quarters when the secretary of legation at the Italian consulate in Cairo, Count Carlo Arrivabene Valenti-Gozanga, issued his own assessment of the Sanusi *ṭarīqa* and its influence in a booklet intended to inform functionaries and policymakers in the Ministry of Foreign Affairs in 1906. Arrivabene's study of the Sanusiyya perpetuated the heightened estimation in nineteenth-century French portrayals of Sanusi authority as highly centralized with immense influence. Citing ʿAbd al-Rahman ʿIlaysh as the source of his information, Arrivabene characterized the Sanusi *ṭarīqa* as a military theocracy with a base of over three million adherents "that could be considered to form a united population obedient to the will of the supreme head alone."[35]

Like Insabato, however, Arrivabene argued that the authority of the Sanusiyya could be wielded for Italy's benefit. For Arrivabene, the Sanusi elites opposed all central authorities—Christian and Muslim alike—insofar as their presence threatened to encroach upon territories under Sanusi control or squelch what he reckoned amounted to Sanusi imperial goals. Italy, he claimed, had been the only state power that managed to maintain a positive relationship with the Sanusi elites. Arrivabene differed from Insabato in that he did not cite a particularly accommodating attitude toward Islam as the secret to Italy's relative success in maintaining a positive relationship with the Sanusi elite; instead, he understood Italy to be in possession of a strategic advantage in the geographic distance between Italian seats of power on the coast and the Sanusi *zawāyā* of the interior, to which French and English expansion posed a more direct threat. Without a hint of irony, Arrivabene suggested that "the friendly attitude of the Sanusi in our regard derives from the fact that we are farther from their zone of influence than the French and the British and thus much less formidable to them, it is no less certain that the Sanusi seem for now to view favorably an eventual Italian occupation of Tripoli and of the Tripolitanian hinterland." Arrivabene's study served as a confirmation of Insabato's understanding of the Sanusiyya as a potential commercial partner, but it came with a strict warning: an eventual occupation needed to respect the geographical boundaries of Sanusi *zawāyā* to prevent this crucial ally in economic imperialism from becoming hostile. Arrivabene included a map indicating the locations of Sanusi strongholds and trade routes to reinforce the lesson.[36]

Besides sharing an interest in pursuing a relationship with Sanusi elites, Insabato and Arrivabene were also both vocal advocates of promoting the interests of Mohammed Ali ʿAlawi within the Italian administration. ʿAlawi's involvement in Italian preparations for the eventual occupation of the Libyan territories became a point of friction for Italian imperialists in Cairo in a ministerial battle for control over communication with the Sanusi elites. Insabato stood firmly on the side of ʿAlawi. In the autumn of 1905 he began to campaign for the Italian government to grant the interpreter citizenship status along with some sort of commemorative medal or title of nobility. The proposal served a practical goal; ʿAlawi needed citizenship status to be eligible for a promotion to the highest rank of interpreter within the Ministry of Foreign Affairs. Insabato also considered it a step toward securing Italian protection for ʿAlawi from any possible retribution on the part of Anglo-Egyptian officials for his involvement in schemes to expand Italian influence.[37] Arrivabene added his more oblique support for the proposal when he wrote to the minister of foreign affairs in November 1905 asking that ʿAlawi be given a raise (which required citizenship status) in recognition of the invaluable services he had rendered the state.[38]

In July 1906 Salvago Raggi agreed to promote ʿAlawi to a second rank interpreter, one step below the highest rank. But he refused to grant ʿAlawi Italian citizenship. The Italian consulate's rejection of the proposal reflected the contempt among diplomatic officials for anyone connected with Insabato. Officially, Salvago Raggi cited a variety of reasons for refusing the request, from bureaucratic difficulties of granting citizenship to an Ottoman subject to personal opposition to the idea of granting Italian titles or official favors to Arabs.[39] But in a memorandum on the subject in October 1906 Gaetano Manzoni, a secretary to the Italian legation in Cairo, made clear the damage his association with Insabato had done to the status of ʿAlawi in the Italian consulate. Manzoni warned that if the Ministry of Foreign Affairs granted favors to ʿAlawi in response to requests made by Insabato, even if ʿAlawi was not aware of Insabato's role in acting on his behalf, it would constitute a threat to the authority and discipline of the ministry itself.[40]

For the consul general, Giuseppe Salvago Raggi—a member of the Italian nobility with extensive experience in the Arabic-speaking world—Insabato's connection to ʿAlawi and his influence over the entire Italian program in North Africa threatened more than diplomatic stability in Cairo. It struck a blow to the heart of the social and political hierarchy of the Italian liberal state. He saw Insabato as nothing more than a dilettante, the son of a railway worker—and suspected of anarchist tendencies at that—pretending to understand issues concerning Islam and politics in North Africa after a few short years in the region.[41] Discomfort with Insabato spread among Italian diplomatic agents as far away as Aleppo when the *Corriere della Sera* reprinted an interview from *Il Messagero* in which Insabato—cited in the article as a journalist and an expert on Islamic matters—criticized Italian actions in Somalia as inciting anti-Italian sentiment. In reaction to the interview, Ferdinando Sola, the Italian consul general in Aleppo, discounted "the ignorance of this literary knave who claims the right, after a brief sojourn in Cairo, to speak *ex cathedra* of the orientalist discipline, not knowing that in order to rise to that honor, to such dignity, requires many years of serious study."[42] Salvago Raggi squirreled away these criticisms of Insabato as proof of his menace to Italy's standing abroad.

Salvago Raggi's opposition to Insabato also reflected a difference in approach to Italian imperialism. To a certain extent Salvago Raggi would have agreed with Insabato's interest in collaborating with Muslim elites in Italian imperial expansion; it was during Salvago Raggi's term that the consulate began to send gifts to Ahmad al-Sharif through ʿAlawi's mediation, after all. But Salvago Raggi found Insabato's willingness to embrace native functionaries, and ʿAlawi in particular, distasteful. Insabato's proposal to grant ʿAlawi citizenship, for example, rankled with Salvago Raggi's sense of propriety. That is not to say that Insabato saw Arab Muslims and Italians as cultural or political equals; Insabato's support of cross-cultural collaboration served a strategic purpose to facilitate an expansion of Italian influence in North Africa. But Salvago Raggi demonstrated a commitment to clear racial and cultural hierarchies that he would continue to promote in his tenure as governor of Eritrea from 1907 to 1915.[43] Salvago Raggi welcomed the utility of a collaborative approach to imperial expansion, but only insofar as it left intact a sense of Italian superiority. Suggestions of allowing ʿAlawi to transition from an intermediary to a full citizen with the possibility of promotion in the ranks of the Ministry of Foreign Affairs threatened Salvago Raggi's delicate civilizational hierarchy.

The extent of distrust of both Insabato and ʿAlawi in the ministry can be seen in plans by the minister of foreign affairs to send a mission to the oases of Kufra with additional gifts for Ahmad al-Sharif in 1905. The ministry chose as its emissary Aldo Mei, the head of an Italian medical clinic in Benghazi. Mei brought both experience in the region and additional utility as someone who could offer medical services to his hosts in the Libyan interior. The ostensible objective was to fulfill a request al-Sharif had sent via ʿAlawi for additional gifts of arms and ammunition from the Italians. But the Ministry of Foreign Affairs hoped that Mei's visit would also encourage Sanusi elites to turn to Italian rather than Ottoman assistance in reaction to any increased threat of French *or* British occupation of Sanusi territories—a possibility that seemed increasingly likely in an era of instability along Egypt's western borderlands. The ministry also intended the mission to serve as an opportunity to transfer the center of operations for Italian efforts to connect with the Sanusi family from the consulate in Cairo to the diplomatic offices in Benghazi. Planning for the mission, however, still required the assistance of ʿAlawi in his capacity as Italy's primary contact with the Sanusiyya. ʿAlawi was instructed to get the necessary permissions and protections for the mission to travel to the interior oases, yet the Ministry of Foreign Affairs was eager to limit his knowledge of the scope of the mission, citing his supposed tendency to "talk easily"—running the risk of his leaking the true intentions of the Italian mission—as a source of concern.[44]

Ultimately, Mei's mission to Kufra failed to produce any significant results in terms of increasing direct contact between Italian diplomatic officials and the Sanusi family. The Ministry of Foreign Affairs did officially move the center of activity for Sanusi outreach to Benghazi in March 1907; there followed several years of competition between ʿAlawi and his circle of associates in Cairo on the one hand and the Italian consulate in Benghazi on the other. For many in the Italian Ministry of Foreign Affairs, reliance on ʿAlawi carried the risk that he might provide information on Italian efforts to cultivate a relationship with the Sanusiyya to British and French officials. Given the frequent requests on the part of the Sanusiyya for gifts of arms and ammunition to fight against French forces, Italian diplomatic officials saw the utility in keeping their outreach efforts within a close group of individuals who shared Italy's national and racial identity. Nevertheless, ʿAlawi's apparent success in communicating with Sanusi elites inspired Italian officials to continue to turn to the interpreter in Cairo for intelligence.

At times the opposition to ʿAlawi's involvement in Italian-Sanusi relations took on a more personal tone. When Giacomo De Martino was sent to Cairo as the new consul general in October 1907, he initiated more drastic measures to decrease the Ministry of Foreign Affair's reliance on ʿAlawi. A diplomatic agent with a long history of working in the Muslim world, De Martino proved even more hostile to the activities of Insabato and ʿAlawi than Salvago Raggi had been. Anti-Arab stereotypes suffused De Martino's criticisms of ʿAlawi. He understood ʿAlawi's relationship with Insabato to be indicative of an "oriental tendency" to try to circumvent official channels through personal relationships.[45] De Martino saw in ʿAlawi a combination of insidious efforts to use his relationship with the Italian consulate for personal gain and an inherent incapacity for discretion. De Martino described a breakdown of Italian information services in Cairo with ʿAlawi at the center. All of the efforts to increase Italian influence in North Africa through personal connections and unofficial propaganda campaigns were an open secret to British and Egyptian officials. The problem, in De Martino's eyes, was also the result of the Egyptian interpreter having gained too much power in the Italian administration. His close relationship with Insabato, De Martino complained, gave ʿAlawi's actions an "almost official character" as a police agent, rather than his being a mere interpreter. De Martino pressed for the appointment of an Italian interpreter to the consulate as a means of teaching ʿAlawi the extent of his own insignificance.[46]

Fears that the Italian consulate in Cairo depended too heavily on ʿAlawi reflected anxiety over maintaining racial hierarchies. Both Salvago Raggi and De Martino expressed an interest in keeping ʿAlawi in a subordinate position. When De Martino intensified his criticism of ʿAlawi in the spring and summer of 1908, many of his complaints focused on the inability of the Ministry of Foreign Affairs to control the Egyptian interpreter, especially his interactions with ʿAbd al-Rahman ʿIlaysh and other Italian allies in Cairo. The issue came to a head in March 1908 when the Italian Mutual Aid Society based in Alexandria planned to take a group trip to Cairo to visit the mosque that ʿAbd al-Rahman ʿIlaysh had dedicated to Umberto I. A group of Italians who regularly took classes in Arabic at the mosque organized a day of events that was meant to highlight Italian-Egyptian cooperation for the visitors. De Martino objected to the plan based on a fear that the display of Italian-Egyptian cooperation would meet with anti-European protests in Cairo and exacerbate tensions with the Italian consulate's Anglo-Egyptian hosts. When De Martino pressured the contingent of Italians from Alexandria to cancel the event, the students in Cairo angrily confronted him, ʿAlawi leading the way. Though he managed to convince the Italian students to forego their planned visit, De Martino fumed at what he considered a blatant disregard for hierarchy on the part of the Egyptian interpreter, demonstrated by his involvement in the protest.[47] The incident led to the removal of ʿAlawi from his position as the lead interpreter at the Italian consulate. The Ministry of Foreign Affairs replaced him with Giuseppe Crolla, an Italian interpreter at the Italian consulate in Beirut.

While De Martino was eager to finally deflate ʿAlawi's position in Italian foreign affairs, he also worried that ʿAlawi had the potential to cause real damage to Italy's efforts to portray itself as a friendly European power in North Africa if he was dismissed too abruptly. Under De Martino's advice, the Egyptian interpreter remained in his position for the first month after Crolla's arrival to give the consulate time to reach out to ʿAlawi's closest contacts—especially ʿAbd al-Rahman ʿIlaysh—to try to mitigate any damage ʿAlawi might inflict on Italian relationships with Muslim notables in Cairo. De Martino understood the prospect of losing the support of the mosque ʿIlaysh had dedicated to Umberto I as the most dangerous potential effect of his replacement of ʿAlawi. Crolla, in his new position as the head interpreter, made an effort to establish a direct relationship with ʿIlaysh, but De Martino also enlisted the help of Ugo Lesona Bey, the Italian head of the Egyptian Dante Alighieri Society.[48] In a further attempt to prevent negative consequences, the Ministry of Foreign Affairs never fully fired ʿAlawi; rather, in June 1908 he was demoted to the position of "honorary interpreter." The arrival of Crolla precluded any possibility of further promotion of the Egyptian interpreter, and after a few months ʿAlawi ceased his active work at the Italian consulate. But the decision not to fire him meant that ʿAlawi continued to hold a vague, semiofficial position that allowed him to claim the permanent protection of the Italian government.[49]

ʿAlawi reacted to his demotion by mobilizing his Italian support network. Though Insabato was stationed in Istanbul after being pushed out of Cairo, to determine Ottoman attitudes toward a potential Italian invasion of the Libyan territories, he contributed to the effort to repair ʿAlawi's position at the Italian consulate through his remaining contacts in Cairo. A few weeks after ʿAlawi's demotion, Ivan Aguéli surprised De Martino with a visit to his office, at the request of Insabato. Demanding a reinstatement of the Egyptian interpreter, Aguéli warned of ʿAlawi's intention to turn ʿAbd al-Rahman ʿIlaysh against the Italian government.[50] When threats failed to secure a return to his former position, ʿAlawi attempted to prove his worth as an Italian intermediary by continuing to work on promoting a friendly relationship with Italy among Sanusi elites. In November 1908 ʿAlawi told Italian officials that he had received a favorable letter from Ahmad al-Sharif. Though dubious of the letter's authenticity, the Ministry of Foreign Affairs found the possibility that ʿAlawi had the ear of the "Grand Senusso" enticing enough to demand a full investigation.[51]

The idea that ʿAlawi might have attained some success in establishing direct contact with Ahmad al-Sharif, however, did little to persuade De Martino of the Egyptian interpreter's utility for the Italian consulate. ʿAlawi had already obtained a direct line to the "Grand Senusso" before his demotion in the summer of 1908. One of the roadblocks ʿAlawi needed to overcome was the possibility that Ottoman agents would intercept their communications and the Italian-Sanusi relationship (especially the illegal exchange of arms and ammunition) would be revealed to an international audience. In the spring of 1908 ʿAlawi devised a system whereby al-Sharif could simply send one of ʿAlawi's personal calling cards whenever he needed additional supplies, thus limiting Italian exposure.[52] It was ʿAlawi's success, in fact, that bothered De Martino. He worried that the Sanusi family might think the regular shipments of gifts sent via ʿAlawi came from the intermediary rather than from the Italian government. De Martino believed the Sanusiyya to be incapable of "entering into a relationship with a Christian power."[53] If the communications between Cairo and Sanusi *zawāyā* in Kufra were building a relationship, it was one that benefited ʿAlawi rather than the Italian government. De Martino's suspicions of ʿAlawi's intentions certainly reflected an anti-Arab bias, but they were also the result of a total dependence on ʿAlawi to interpret the Sanusi communications. As the intermediary *and* the interpreter, ʿAlawi composed the letters to Sanusi elites and explained the responses to Italian officials. When the communications involved cryptic messages meant to evade Ottoman interception, the Italian consulate was even less capable of evaluating the validity of ʿAlawi's interpretations. After the invasion of the Libyan coast in October 1911, Italian officials wanted to pursue various possible avenues for circumventing ʿAlawi in communications with the Sanusi elites, but the Ministry of Foreign Affairs (and after 1912, the Ministry of Colonies) remained warily open to the possibility of negotiating a relationship with Sanusi elites with the mediation of ʿAlawi and Insabato.

Expectations of Economic Benefits from the Italian Occupation

The repeated insistence by ʿAlawi and Insabato that the Italian occupation would meet with widespread approval among Sanusi elites contributed to a general expectation that expansion in North Africa would be easy and profitable. Dominant media coverage in the months leading up to the wars of occupation portrayed the Libyan territories as exceptionally fertile and ready for Italian settlement to transform them into an economic and agricultural engine of Italy. A range of nationalist figures contributed to the exaggerated sense of the economic potential of the Libyan territories. Perhaps most famously the poet Enrico Corradini, in his *L'ora di Tripoli* in 1911, misrepresented the agricultural possibilities of the Libyan territories based on a distorted understanding of the region's geography and an inflated estimation of the skills of Italian agriculturalists.[54] The majority of nationalist propaganda in favor of annexation of the Libyan territories focused on the economic potential for Italian settlement and trade in North Africa, but those discussions did not exclude the importance of dealing with the Sanusiyya as a regional force.

In *La nostra terra promessa: Lettere dalla Tripolitania (Marzo-Maggio 1911)*, for example, the journalist Giuseppe Piazza emphasized the potential for an economic relationship with the Sanusi elite in an analysis that added to inflated expectations about the Libyan territories as an agricultural settlement. Sent to Tripolitania by *La Tribuna*, a daily newspaper with a reputation for supporting Giolitti's liberal government, Piazza based his analysis of the economic situation in the Libyan territories on a brief visit through Tunisia and along the Libyan coastline. Piazza identified the key to unlocking the economic potential of the region as negotiating a relationship with the Sanusiyya. Referring to the leading religious figure of the Sanusiyya as a Bedouin "Pope-King," Piazza reflected an image of the Sanusiyya as an all-powerful religious authority that had transformed into an earthly potentate, one the Ottomans understood to be necessary for control in North Africa.[55]

Far from being manned by religious fanatics, Piazza's Sanusiyya seemed an organization focused on financial gain: "If the *zawāyā* are rich," he claimed, "the Grand Senusso is filthy rich."[56] Unlike Insabato's focus on religious traditionalism as a means of appealing to the Sanusi elite, Piazza recommended appealing to a mutual desire for profit. In what would become one of the major themes in Italian perceptions of the Sanusiyya, Piazza presented the Sufi *tarīqa* and its leadership as coldly calculating. Any opposition to the French presence in the region did not reflect the embers of a growing nationalism (the Sanusi family, Piazza was quick to point out, did not originate in the Libyan territories—*"nemo propheta in patria!"*).[57] Rather, the opposition of Sanusi elites to the French presence had more to do with the threat the French posed to Sanusi commercial interests. Piazza identified that desire to protect its economic standing as the best hope for Italy to secure this key ally in the Libyan territories.

Giuseppe Piazza and Enrico Insabato spoke to different audiences. Insabato communicated with officials in Giolitti's administration, while Piazza wrote for a wider public, funded by a liberal daily newspaper.[58] But they both emphasized the possibility of establishing an alliance with the Sanusiyya as a key to Italian expansion in North Africa by harnessing the Sufi *tarīqa*'s combined religious and political authority, albeit through different means. In their own ways, they both contributed to a sense of inevitable success for the imperial project in Rome in 1911 that brought together a wide range of interests in Italian politics and society. Giolitti's decision to invade the Libyan territories helped to secure support for his government from a growing nationalist movement, formalized in the establishment of the Associazione Nazionalista Italiana (ANI) in Florence in 1910. Piazza's small book contributed to a pro-imperial chorus of liberal and nationalist newspapers in the early months of 1911.

In nationalist celebrations of the plan to invade the Libyan territories, few voices of opposition to Italian imperialism rang through. A rare exception was Leone Caetani, the Duke of Sermoneta and Prince of Teano. A liberal member of the Italian Chamber of Deputies from 1909 to 1913 and a noted scholar of the history of Islam, Caetani made up part of a small group of liberal opponents to the occupation of Libya in the public sphere that included the historian Gaetano Salvemini and the economist Luigi Einaudi. They mounted their opposition based primarily on economic and scientific arguments that refuted the exaggerated reports in the Italian press of the agricultural and mercantile potential of the Libyan territories. In the pages of Salvamini's anti-imperial journal *L'Unità* or in debates on the floor of parliament, Caetani also laid claim to a unique perspective in the liberal opposition to the occupation of the Libyan territories, based on his reputation as a scholar of Islam and as someone with relatively extensive experience traveling in North Africa.[59] Caetani disputed favorable portrayals of the economic potential of the Libyan territories as nationalist fantasies founded on insufficient familiarity with the Arabic language, Islamic culture, and the geography of North Africa. Caetani voiced his most stringent opposition to the colonial project in a meeting of the Chamber of Deputies on June 7, 1911. In discrediting the idea of occupying the Libyan territories, Caetani was careful not to oppose the concept of Italian imperial expansion in general. Rather, he questioned the value of the Libyan territories as a suitable destination. Caetani ridiculed the characterizations of the Libyan territories in the nationalist press and among members of the Italian parliament as a fecund land of mineral and agricultural possibilities. Anyone who had traveled to the region, he remarked, would know the Libyan territories to be a poor desert region with little opportunity for development. He also lamented Italy's inability to seize Tunisia before the French, making it clear that he did not oppose the principle of Italian expansionism, just the target location.

In support of his opposition to the occupation, Caetani called on his orientalist expertise to formulate a reinterpretation of the Sanusiyya as a religious and political authority. In a presentation on the issue in the Chamber of Deputies, Caetani argued that the proposal to occupy the Libyan territories ran the risk of damaging Italy's reputation in the wider

Muslim world, a reputation he characterized as already injured by the lack of education in Arabic or Islamic culture among Italy's consulate officials (a frequent source of complaint from Caetani). More immediately, the occupation would pit Italy against populations that he counted as "among the most fanatical of the Muslim world," due to the presence of the Sanusiyya. Caetani referred to Ahmad al-Sharif, the recognized leader of the Sanusi *ṭarīqa*, as "the black Pope, the pontiff of the Muslim Vatican," and the head of an organization he chose to call an "ecclesiastical Masonry"—thus combining two diametrically opposed institutions: the church and the Freemasonry. Caetani attributed an empire on a massive scale to the Sanusiyya, one that could unite all inhabitants of North Africa, ready to "sacrifice their lives for an order from the pontiff."[60]

Caetani intended his characterization of the Sanusiyya as religious fanatics to add further weight to economic arguments against occupation; not only would Italians find little of economic value in the region, but they would also pit themselves against an intractable Islamic resistance. The interpretation of the Sanusiyya in Caetani's opposition to the occupation of the Libyan territories also reverberated in his publications on Islamic history from the same era, revealing a perspective entirely antithetical to Insabato's concept of calling on a shared sensibility of religious traditionalism to establish common ground in the Muslim Mediterranean. In 1911 Caetani published his *Studi di storia orientale*, which along with the ten-volume *Annali d'Islam* (published between 1905 and 1926) cemented his status as one of Italy's premier orientalists. In an introductory article to the first volume of *Studi di storia orientale*, entitled *Islam e Cristianesimo*, Caetani warned Italians against seeing Islam and Christianity as compatible. Islamic civilization, he argued, presented "the big, the only rival of Christian civilization." The clash, he argued, originated in the missionary objectives of two religions intent on expanding the faith:

> Islam and Christianity have this special point of contact, that both have a catholic, universal character. Islam, in fact, rises with gigantic force and with vitality so intense, that for over a century it seriously threatened the very existence of Christianity. No other religion can brag of so much, none other can inflict such disastrous and lasting damages on the faith of Christ, exactly where it reigned for centuries as recognized sovereign and in the very cradle where it was born.[61]

In a clash between the two evangelizing missions, Caetani argued, Christianity stood at a disadvantage, at least outside Europe. Wherever Islam had established roots, he claimed, there was little chance of conversion to Christianity, and without conversion there was little hope of friendly relations. While he broached neither the issue of Italian plans to occupy the Libyan territories nor the specific subject of the Sanusiyya in his piece, Caetani's warning refuted expectations of an easy victory through Italo-Sanusi alliances.

Caetani's public opposition to the occupation of the Libyan territories provoked remonstrations from the full gambit of nationalists and liberal democrats who advocated the expansionist program, but his comparison of Islam and Christianity—and the implication that Catholic evangelism would meet with disaster in the Muslim world—incited the particular disapproval of the Catholic press. In September 1912 *La Civiltá Cattolica*, a semiofficial newspaper of the Vatican, reviewed Caetani's *Studi di storia orientale*, accusing him of antinationalist admiration for the enemy that blinded him to the true strength and superiority of Christianity. The root of Caetani's objections, the article claimed, could be found in his anticlericalism.[62] In fact, Caetani was known as a secularist; he entered the Italian parliament as part of a secular "popular bloc" led by the mayor of Rome, Ernesto Nathan.[63] In a polarizing speech to the Chamber of Deputies on June 7, 1911, Caetani revealed an underlying factor in his objections to the plan to occupy the Libyan territories: his suspicion—not without solid foundation, as we will see—that the entire move in favor of imperial expansion was driven by the interests of the Banco di Roma, "which we all know is the bank in which the Vatican places all of its savings." Caetani objected to the idea that the interests of the Banco di Roma and the interests of the Italian nation might be the same. During a time when church officials boycotted Italian national holidays—as he was eager to point out—the connection violated Caetani's sense of Italian nationalism as a strictly secular identity.

Caetani's opposition to the occupation of the Libyan territories cost him his political career. Accused of anti-Italian sentiment, he was politically isolated after the occupation began, leading to the loss of his seat in parliament in the election of 1913.[64] Soon after he left public office, however, Caetani joined the imperial project by accepting an invitation to serve on a board of advisers for the Ministry of Colonies. Established by royal decree in December 1914, the Commissione per lo studio di questioni islamiche, or the Commission for the Study of Islamic Issues, convened under the leadership of Giacomo Agnesa, the general director of political affairs in the Ministry of Colonies. A variety of religious and legal scholars with expertise in the Italian colonies of North and East Africa served on the commission as consultants on legal and cultural issues facing the Italian administration. Designed to assist the Ministry of Colonies in understanding how best to nominate qadi and deal with *awqāf* properties in the Libyan territories, the commission, Agnesa hoped, would help the colonial administration navigate rocky political waters among a Muslim population.[65]

Caetani's involvement on the commission offers evidence of the popularity of the colonial project across a wide political spectrum in Italy; even one of the most vocal opponents of the invasion of the Libyan territories joined the program once the occupation began. Indeed, if we look carefully at Caetani's opposition to the initial invasion, he never posed an explicit aversion to imperialism in general. His opposition was based on a conviction that Italians were ill prepared for the challenges of colonial rule, especially in a region with a predominantly Muslim population. Given the right opportunity to educate Italian officials destined to perform functions in the Italian colonial rule, Caetani seemed optimistic that the imperial project could redeem Italy's standing in the wider world. All it required, Caetani argued in the *Annali d'Islam* of 1912, was that they "prove that we know how to rule our new subjects with tact, intelligence, and firmness, respecting their age-old customs of social life and their profound religious faith."[66]

Catholic Nationalism in Support of Empire

The criticism of Caetani's depiction of Islam in the pages of *La Civiltà Cattolica* reflected a heightened interest in the prospect of expansion into Libya among the Catholic press. Some of the earliest and most consistent enthusiasm for an aggressive foreign policy and imperial expansion in Italy stemmed from Catholic interest groups. Support for the occupation of the Libyan territories in publications linked to the Holy See reflected the involvement of Catholic financial interests in North Africa and a sense of shared goals for expanded missionary activities in an Italian occupation. In the long term, the enthusiasm for the imperial project in the Catholic press contributed to the development of a specifically Catholic sense of Italian nationalism and the integration of Catholics into political life in Rome after decades of tension.

Not surprisingly, much of the support the Catholic press expressed for an expanded involvement of the Italian state in the Libyan territories focused on the issue of Catholic missionaries. Publications linked to the Holy See complained frequently that Catholic missionaries faced difficult conditions in the Ottoman territories during the nineteenth century, but suspicions about the death of Giustino Pacini in Libya in March 1908 increased support for state intervention on behalf of church interests in North Africa. Pacini died in the coastal city of Derna, where he had been sent to build a new station on behalf of the Franciscan order of the Frati Minori di Lombardia. One of two semiofficial media outlets of the Holy See, *La Civiltá Cattolica*, joined a spectrum of popular Catholic newspapers that reacted to his death by launching accusations that Ottoman officials had ordered the murder of the Franciscan missionary. The paper argued that his murder was part of a pattern of persistent anti-Christian behavior in regions under Ottoman control that demanded a reaction from the Italian state.[67]

Though nationalist movements at the time would have denied it, the Catholic press actually anticipated a burgeoning nationalist press in expressing public support for expanding the Italian presence in North Africa.[68] With public sympathy for the plight of Catholic missions at its height, Catholic publications saw the possible murder of the Italian missionary as an opportunity to extol the benefits of a Catholic form of Italian national identity in facilitating imperial expansion. In their outcry, these publications often expressed an expectation that projecting a shared interest in protecting religious traditionalism would secure the support of local populations (and at the same time would promote cooperation between Catholics and liberals against the influences of socialism and Freemasonry).[69] In contrast to Insabato's understanding of Sufism as a conservative religious force and a potential ally in Italian expansion, however, church interests focused on the potential to align with urban elites against rising secularism in Istanbul, especially following the rise to power of the Committee of Union and Progress (CUP) in 1908. Having developed ties with the Qaramanli and Muntasir families—prominent merchants and political elites who complained of a loss of influence under the CUP—the director of the Banco di Roma in Tripoli reported widespread support for an Italian occupation. He argued that Catholic Italy would be welcomed as protection for elites in the Ottoman world from the modernizing reforms of the new political order in Istanbul.[70] *La Civiltá Cattolica* went further in likening opposition to the CUP in Ottoman territories to

the beleaguered church in the era of liberal Italian state building immediately after Italian unification. The comparison drew political parallels
across the Mediterranean and suggested that any failure to foreground the
Catholic Church in nationalist expansion would weaken Italy's position.
"The lack of religion is not in fashion in the Orient," *La Civiltá Cattolica*
claimed, "and they know well of the burning of the churches and of those
who scoff [at] the clergy in Italy, [that] their sacrilege dissolves the patria at
its frontiers and defames it abroad, stopping its impulses and initiatives."[71]

The Catholic press also connected opposition to the CUP to opposition
to the influence of Freemasonry, a cause that often galvanized conservative popular opinion in Italy. In January 1911, for example, the Catholic
daily of Turin, *Il Momento*, claimed to have uncovered a plot involving
members of the CUP and officials in the Italian government who agreed
to refrain from challenging Ottoman sovereignty in North Africa out of
loyalty to their mutual ties to Freemason lodges. The editors of *La Civiltà
Cattolica* cited the story as evidence of a confluence of international and
national interests pitted against increased Italian presence in Ottoman territories.[72] The influential Catholic daily *Corriere d'Italia* also sounded the
alarm in September 1911, depicting an international meeting of Masonic
lodges in Rome as a sign of attempts to prevent the Italian occupation.
Corriere d'Italia expected the work of missionaries to provide an effective
defense against Freemason activity. Popular support for the Catholic mission in Libya was meant to discredit attempts by the Freemasons to "create
a public opinion opposed to and adverse to any of our most just and civilized influence in the countries subject to and tyrannized by the crescent
moon."[73]

The identification of a shared interest in protecting religious traditionalism against the influence of Freemasonry did not lead the Catholic press
to support the "pro-Islamic" approach of Enrico Insabato; the Catholic press
had no interest in projecting an image of Italy as the protector of Islam.
Even the mild declaration of General Caneva in the initial occupation—
promising to defend Islamic sensibilities in the Libyan territories and the
right to continue Muslim traditions and practices under Italian rule—
provoked an immediate response from the Catholic press. An article in *La
Civiltá Cattolica* criticized Caneva's attempt to appease the religious sensibilities of the local population as a false representation of Italian culture
and a denial of Italian religious identity. "The Italian authorities tried, and
please excuse the term, to 'muslimize' themselves, using phrases from
the Qurʿan and appropriating Muslim religious sentiments that in their

mouths are a fiction and an ugly and misleading political action."[74] If state officials hoped to appeal to the religious sensibilities of a predominantly Muslim population, the editors of *La Civiltá Cattolica* implied, they would do better to foreground Catholicism in the process of national expansion as an authentic expression of Italian religious identity.

Many politicians in Rome were willing and even eager to embrace some Catholic components of the expansionist enterprise. The occupation promised to integrate Catholic interests into national politics to the benefit of the liberal ruling party in a new era of mass politics. The general election of 1913 seemed to confirm their expectations. The popularity of the expansionist project drove Catholic voters to the polls and contributed to the success of the Gentiloni Pact—the formation of a liberal and Catholic bloc united against a socialist party that was already weakened by its divided reactions to the imperial project.

The increase in Catholic participation in national politics supporting the invasion of the Libyan territories represented a significant shift after decades of public disputes between the Catholic Church and state officials in Rome. The nationalization of a large portion of papal lands in 1860 and the dismantling of the Papal States in 1871 had pitted the church against Italian national unification. Starting with Pope Pius IX's encyclical *Syllabus Errorum* in 1864, church officials declared Italian nationalism anathema to Catholic interests and recommended against Catholic participation in national elections. The 1868 *Non Expedit* turned the recommendation into a prohibition against voting in Italian national elections that lasted until Pope Benedict XV declared an end to the ban in the election of 1919.[75]

The inflammatory rhetoric of Catholic intransigency masked a gradual incorporation of moderate Catholics into national politics. Catholic financial interests were already deeply intertwined with the fortunes of the Italian state. The loss of revenue from papal lands confiscated during the wars of unification found church officials looking for lucrative investment opportunities. As Rome pursued nation-building policies, investments in state infrastructure and in those foreign markets where Italian investments were particularly welcomed offered an easy solution.[76] Church finances largely funded Rome's building boom in the 1870s and early 1880s and became a central part of an expanding banking system through the founding of the Banco di Roma in 1884, which began with a sizable investment from the coffers of the Holy See.[77] Following the crash of the building boom in Rome in 1887, the church began to look for investment opportunities in North Africa. In 1905 the Banco di Roma opened a new branch in Alexandria with papal funds. The Banco di Roma subsequently began investing in shipping lines, agricultural projects, and commercial enterprises on the Libyan coast with the explicit support of the Italian Ministry of Foreign Affairs.[78] By the beginning of the Italian invasion in 1911, the investments of the Holy See were so deeply intertwined with the imperial project that they influenced diplomatic language; John Pollard has noted that the terms of the ultimatum the Italian state issued to the Ottoman Empire upon the invasion of Tripoli and Benghazi implied that Italy had initiated the military action at least in part to defend the interests of the Banco di Roma.[79]

Since unification, church and state interests had often aligned on issues of expansion abroad. This convergence of interests was especially evident in periods when aggressive military campaigns fell out of favor (e.g., after the losses in Dogali and Adwa) and Italian imperialists focused instead on emigration as a less risky form of demographic imperialism. At the end of the nineteenth century, for example, Italian political leaders of the Crispi administration had enlisted the help of Catholic missionary networks to maintain a sense of Italian identity among emigrant communities around the world.[80] Missionary groups also collaborated in Crispi's more aggressive expansionist programs in East Africa, though the relationships between colonial officials overseeing the tentative extension of Italian influence and the missionaries often depended more on the political and religious persuasions of the particular individuals working in the region than on an overarching plan dictated from Rome.

Despite these realms of cooperation, the tensions of unification remained close to the surface in church-state relations. In the early years of Italian expansion abroad, conflicts over Catholic involvement in national politics reverberated in the personal attitudes of officials on a local level. When Crispi declared Eritrea an Italian colony in 1890, he appointed Oreste Baratieri—known for advocating a favorable attitude toward the church—to be its first military governor. Baratieri promoted the involvement of Catholic missionaries in the Italian colonial project throughout his tenure. It helped that he found a willing partner in that endeavor in Geremia Bonomelli, a moderate bishop who had founded the Associazione nazionale per soccorrere i missioni cattolici italiani (National Association to Aid Italian Catholic Missions) in Florence in 1886. Bonomelli's association embraced a nationalist message. Practically speaking, he sought to end the reliance of Italian missionaries on subsidies from France, which had sustained Catholic missionary activity for much of the nineteenth century.[81] In 1890 the Catholic missions in Eritrea fell under the jurisdiction of the Vicariate of the French Lazzarists in Ethiopia, and Baratieri and Bonomelli worked together to remove French control as a means of solidifying Italian claims to the region. Citing concerns that the disparity in language between the missions and state officials would confuse the native populations, Baratieri enlisted Bonomelli's assistance to request that the Holy See transfer the mission in Eritrea to Italian control. Initially, Propaganda Fide refused out of deference to the Missionary Institution of Lyon, but in 1894 the Holy See finally placed the missionaries in Eritrea under the control of Italian Capuchins.[82] Having achieved their initial goal of nationalizing the Catholic mission, Baratieri and Bonomelli organized a Catholic settlement program to bring Italian agriculturalists to Eritrea in 1895. Their project competed directly with a similar parliamentary project under the direction of the conservative baron Leopoldo Franchetti.[83] Both projects ultimately failed after the defeat at Adwa in 1896 led to the withdrawal of Italian troops and settlements, but the state-church cooperation established a blueprint of sorts for future Catholic involvement in Italian imperial expansion.

The collaboration between Baratieri and Bonomelli in Eritrea stemmed in part from their dedication to church-state reconciliation in national politics through a mutual interest in expansion abroad. In 1889 the journalist Filippo Tolli founded the Societá antischiavista d'Italia (The Italian Anti-Slavery Society) in Rome and similarly began to advocate for the establishment of Italian missions in East Africa as a means of promoting the unification of church and state interests in Rome while also defending the region against the perceived threats of the slave trade and Muslim expansion.[84] Lucia Ceci has pointed to the language of the vice secretary of the Societá antischiavista d'Italia, Gennaro Angelini, on the occasion of its first meeting in 1892 as speaking to hopes for the potential of colonial expansion to unify church and state interests:

> Convinced that colonial expansion in Africa will be providential for opening the black continent to the Christian civilization and to rescue it from the predominant and fatal Islamic influence, frankly I declare myself happy that for Italy as well, more faithful for the most part to the old religion, there has been reserved a part of this glorious crusade against barbarity offering thus to our valorous

Missionaries a most extensive field of action for the benefit of the civilization of the Patria.[85]

Given the tension of the Roman question in national politics, Angelini's support for Italian state expansion represented a shift in perspective, albeit on a limited and individual basis. It was an opening for increased cooperation based on an idea of Italy projecting a Catholic identity in colonial expansion overseas. Based on his recommendations, Propaganda Fide established an Italian mission in Benadir in 1904, with the intention of supporting the expansion of Italian communities along the coast of Italian Somaliland.

Unlike the friendly collaboration between Baratieri and Bonomelli in Eritrea, however, Angelini's project faced stiff opposition in Italian Somalia on the part of the commissioner general, Luigi Mercatelli. Mercatelli blocked the entry of the man meant to organize the mission, Father Leandro, and convinced the minister of foreign affairs that the presence of a Catholic mission in the colony would inflame anti-Italian sentiment by provoking Islamic fanaticism. The subsequent standoff between Mercatelli and Leandro inspired bitter disputes in ministerial communications, the popular press, and parliament over the relationship between colonial expansion and missionary activities. When Father Leandro moved his mission to just over the border of British Somaliland, critics pointed to the absence of an Islamic backlash as a sign that Mercatelli's obstruction was driven by the anticlericalism of a known Freemason.[86] In Rome, political opponents seized on the events to denounce Mercatelli and, by extension, a secular liberal approach to Italian colonial administration. The introduction of a new minister of foreign affairs, Antonino Di San Giuliano, in December 1905 marked a general shift in attitude among central officials in Rome in favor of using missionaries for the benefit of Italy's imperialist ambitions, although the relationship between Italian missionary activity and colonial expansion would never be easy.[87]

Missionaries and Nationalism in the Libyan Territories

The personal attitudes of the church and state officials involved in the annexation of the Libyan territories facilitated cooperation, at least at the beginning of the colonial occupation. Giolitti's foreign minister, Tomasso Tittoni, learned from the public debacle caused by Mercatelli's conflicts with Father Leandro in Benadir. This time around, Tittoni advocated state support of Catholic missions in the Libyan territories as a reliable and relatively inexpensive source of education and health care. In the Libyan territories, that meant increased state support for the mission of the Frati Minori di Lombardia. Present in the region since the mid-seventeenth century, the mission could call on its long history in the region as evidence of its utility in emphasizing a Catholic identity in Italian expansionism. The mission possessed the further advantage of having secured a monopoly on missionary activity in the region after establishing its first school in Tripoli in 1810. Like other Catholic missions, the Frati Minori received political protection and financial subsidies from France during this period of its monopoly in the nineteenth century. With French funding, the Frati Minori opened a girls' school in Tripoli and a second boys' school in Benghazi. The formation of a new government in France in 1899 under the republican Pierre Waldeck-Rousseau put an end to France's official protection of Catholic missionaries. His government severed ties between church and state, expelled religious orders from France, and severely curtailed subsidies to Catholic missionaries abroad.[88]

The repeal of French political and economic support at the turn of the century left the Italian Franciscans in Tripolitania and Cyrenaica in search of new patrons for both financial and diplomatic assistance, and the mission turned to Italy for support. At the beginning of 1901 the apostolic prefect of Tripoli, Giuseppe Bevilacqua, complained of lack of funds in his annual report to the Holy See. He also complained of continuous clashes with Ottoman officials. The point of contention centered on the prefect's request for permits from the Ottoman government for the mission to buy land and construct a new church in al-Khums, a city about one hundred kilometers southeast of Tripoli.[89] Bevilacqua blamed Ottoman obstruction for delaying the process by three years, and once it had received permission, the withdrawal of French funding left the mission without the means to complete the project. In 1904 the prefect reported a dire financial situation.[90] Bevilacqua pursued an aggressive tactic of nationalizing the mission and promoting increased Italian presence in the region. In November 1905 he sent requests to the consulate in Tripoli asking for Italian protection of the mission. When the mission renounced French backing in 1908, the minister of foreign affairs agreed to grant Italian protection and promised to pay the Franciscan mission an annual sum of 12,000 lire in exchange for an increased emphasis on teaching the Italian language in missionary schools and promoting a positive image of Italy through the provision of medical services.[91]

With state funding secured, the Franciscan mission proved eager to show its commitment to state objectives in the region, even when that meant putting aside the core interest of spreading the faith. The Frati Minori di Lombardia, after all, faced competition for influence among North Africa's small—but potentially growing—Catholic population. As part of a strategy for securing the Franciscan mission's position in the Libyan territories, a new prefect, Buonaventura Rossetti, appointed in 1907, assured officials in Rome that the Frati Minori would respect the difficulties the Italian administration faced in governing a Muslim population by lowering the mission's profile. In exchange for a promise to abstain from active proselytizing, at least in the initial phases of the Italian occupation, Rossetti secured state support with an increase in Italian funding and a monopoly over the region's schools.[92] This agreement did not introduce a new constraint on the activities of the mission; since its establishment in the seventeenth century, Ottoman authorities had tolerated the presence of the mission based on the understanding that the Franciscans would restrict their work to ministering among the small European population and communities of former slaves.[93] Though the restrictions on proselytizing were not new, they did signal recognition that a change in state authority from Ottoman to Italian would not correspond to a shift in policy toward the mission, at least not immediately.

The restrictions on missionary activities did little to dampen the enthusiasm of missionary leadership for the idea of Italian expansion in the Libyan territories. It was an attitude that threatened to alienate non-Italian elements of the mission's small community of believers, especially the Maltese fishers and their families who made up the majority of the mission's congregation.[94] Bitter disputes broke out within the Catholic community over language, both in terms of the dominant language of instruction in the mission schools and the languages available for confession. Complaints over the use of Italian as a language of instruction reflected longer held tensions over the Franciscans' control of the Catholic mission in the Libyan territories. The Franciscans established Italian as the primary language of instruction when they founded their first schools, but for much of the nineteenth century the financial support of the French government and pressure from French consular agents in the region challenged that principle.[95] Complicating matters, the Franciscan mission signed a contract in 1882 with the Frères

Maristes, a French lay order dedicated to educating young Catholics, that brought them to North Africa as the primary instructors and managers of the mission's schools. Turning to the French order was fitting in the context of bitter disputes over the Italian wars of unification, and it reflected the dominance of the French in Catholic missionaries around the world in the late nineteenth century. With the arrival of the Fréres Maristes, instruction in the schools was conducted primarily in French, much to the delight of Maltese inhabitants of the region. Conflicts over the primary language of instruction, however, would reemerge as the Frati Minori embraced an Italian identity in the years leading up to the Italian occupation.[96]

When Giuseppe Bevilacqua replaced Maltese confessionals with Italian and replaced French language education in the mission schools with Italian language education in 1906–1907, a new round of debates was sparked over language and national identity in the Franciscan mission.[97] Unhappy with these signs that the mission had embraced an Italian national identity, the Maltese community lodged formal complaints with the Holy See. Bevilacqua took a long view in response, assuring his superiors in Rome that the issue would resolve itself naturally with time as the Maltese children came of age in an era of Italian dominance—and came to think of themselves increasingly as Italians. The prefect called the desire of the Maltese community to maintain services in their language "pure fanaticism" because, he claimed, the most common language in the region after Arabic was Italian. "If the mission has Maltese priests," he added, "it is just to satisfy these fanatics and maintain peace in the Christian colonies."[98]

Complaints from the Maltese community against the prefect from the summer of 1904 through 1906 contributed to a measure of hesitation on the part of the Italian Ministry of Foreign Affairs to provide state funding to the Franciscan mission as it tried to minimize local opposition to expanding Italian influence in North Africa; if the ministry could not count on a population of Maltese Catholics to support the eventual annexation, surely there would be little hope of gaining support among the region's Muslim inhabitants. The upheaval in the Catholic community was instrumental in the decision to replace Bevilacqua with the new apostolic prefect, Bonaventura Rossetti, in the summer of 1907. The new appointment was timed to coincide with the extension of official Italian protection over the mission, with the hope that the change of leadership would ease tensions in the Catholic community.[99]

Any reprieve Rossetti's arrival might have secured soured when he began to edge the Fréres Maristes out of the mission's schools.[100] Initially, Rossetti called for a mix of teachers from the Frati Minori and the Fréres Maristes to gradually introduce more Italian instructors into the system, but in 1909 the French order accelerated the process by volunteering to leave the colonies rather than accept a reduction of its control over the mission schools.[101] The changes provoked further protests from the Maltese community; the mission's students even declared a general strike against the schools. In a failed attempt to appease the Maltese, Propaganda Fide issued new regulations for the mission, including a clause warning against overnationalization of the mission's work. The regulations admonished the missionaries to "avoid every discourse of nationality and do not get involved in things that are even broadly political; but instead concern yourself with the politics of Jesus Christ . . . looking on those near you as brothers no matter what nationality they belong to."[102] The new regulations also called for new missionaries to learn both Maltese and Arabic to make themselves useful to the Maltese Catholics in the colonies. Despite these measures, the Maltese attempted to break away from the Italian mission by signing a petition in 1909 asking for the archbishop of Malta to fund the construction of an exclusively Maltese church.[103] When the Holy See sent a representative to Tripoli to consider the possibility, he supported the claims of the Maltese community. In his report the representative emphasized the official status of the Maltese as British subjects in an Ottoman territory, as a sign of the limits to Italian claims over the region or over the Catholic mission: "The Church is not *Italian, much less the land*," he wrote. Then he argued, "If Propaganda really wants to save its sons, it should give [the mission] to the Maltese Franciscan Province."[104]

This warning corresponded with an effort among some in the Catholic mission and in the central offices of Propaganda Fide to distance the missionary work of the church from the Italian colonial project. There was an underlying tension between the objectives of the mission and the often secular identity of state programs during the occupation. The arrival of the occupying forces in the fall of 1911 put an end to the debates over the national identity of the mission and the dominance of Italian as the language of instruction in its schools as the mission sought to serve a new influx of Italian soldiers and settlers. But the occupation introduced a new set of challenges. For the missionaries, the biggest threat the Italian administration posed was the prospect of establishing a competing state-run system of education that could diminish Catholic influence and detract from the mission's services. As early as 1910, Rossetti proposed a solution whereby the mission schools would be responsible for elementary education while the state schools would take the lead in education after the sixth grade.[105] State officials advocated maintaining both types of schools to allow a choice between the two parallel systems, but in 1911 Rossetti complained that the Italian consulate had pressured Italian families to attend the state schools. Competition for students in the classrooms revealed what Rossetti characterized as a pervasive obstruction of the Catholic mission, including efforts to foment the long-standing discord among the Maltese community in order to attract Maltese students to state schools.[106]

After having spent considerable time and effort linking the Franciscan mission to an expansion of the Italian presence in the region, the prefect was determined to maintain dominance of the mission in an era of Italian state control that promised to bring an increase in the Catholic community.[107] Even the introduction of Catholic chaplains as part of the occupying forces seemed a potential threat to the mission's control over Catholicism in the Libyan territories.[108] In official correspondence, Rossetti complained about the quality of some of the chaplains, claiming that many of them seemed to have gone to Libya "more to take a pleasure jaunt than to lend their spiritual work for the benefit of our soldiers." Lacking any control over the selection of military chaplains, Rossetti required them to present themselves to the mission upon arrival in the region as recognition of the Franciscans' authority among Catholics in the Libyan territories.[109] Rossetti's determination to preserve the position of the Frati Minori di Lombardia reflected the sizable increase in the Catholic community under the Italian occupation. According to the mission's data, the number of Catholics jumped from four thousand in November 1911 to fifteen thousand in December 1912.[110] The increase in the size of the Catholic community promised to bring increased funding and a higher profile to the mission. The benefits were not immediate, however. The mission and its properties incurred extensive damages during the initial wars of occupation. The mission's school in Benghazi suffered in particular. By March 1912, however, the immediate danger to missionary properties in the coastal region seemed to have quieted, and Rossetti asked the Holy See for permission to travel to Rome to secure permits and funding from both church and military coffers to build new missionary stations in Ṭubruq, Misrata, and Zlitan to prepare for serving military personnel and the expected increase in Italian settlers.[111] The prefect's excitement over the mission's potential for expansion and his enthusiasm for state programs of colonization infused his official correspondence as he formulated programs in line with expectations for the Libyan territories to become a fully Italian space with an influx of Italian settlers.[112]

Conclusion

Italian imperialists considered pursuing a power-sharing relationship with Sanusi elites in the years leading up to the occupation of the Libyan coast in 1911 through a process of reimagining what sort of religious and political authority the Sanusiyya represented. They characterized the Sanusiyya variously as a rational organization driven by economic and strategic interests or a religious force involved in a civilizing mission among the Bedouin tribes of North Africa. But the concept also involved debates over the role of religion in Italian expansion in overseas colonies. Contested understandings of the relationship between the Catholic Church and the Italian government shaped debates over the attitudes of Sanusi elites toward Christian powers. In the enthusiasm over the prospects of Italian colonialism in the years leading up to the invasion of the Libyan territories, the possibilities of state and church collaboration in expanding the Italian presence overseas seemed enticing. But in the aftermath of the wars of occupation, the prospect of governing a Muslim population took precedence over an effort to involve Catholic interests in overseas expansion for the newly formed Ministry of Colonies. The establishment of a colonial administration—and the failure of Insabato and ʿAlawi to procure a real accord with Ahmad al-Sharif—introduced a sense of urgency in efforts to forge a relationship with the Sanusi family in the interests of stability. It was an imperative that would lead to an effort to redefine the Sanusi *ṭarīqa* through a shift in leadership from al-Sharif to his more amenable cousin, Idris al-Sanusi, as we will see in chapter 3. The focus on security through an alliance would cause the relationship between the colonial administration and the Franciscan mission to sour in the years following the initial occupation, as Italian colonial officials made an effort to reassure the Muslim population of their newly acquired territories that the Italian presence would not lead to an effort at mass conversion.

Attempts to lessen the appearance of Italian expansion as a Catholic mission must have been of small consolation to the populations of Cyrenaica. Famine, mass deportations, and the military rule of Italian occupying forces surely posed a greater threat than the activities of nationalist missionaries. But public denunciations of the Italian occupation often accused Italy of an attack on Islam; Ahmad al-Sharif, for example, would appeal to solidarity with urban notables in Benghazi by arguing that the Italian occupation was an attempt to "annihilate Islam." For Ferdinando Martini, the minister of colonies during World War I, the correct response was to aggressively pursue a relationship with al-Sharif. His objective was to reach a point of relative stability, but a relationship with al-Sharif would carry with it the added bonus of demonstrating Italian exceptionalism in the Muslim world. Martini called for an effort to distinguish an Italian approach to colonial rule from that of the British. "The English treat their Muslim subjects rudely and bully them," Martini claimed. A friendly relationship with Ahmad al-Sharif would prove the superiority of an Italian approach to colonial rule.[113]

3

Occupation, War, and the Transformation of the Sanusiyya

IN JANUARY 1912, three months after the initial Italian invasion of the Libyan coast, a group of Italian soldiers made a public display of baptizing a ten-year-old girl in Tripoli. Orphaned during the Italian occupation, the young girl was adopted by what the newspaper *La Tribuna* described as "a group of officers." They conducted the baptism at a provisional altar in the open air of a market; the girl, according to the newspaper, acted "affectionately" toward her new spiritual protectors.[1] News of the event provoked immediate condemnation from the Italian consulate in Cairo, which complained that with the baptism, "we risk making those few Muslims who do not attribute a religious character to our war doubt us."[2] The Ministry of Foreign Affairs responded to the complaint with hurried assurances that the incident violated military policy, the officers in question would be punished, and mass conversions would not become a tactic of warfare under the occupation. Soldiers had "strict instructions not to do anything that might offend religious sentiment."[3]

The public baptism rankled with the Italian diplomatic officials who had been working toward an agreement with Sanusi elites in the years leading up to the invasion of Libya. This was not a story that would endear Italian rule to the region's Muslim inhabitants. The immediate punishment of the soldiers responsible for the baptism set the tone for directives from Rome during the first decade of the occupation. In administrative circles, any idea of projecting a Catholic identity in the occupation was muted during this first decade. The story of the baptism, however, shows an undercurrent of tension between a popular idea of Italian expansion as a Catholic civilizing mission on the one hand and the liberal dictates of expressing respect for local religious customs on the other. Relations with the Catholic mission grew uneasy as military and civil officials of the colonial administration focused on molding an image of Italy as particularly friendly to Islam in general and to the Sanusiyya in particular.

Their efforts bore fruit when colonial officials finally realized their ambition to establish a power-sharing relationship with Sanusi elites during World War I. Despite the formal renunciation of sovereignty over the Libyan territories by the Ottoman sultan in 1912, the wars of Italian occupation bled seamlessly into the conflicts of World War I in the Libyan interior. Italian forces faced continuous armed opposition of combined Sanusi and Ottoman forces. Years of warfare, disruption to agriculture, and restricted access to trade routes constrained both the Italian military capability in Libya and the tenacity of anti-Italian forces until, in 1917, the two sides were able to agree on an armistice. The negotiations, however, were not with Ahmad al-Sharif, despite the fact that he was recognized as the "Grand Sanuso" (al-Sanuso al-Kabīr); the process of negotiating an alliance with the Sanusiyya involved a restructuring of the Sufi *ṭarīqa* and a transfer of power to al-Sharif's younger cousin, Idris al-Sanusi. The new arrangement transformed the Sanusiyya from a source of resistance into an extension of Italian state control. But after negotiating a treaty with Idris, some Italian officials began to recognize the inherent instability of a power-sharing relationship that seemed to require them to empower Sanusi elites at the expense of Italian claims to sovereignty.

Reassessments of the Sanusiyya

For Italian occupying forces, the attitude of Ahmad al-Sharif and the Sanusiyya remained hazy in the early months of the invasion.[4] The uncertainty bred a new round of competition to claim the ability to communicate with the Sanusi family on behalf of the Italian state. Enrico Insabato reemerged along with Muhammad ʿAli ʿAlawi as confident proponents of Italo-Sanusi collaboration.[5] Sent back to Cairo in the spring of 1910, Insabato journeyed through Cyrenaica and Tripolitania in 1911 to gather information. During his trip Insabato reported on evidence of "the immense influence of Mohammed Ali Elui [*sic*] among Muslims" in Tripoli.[6] In October 1911 ʿAlawi claimed to have received a series of letters from al-Sharif promising Sanusi neutrality, at the very least, in the upcoming Italo-Turkish War over the Libyan territories in exchange for the promise of a healthy shipment of arms. He presented the most compelling evidence of a favorable attitude in messages passed along to various shaykhs in charge of Sanusi *zawāyā*, who were instructed not to oppose the Italian occupation. Insabato passed along the following quote from Ahmad al-Sharif in one such message: "If the Italians occupy Tripoli and take it from the Sultan, we will not impede or hinder them, because we believe that their friendship is the most appropriate for Muslims: they will not attack our *zawāyā* because they are Christians and they have a Holy Book."[7] Requests from Sanusi family members for medical supplies, arms, and ammunition suggested a return to the mutually beneficial relationship established through ʿAlawi's mediation prior to 1908. In light of these messages, Insabato began to imagine the possibility of flying an Italian flag in Sanusi oases of the Libyan interior, albeit a flag altered to include the insignia of the Star of Italy in place of the usual cross on the middle white section of the *tricolore*.[8]

Insabato and ʿAlawi's return to diplomatic initiatives to secure an alliance with Ahmad al-Sharif stirred up the previous antagonism with Giacomo De Martino and the Italian consulate in Cairo. Ever a critic of ʿAlawi, De Martino preferred sending gifts (especially gifts of arms) to Sanusi elites through the Italian consulate of Benghazi; if they excluded the talkative Egyptian from the plan, De Martino suggested, British and Ottoman officials would be less likely to learn about their initiatives.[9] Insabato's return to Cairo did invoke the ire of Anglo-Egyptian officials, particularly when he fired up the dormant printing presses of his pro-Italian publication, *Il Convito/al-Nadi*, to publish a pamphlet (poorly written in Arabic) that he meant to use as pro-Italian propaganda throughout the Arab Muslim world. Insabato intended to distribute some 100 copies of the rather long treatise, in which he extolled Italian intentions to promote Islamic practices and correct supposed shortcomings in Ottoman efforts to maintain religious properties, to Muslim shaykhs.[10] Accusing Insabato of violating censorship laws (due to his criticism of the sultan as the Muslim caliph), Anglo-Egyptian authorities seized the pamphlets. The Italian consulate sought to distance itself from Insabato yet again, refusing to defend his right to publish the pro-Italian tract due to his supposed leanings toward anarchism.[11]

ʿAlawi also faced increased hostility in Cairo because of his involvement in promoting Italian expansion during the Italo-Turkish War. In February 1912 a series of articles in Egyptian newspapers denounced both ʿAlawi and ʿAbd al-Rahman ʿIlaysh as pro-Italian agitators against the Ottoman sultan. Insabato stressed the importance of protecting both of them from Egyptian hostility to prevent them from turning to other European powers for protection, especially France.[12] Students in the *ruwaq* at al-Azhar University, managed by ʿAlawi, also faced increased hostility. In January 1912, for example, one student from Tripolitania accused another student from Morocco of robbing him and then complained of officials at the university showing favoritism toward the Moroccan because the Tripolitanian was known to accept subsidies from ʿAlawi and Insabato—thus demonstrating a pro-Italian attitude.[13]

The disruptive effects of the men's activities, however, did not lead to a second expulsion of Insabato from Cairo, at least not immediately. The context of the Italo-Turkish War made the Italian consulate in Cairo more receptive to potential avenues to a negotiated peace in the Libyan territories. Of course the Ministry of Foreign Affairs continued to look for ways to circumvent ʿAlawi in communicating with the Sanusi family. Giacomo De Martino was particularly keen to foster a relationship through the mediation of either Prince Fuʿad—who vehemently refused to have anything to do with Insabato or ʿAlawi—or Khedive Abbas II.[14] While khedival involvement in the Italo-Sanusi relationship would become important during World War I, however, these attempts failed to achieve any significant gains in attracting the support of Ahmad al-Sharif.

Insabato and ʿAlawi claimed to have received a letter from the Sanusi leader in February 1912 confirming his support for the Italian occupation. Additional letters from Ahmad al-Sharif's brother, Mohammed al-Abed al-Sanusi, soon followed, full of praise for ʿAlawi and Insabato and declaring his intention to hang a photograph of the Italian king in the Sanusi *zawāyā*. Later that year Insabato arranged a celebratory trip of four Sanusi shaykhs to Rome, designed as a full display of Italian influence in Muslim North Africa in a new era of imperial expansion.[15]

However, when news reached Italian agents that Ahmad al-Sharif had moved a contingent of Sanusi troops to the oases of Jaghbub to join Ottoman forces in August 1912, it raised new doubts about Sanusi attitudes toward the Italian occupation.[16] Insabato and ʿAlawi faced a fierce backlash in Cairo and Italy. Accused of having provided the Italian government with fake letters from al-Sharif, ʿAlawi was dismissed entirely as an intermediary. Insabato faced accusations from the newspaper *Il Secolo* of having passed off "regular" Arabs as "phony" Sanusi leaders during the organized trip to Rome in 1912. The newspaper threatened legal action and called on ʿAlawi to travel to Rome to testify on his behalf.[17] To distance him from the Libyan territories, the Ministry of Foreign Affairs stationed Insabato in Istanbul starting in 1914 to monitor events in the city during World War I; he never held an official position in the Italian administration in Libya.[18] But Insabato would remain a marginal force in the occupation of the Libyan territories. On occasion, the Ministry of Colonies continued to contact him in Istanbul (albeit reluctantly) to seek his advice about communicating with the Sanusiyya.

Once Insabato's claims to have secured the neutrality—if not the alliance—of Ahmad al-Sharif were proven false, speculation flourished among Italian, French, British, and Ottoman agents about al-Sharif and his position in relationship to the interimperial rivals. The debate was carried on in the realm of an odd assortment of military reports, expert studies, and interviews with local informants. In these discussions the likelihood of an alliance between the Sanusiyya and any centralized state power was called into question, but so too was the actual extent of the religious and political authority of al-Sharif. These analyses of Sanusi authority expressed a common paradox in the power-sharing relationships of the era of high imperialism; it was feared that the act of recognizing al-Sharif as a political figure would exaggerate the importance of the Sanusiyya at the expense of state authority. Despite that fear, European authorities tried time and again to negotiate an understanding with al-Sharif in the hope of harnessing his influence for Italian objectives. Even when plans were introduced that were meant to circumvent his authority, such as by dealing directly with a variety of Sanusi shaykhs, the ultimate goal remained an alliance with al-Sharif.

Early in the initial invasion, officers from the Political Office of the Occupying Forces generated official reports meant to clarify the general political situation in the Libyan territories and the prospects for negotiating with Ahmad al-Sharif in particular. In contrast to Insabato's characterization of the Sanusiyya as a natural ally of an Italian civilizing mission, military accounts portrayed the Sufi *ṭarīqa* as a parasitic organization, suggesting that Sanusi elites used their religious authority among Bedouin tribes primarily for personal financial gain. Though it did not deny the utility of an initial alliance with al-Sharif to promote stability, the military command advocated a gradual process of weakening Sanusi authority and replacing it with a strong Italian state presence. This perspective on the Sanusiyya reflected heightened contact with a greater variety of individuals from the region during the initial occupation, including people outside of a Sanusi sphere of influence. In March 1912, for example, the commander of the Second Division of the Italian Occupying Forces, Captain Bianco, wrote a report on Sufi *ṭuruq* in Cyrenaica based primarily on information from members of the Madaniyya, another Sufi *ṭarīqa* that had developed in North Africa in the nineteenth century. Bianco's report questioned the dominant characterizations of the Sanusiyya that portrayed the *ṭarīqa* as a unified source of centralized authority in the region with the potential to generate political consensus; according to Bianco's Madani informants, this representation reflected the influence of Sanusi adherents who hoped to convince European authorities to value the Sanusiyya in order to bolster their own profile. Bianco's report also criticized European depictions of the individual figure of al-Sharif as having absolute authority over the *zawāyā* and through their adherents, over the entire region. "Around this individual has been created a proper legend that depicts him almost like a star around which moves, in a fixed, immutable orbit, this entire world. This simplistic and almost mechanical idea of the society in which we live does not correspond to the truth of the matter."[19]

The Bianco report instead suggested that Ahmad al-Sharif's authority, even among Sanusi shaykhs, had clear limitations that Italians could exploit for the benefit of state expansion. As evidence, Bianco cited inconsistency in reactions among the Sanusi *ikhwān* to the Italian invasion. ʿAbd al-Aziz, a shaykh of the *zāwiya* of Benghazi and one of the few Sanusi notables with whom the Italian military command developed a positive relationship during the initial occupation, confirmed Insabato's claims that al-Sharif had assumed a position of neutrality toward the Italian occupation, but noted that his neutrality had generated a variety of responses from individual Sanusi shaykhs. Bianco suggested that al-Sharif's call for noninterference "did not induce all the heads of the *zawāyā* to a position of neutrality, but rather prompted several leaders to rule differently, some in a sense weakly favorable, others in a sense of open hostility."[20] The variety of reactions, Bianco claimed, reflected dissatisfaction with the leadership of al-Sharif, whom many compared unfavorably to his predecessor at the helm of the Sanusi *ṭarīqa*, Muhammad al-Mahdi al-Sanusi. The disparity in reactions to al-Sharif's neutrality also indicated a level of relative independence of individual *zawāyā* that contrasted with the highly centralized model of the Sanusiyya. Bianco even pointed out that some of the Sanusi shaykhs had accumulated such wealth and authority around their individual *zawāyā* that al-Sharif depended more on their support for his position of authority rather than the other way around.

Bianco's report aimed at a clear objective of identifying possible meth-ods to circumvent Ahmad al-Sharif while promoting the rapid expansion of a strong Italian state presence. In addition to finding signs of internal dissent among Sanusi elites, Bianco identified opposition to the Sanusiyya among what he referred to as "healthy" populations of the Bedouin tribes, which in the lexicon of the colonial era meant settled agricultural tribes. In this context, Bianco characterized the Sanusiyya as a "parasitic organi-zation" in the region that had served as an unwelcome proxy for Ottoman control in local tribal affairs. Assistance from the *zawāyā* to those in need and resting points along trade routes, Bianco suggested, were the only benefits most people in the region gained from the presence of the Sufi *ṭarīqa*: "The true friends of the *zawāyā* were the Turkish government and the bullies who leaned on it to govern and misgovern, the poor who found aid there, the troublemakers and thieves who took advantage of the right of asylum and the camel drivers who went undisturbed under their watch along their long travels."[21] Bianco called for the Italian state to undermine the Sanusiyya by replacing the *zawāyā* in the role of providing benefits and protection. Doing so, he suggested, would foster a strong state pres-ence that would eventually "annihilate all of the parasitic institutions [in the region] including that of the Sanusiyya."[22]

Bianco's assessment of the Sanusiyya echoed throughout a series of reports from the Political Office of the Occupying Forces. The school of thought that emerged out of these reports carried with it a message con-cerning the role of religion in Italian imperial expansion. In contrast to Insabato's interest in promoting religious traditionalism as a foundation for an Italo-Sanusi alliance, the military command projected a secular identity in an Italian style of colonial rule. For example, a handbook for colonial officials informed by the Bianco report called on an image of the Italian nation as a secular civilizing force that would save the Bedouin tribes from the perils of religious fanaticism. A secular approach to colo-nial rule, the handbook suggested, would provide the only means of secur-ity against the threat of Islamic unity against the European presence in North Africa. "We must put our hearts at rest against the fear of this pan-Islamism of which the *ṭuruq* would be at once the foundation and the keystone. We must not lull ourselves into a false state of tranquility; cases may occur at any moment that these orders forget their dissension to take up a common cause against a common enemy. But it is the task of the secular colonial policy to know how to make this impossible."[23] Beyond expressing a reaction against the prospect of united Muslim opposition, the handbook asserted a secular position in Italian state expansion that implicitly excluded the utility of supporting either Islamic or Catholic traditionalism in Italian colonial rule.

The theme of secular expansion also featured in *L'Islamismo e la Confraternita dei Senussi*, by Captain Giuseppe Bourbon del Monte Santa Maria. Published in 1912 for the Italian armed forces as part of the effort to prepare colonial officers for the task of governing the Libyan territories, Bourbon del Monte's analysis of the Sanusiyya was based on his reading of a variety of unpublished reports, published books, and newspaper articles. This work was meant to make information from previous European studies of the Sanusiyya available to an Italian audience; as such, it reflected the full confusion of European opinions about the Sanusiyya at the beginning of the twentieth century. Heavily influenced by the writings of Duveyrier, much of Bourbon del Monte's book mimicked the French depiction of the Sanusiyya as composed of intransigent anti-Christian fanatics and as "the most active propagator of the idea of pan-Islam—which, in essence, associates the religious power with the political."[24] The Sanusiyya of Bourbon del Monte, like the Sanusiyya of Duveyrier, intended to use religious authority as leverage to create a vast Islamic empire in North Africa. It was, his study suggested, an idea that stemmed from the founding doctrines of the *ṭarīqa*, which prohibited any contact with the Christian world.

Bourbon del Monte's study also echoed the Bianco report in its portrayal of the contingent nature of Sanusi authority. Unlike the nineteenth-century French literature on the Sanusiyya, Bourbon del Monte's work found evidence of a weak center in the Sanusi *ṭarīqa*. Citing evidence from British intelligence from the early twentieth century, Bourbon del Monte found the Sanusiyya too "diffuse" and divided by tribal concerns to mount a unified resistance to European expansion. He suggested that the Sanusiyya—and the Islamic world in general—was undergoing a moment of transition that would allow the Sanusi elites to appreciate the benefits of Italian rule. It was a period of reforms, he claimed, that mirrored an earlier transition in Catholic Italy in the separation between church and state. Calling on a "Cavour-ian formula," Bourbon del Monte saw a solution to the problem of the Sanusiyya in a republican ideal that would allow Sanusi authority to exist distinct from the authority of the Italian colonial state. Bourbon del Monte finished his work with a quote from a professor of constitutional law, Luigi Luzzatti, in support of an approach to Italian colonial rule based on republican ideals:

Our respect for religious liberty will arise now to the ordeal, in regulating the relations of the Italian state, with a new God, that of Islam, in our Mediterranean Africa. It will not be an easy task because the Arabs of Tripoli and Cirene [*sic*] pray, other than for Mohammed, also for the Caliph, who contains in him the two regiments, the spiritual and the temporal. We find ourselves facing a holy rebellion, and we must invoke all of the knowledge of our ancestors, the Romans, and the worthy successors who prepared the incomparable laws on the prerogatives of the Supreme Pontiff and the Holy See.[25]

Bourbon del Monte lauded the principle of religious liberties as the greatest achievement of western European states and Italy's most important export to the new colonies. He therefore understood a republican ideal of the separation between religious and political authority modeled after the modern unified Italian state as the best answer to the question of how Italy should deal with the presence of the Sanusiyya.

Due to their emphasis on the desirability of a secular state expansion, these perspectives on the Sanusiyya from the Political Office of the Occupying Forces suggested the benefits of the Italian administration turning away from Insabato's emphasis on religious traditionalism, preferring an appeal to rational economic motivations. Bourbon del Monte, for example, argued that the economic benefits of an Italian administration would gradually attract the loyalty of the inhabitants of the region and allow the Italian state to expand beyond the immediate coastal urban centers to the interior by invitation rather than intimidation. But the perspective of the occupying forces also fundamentally questioned the utility of Ahmad al-Sharif's religious and political authority as officials began to look instead at the possibility of exploiting points of weakness and division that could serve to undermine the Sufi *ṭarīqa*.

The Ministry of Colonies and the *Politica dei capi*

The Political Office of the Occupying Forces represented only one perspective that emerged after the invasion of the Libyan territories. After its creation in November 1912, the Italian Ministry of Colonies—an administrative symbol of Italy's arrival as one of Europe's imperial powers—became the new authoritative source for formulating an Italian approach to colonial rule. In January 1913 the first minister of colonies, Pietro Bertolini, began the year eager to prove Italy's ability to govern a civil administration in the colonial territories. A conservative element in Giolitti's cabinet, and a former minister of public works, Bertolini declared his commitment to securing pacification in Libyan territories through political rather than military means. Though he left open the possibility of using force in situations that seemed to require it, Bertolini advocated political and economic measures to generate cooperation among Libyan notables whenever possible.[26] Bertolini did not focus exclusively on the prospect of negotiations with the Sanusiyya, but his attitude signaled a direct line of thought between the founding principles of the Italian Ministry of Colonies and the "pro-Islamic" approach of Enrico Insabato by establishing a goal of political appeasement.

Bertolini's insistence on conciliation, however, also reflected the influence of the Bianco report, in that it represented an attempt to bring a wider range of individuals into an Italian orbit with the possibility of circumventing the authority of Ahmad al-Sharif. The concept became formal policy in royal decrees issued in January 1913 and January 1914 that prescribed a "politics of chiefs"—or *politica dei capi*—that centered on collaboration with local notables. Through this policy, the Italian administration identified tribal and village chiefs to rule the broader population in exchange for a payment of regular stipends from colonial state coffers.[27] The Ministry of Colonies, however, faced a daunting task in identifying viable chiefs. During the wars of occupation and World War I an increased flow of funding in the region, especially from Ottoman and German sources, led to a proliferation of regional power brokers.[28] The question of how to identify appropriate individuals to incorporate in the Italian administration led the separate administrations of Cyrenaica and Tripolitania to generate detailed charts tracing tribal affiliations. Their strategy evolved into a creative and strategic process. Those notables who were willing to declare their formal submission to colonial authority gained a title, funding, and a claim to political authority. The end goal for Italian officials was to form new alliances while accentuating divisions and rivalries to prevent the potential for a concentration of power in any one individual or the formation of a unified front against the Italian presence.[29]

In the first two years after Italy gained official sovereignty over the Libyan territories, the *politica dei capi* seemed to be working. This was especially true in the coastal cities of Tripolitania, where the Italian administration established alliances with high-ranking individuals, including

ʿUmar Pasha Muntasir and his extended family in Misrata. Having gained prominence during the reign of Abdulhamid II, their relative marginalization after the Young Turk Revolution of 1908 led members of the Muntasir family to support the Italian occupation, and their relationship with the Italian state provided them with immediate benefits to employ against political rivals.[30] With the coastal area more or less secure, the Italian administration considered the possibility of extending the occupation into the Fezzan. The ultimate goal was to use the position as a base for operations into territories they recognized as under the control of the Maghārba tribes in western Cyrenaica, affiliates of the Sanusiyya with ties to crucial trade routes through their networks that extended to Kufra.[31] With the shift in objectives, the Italian administration abandoned the alliance with the Muntasir family to cultivate an alliance with the Sayf al-Nasr, a rival family from the Awlad Sulayman tribes in the interior region of Sirte and the Fezzan.[32] In the summer of 1913 Colonel Antonio Miani arrived with Italian troops on the coast, and for six months he stationed his troops in the oasis of Sawkna, a stronghold of the Sayf al-Nasr family and a staging ground for military operations in the Fezzan.

During his campaign Miani also relied on the assistance of ʿAbd al-Nabi Belkhir, a leading figure of the Warfalla tribe who accepted Italian state money in exchange for his services as a political guide and for obtaining supplies and local troops. Though both the Sayf al-Nasr family and ʿAbd al-Nabi Belkhir helped the Italian mission in the initial occupation of the Fezzan, they later used their resources and political influence against the Italian state presence: ʿAbd al Nabi Belkhir in 1915 and the Sayf al-Nasr family in the 1920s. But in December 1913 and January 1914, Miani and his troops occupied a succession of oases in the Fezzan with their assistance and declared the region pacified, resulting in formal acts of submission or *sottomissione* to Italian state authorities by state-recognized tribal leaders.[33]

The act of submission merits a moment of attention. The ultimate goal in most Italian negotiations or armed battles was to gain the submission of the region's elites. In the first years of the Italian occupation, the act of submission offered the illusion, at least, of an expanding network of alliances through the *politica dei capi*, and it loomed large in popular Italian imagination as a sign of national strength and imperial expansion. Acts of submission determined where to draw the boundaries of effective state control on maps of the Libyan interior. Representations of the act of submission became a symbol of empire for a broader public, especially as images on children's school notebooks during the occupation of Ethiopia in the 1930s, as pictured in figure 3.1. But what did the act of submission involve? In May 1912 Enrico Insabato created what he intended to be a template for the submission of tribes to Italian sovereignty. Insabato's proposal listed a series of obligations the Italian colonial administration would promise to fulfill in exchange for promises to end anti-Italian hostilities. The ten-point list included a commitment to uphold Islamic practices in all government functions, assurances of Italian intentions to build hospitals and infrastructure, and even a promise to include tribal leaders

FIGURE 3.1 "Submission" depicted on a school notebook.

Source: Il Laboratorio di Ricerca e Documentazione Storico Iconografica, Università degli Studi Roma Tre.

on advisory councils that would meet with government representatives to make decisions concerning tribal affairs jointly.

Insabato's template for submission also included a provision that would guarantee a substantial role for Ahmad al-Sharif; the proposed contract stipulated that all acts of submission would be subject to review by the head of the Sanusiyya and reserved to him the right to modify such agreements as he deemed necessary. This provision foreshadowed the essential elements of the power-sharing agreements the Italian Ministry of Colonies would establish with Idris al-Sanusi after 1916. But in 1912 the idea provoked the unstinting condemnation of Pier Luigi Grimani, the Italian consul general in Cairo, who considered the concessions an extreme renunciation of state power. Grimani noted that the arrangement would recognize al-Sharif's authority over tribes that were not already among the adherents of the Sufi *ṭarīqa*, thus undermining the original intention of the *politica dei capi*: to circumvent the authority of the Sanusi leader.[34] Giolitti—acting as both prime minister and minister of the interior—agreed with Grimani and denounced the very idea of establishing a written template for acts of submission. Giolitti thought it preferable to rely on the vague assurances of Caneva's proclamation of Italy's promises to protect Islam in the Libyan colonies. The goal, his telegram suggested, should be to avoid making any specific promises in writing in order to strengthen Italy's hand in any individual negotiations with tribal leaders.[35] The act of submission, therefore, lacked a standard form, but it usually included a written statement requiring Libyan signatories to recognize the Italian colonial state. The written document was accompanied by a ritualized presentation of tribal leaders in front of Italian colonial officials, captured in a series of photographs from Miani's campaign.[36] Submission often required a relinquishment of weapons, though some tribal forces who agreed to join the Italian colonial war effort kept their weapons after registering them with state officials.

Acts of submission to Italian rule increased during the implementation of the *politica dei capi*. Despite relatively small territorial gains through military conquest during 1913, the governor of Cyrenaica, Giovanni Ameglio, recorded an increasing number of acts of formal submissions to Italian rule, especially among tribes near Benghazi and Derna.[37] By the end of the year the Italians calculated that 135,200 out of a total population of 351,600 in Cyrenaica had submitted to Italian rule. Most submissions occurred en masse, with tribal elders declaring submission on behalf of those they represented. But there were also instances of individuals choosing to submit,

particularly after the wars of occupation bled into the wider regional hostilities of World War I. These individual acts of submission gave Italian
military officials an opportunity to interview former enemies about the
structure and location of opposition forces. Those interviews also provide
some insight into the issues that informed individual decisions to switch
allegiance to the colonial state.

Hunger was a powerful motivation for individual submission. At least
one individual submitting to Italian rule noted the refusal of Ottoman-
Sanusi commanders to allow him to return to his land to tend to crops as
a motivation for changing allegiance.[38] Agricultural concerns were particularly urgent given the shortage of food throughout the region when
the battles of World War I prevented supplies from arriving across the
Egyptian border, and individual acts of submission increased in times of
food shortages.[39] Separation from family members who lived in regions
that had submitted to Italian authority inspired some to abandon the
Sanusi-Ottoman forces, especially when they received news from relatives
suggesting that they would find gainful employment in the Italian armed
forces after submission.[40] Those making the transition also cited the
refusal of Sanusi elites to allow troops to leave armed camps for the plant-
ing season as contributing to their decisions. Though limited in impact,
these individual acts of submission seemed to show a way forward for
an Italian campaign to win loyalty away from the Sanusiyya—or at least
away from Ahmad al-Sharif—through the attraction of familial stability
and gainful employment.

Broad regions where Italians failed to record acts of submission, however, indicated the limits of Italian influence. Areas where the Maghārba
tribe was dominant in the oases of Kufra, Jalu, Jaghbub, and western
Cyrenaica were the largest holdouts. The refusal of these highly influential affiliates of the Sanusiyya to recognize Italian sovereignty indicated
the development of centers of opposition based on a unified Sanusi identity that suggested the imperative of either negotiating an alliance with
the Sanusi family or cultivating alternative sources of political and moral
authority to support the expansion of the Italian state presence in the
region.[41] After the increase in the number of submissions to Italian rule
among Cyrenaican tribes in the spring of 1913, the Ministry of Colonies
and Governor Ameglio saw an opportunity to convince the Sanusi family
to align with Italy. In the Ministry of Colonies, a theory developed that if
Italy could win the submission of enough tribal leaders in the interior,
Ahmad al-Sharif would be forced to follow their lead.[42] As part of that

effort, the governor of Tripolitania offered to provide armed forces to the Sayf al-Nasr family in exchange for their help in pressuring Maghārba leaders to submit to Italian authority, but representatives of the Sayf al-Nasr family refused to comply.[43] Thus, despite limited success in developing an alternative network of alliances through the *politica dei capi*, the goal of forming a power-sharing system with the Sanusi elite remained a focal point in the Ministry of Colonies. The concept would continue to direct colonial policy even after Ahmad al-Sharif followed calls from Istanbul to declare jihad against the Italian presence in 1914. From a practical standpoint, the goal of an alliance with the Sanusi family cut through the confusion of shifting regional alliances.

The continued emphasis on negotiations with the Sanusiyya also reflected the influence of individuals who shared Insabato's optimism about the possibilities of a special Italo-Sanusi relationship. An ideological continuity can be seen in the career of Insabato's friend Aldobrandino Malvezzi di Medici as a high-level functionary, first in the Ministry of Foreign Affairs and then in the Ministry of Colonies. Childhood classmates, the two worked together in Cairo when the foreign ministry sent Malvezzi there as an official representative to prepare for the occupation of Libya by contacting the heads of the Sufi *ṭuruq* in the region, alongside Insabato.[44] Malvezzi shared Insabato's opinion about the necessity of negotiations with the Sanusiyya for a successful Italian administration, and he remained in an official position in the Ministry of Colonies until the fascist era. Malvezzi faced his fair share of hostility within the Italian consulate in Cairo as a close associate of Insabato. In May 1910 Malvezzi published an article in the prestigious journal *Nuova antologia* in which he espoused a collaborative approach to Italian colonial expansion: "Italians enjoy a privileged position in the Muslim world: the English are respected, the French feared, the Italians attract great sympathy; we have the reputation of being tolerant of the practices and customs and above all of the religion."[45] More damaging was Malvezzi's insistence that the path toward a collaboration with Sanusi elites could best be forged from Cairo rather than Benghazi. His recommendation amounted to a call to return to the alliances the Ministry of Foreign Affairs had formed through the mediation of Insabato and Muhammad 'Ali 'Alawi. Giacomo De Martino (at that point Italy's diplomatic representative in Cairo) denounced Malvezzi's suggestion of a pro-Islamic approach to Italian colonial rule for demonstrating "the insidious influence of Insabato."

Malvezzi also published a study of religion and society in the Libyan territories in 1913, *L'Italia e l'Islam in Libia,* which expressed his support for the efforts to negotiate with the Sanusi elite. As the Bianco report did, Malvezzi attributed signs of political ambition to Sanusi elites, but whereas the reports of the occupying forces considered those ambitions dangerous and "parasitic," Malvezzi argued that the Italians should accommodate the interests of the Sanusiyya and use the ambitions of its leaders as an effective tool for forwarding Italian interests. "We suggest for our native policy not only to make use of the natural tendencies for autonomy of the Libyan populations, but above all to gain all the advantages that we can from supporting the aspirations for dominance of the religious congregations"[46] In Malvezzi's analysis, Sanusi elites were not figures at the center of a hierarchy of politico-religious authority, but they did want to obtain such a position. And yet rather than trying to undermine Sanusi ambitions as a threat to state control, Malvezzi argued in favor of supporting the centralization of political control under Sanusi leadership. Promoting the authority of the Sanusiyya, he suggested, would help the Italian state govern a Bedouin population that he depicted as inherently violent and in need of strong leadership. A positive relationship could also improve Italian standing in the Muslim world and mark Italy as distinctive from other European colonial powers.[47] Malvezzi's study was one in a small but vocal constellation of opinions in the burgeoning civil administration of the Italian colonial system that continued to focus on the Sanusiyya.

World War I and the Sanusiyya

Malvezzi's model of empowering the Sanusiyya in order to use it as an instrument of Italian state rule posed a paradox for Italian colonial administrators: Depending on the authority of the Sanusi elites offered the potential for immediate stability, but it also carried the risk of either overestimating the authority of Sanusi elites (thereby undermining state control) or empowering the Sanusiyya to the extent that it could pose a challenge to the colonial state. This was a common concern for colonial powers in the era of liberal imperialism. And it was a concern that only heightened with evidence of the militarization of the Sanusiyya during the wars of Italian occupation and the associated battles of World War I in the Libyan interior.

Documents that the Italian Occupying Forces found in the offices of former Ottoman representatives in Tripoli and Benghazi in September 1912 suggested that Istanbul struggled with these same issues in the years leading up to the Italian invasion of the Libyan coast. In communications with the central administration, the Ottoman *vali* of Tripoli suggested that the recognition of Ahmad al-Sharif as a religious figure and Istanbul's reliance on his political authority to govern the remote interior of Cyrenaica had the perverse effect of increasing his power in such a way that it could undermine state control. He suggested that Istanbul should work against rather than with the authority of the Sanusi elites.[48] The Ottoman minister of the interior chose instead to follow the recommendations of the *mutaṣarrif* of Benghazi, Muraf Fuʿad, who favored cultivating the authority of al-Sharif. He hoped to use Sanusi influence to establish an administrative center and military garrison in the oases of Kufra to defend against French incursions in the region. To achieve that end, Istanbul began to pay al-Sharif a monthly salary. Local Ottoman officials in al-Khums and the Jabal al-Akhdar disagreed with the increased reliance on the Sanusiyya, claiming that certain Sanusi elites were taking advantage of Ottoman resources to bolster their authority against the interests of the central state. The cache of Ottoman documents in Tripoli and Benghazi served as a warning to some Italian colonial administrators, calling into question the characterization of the Sanusiyya as a centralized hierarchical power.

The uncertainty about the authority of the Sanusiyya illustrated in these Ottoman documents compounded the confusion among Italian colonial officers, especially in the face of evidence that a transformation of the Sufi *ṭarīqa* in relationship to Ottoman authorities took place during the initial wars of Italian occupation. As we have seen, the Sanusiyya and its associated trade networks facilitated a market in weapons and ammunition in the region. French and British agents in North Africa began to track the arms trade in the Libyan territories before the Italian occupation. They found that weapons from conflicts around the world, including guns from the Russo-Japanese War (1904–1905) and conflicts with Mahdist forces in the Sudan, reached the Sanusi *zawāyā* and from there made their way into the hands of anti-French forces in Wadai, Darfur, and the Central Sahara.[49] The arms trade quickly supplanted the disappearing slave trade as a driving force in the region's economy and contributed to a militarization of the Sanusi *zawāyā*.[50]

During the initial Italian occupation, Istanbul contributed to the militarization of the Sanusi infrastructure by relying increasingly on the networks of the Sanusiyya *zawāyā* to organize defensive forces. When Italian forces attacked the Libyan coast, British neutrality prevented the sultan from sending a large army through Egypt, and Italian naval superiority limited the options for a counterattack via the Mediterranean. Facing these constraints, the Ottoman Ministry of War sent officers from the military agency of the CUP, the Teskilet-i Mahsusa, to organize defensive strategies among local populations. The defense of the Libyan territories proved a popular cause among a cohort of elite officers in the CUP, many of whom later became important figures in Turkish nationalism, including Enver Pasha (director of the Teskilet-i Mahsusa and later minister of war) and Mustafa Kemal.[51] In Cyrenaica, Sanusi *zawāyā* served as training grounds and arms depots for a coalition of regional forces under the leadership of these CUP officers. The efficacy of the anti-Italian forces provided clear proof of the potential strength an alliance with the Sanusi elites could offer, while at the same time the militarization of the *zawāyā* added urgency to the desire of Italian officers to neutralize the Sanusiyya as a threat.[52]

Istanbul turned away from the war over the Libyan territories in 1912 when it faced other crises in the empire due to Italian aggression in the Balkans and the revolt of Muhammad al-Idrisi against the Ottoman government in Yemen, funded in part by Italy as a distraction from the war in the Libyan territories. The multiple conflicts weakened the resolve of Ottoman authorities to continue providing military supplies and training in the Libyan territories and led to the relinquishment of Ottoman sovereignty in the Treaty of Lausanne in October 1912. Italian imperialists hailed peace with Istanbul as Italy's arrival in the league of Europe's great powers, but the official end of the war did not mean an immediate cessation of Ottoman influence in the region.

The treaty ending the Italo-Turkish War assured the continued influence of the Ottoman sultan by recognizing his religious authority in the Libyan territories as caliph. In this position the Sultan retained a representative in the region to deal with a religious-judicial system, allowing Istanbul to have a say in the nomination of qadi and in dealing with *awqaf* properties—religious properties like the Sanusi *zawāyā* that qualified for tax exempt status. For the Italian administration, the continued influence of the sultan compounded the difficulties in untangling the relationship between religious and political authority in Italy's new Muslim territories. This state of affairs would prove a constant source of anxiety for Italian colonial officials until the declaration of war against the Ottoman Empire in World War I enabled them to annul the arrangement.[53]

Despite expectations that the Sanusiyya—along with other regional elites—was eager to rid the region of the CUP, Istanbul also maintained influence in the Libyan territories through contact with Ahmad al-Sharif. With the formal end to the Italo-Turkish War, most Ottoman officers, including Enver Pasha, left the area for the Balkans, but a handful stayed to fight under the leadership of ʿAziz ʿAli al-Misri, the former commander of Ottoman forces in Cyrenaica. The remaining Ottoman officers trained Bedouin troops in the Sanusi *zawāyā*. Their ultimate objective was to eject the Italian occupation forces and establish a semi-independent government under al-Sharif with military support from Istanbul.[54] The collaboration between al-Sharif and al-Misri derailed in the spring of 1913 when the discovery that the military commander had accepted funds from Italian officials in exchange for providing geographical information that helped them make territorial advances into the Cyrenaican interior led to his ouster.[55] The departure of al-Misri signaled a possible break in Ottoman-Sanusi relations, and in the summer and fall of 1913 renewed attempts were made by European officials throughout the region to acquire a strategic advantage in Cyrenaica through an alliance with al-Sharif. But the ties between al-Sharif and Ottoman forces, forged in the militarization of Sanusi *zawāyā*, remained an organizing principle of regional politics throughout World War I. [56]

World War I contributed to the armament of the Sanusi *zawāyā* with the regular arrival of weapons, supplies, and advisers from the Ottoman and German militaries. Estimates of the number of arms in circulation in the Cyrenaican interior after the Italian invasion varied widely, from around 40,000 up to 150,000.[57] The war also led to the dissolution of the shaky network that Italian military commanders had built up through the *politica dei capi* during their earlier operations in the Fezzan and the interior of Cyrenaica. Regional elites chose instead to align with Ottoman and German interests in exchange for an influx of military supplies. The Italian expansion into Cyrenaica beyond the immediate surroundings of Benghazi halted as armed forces attacked Italian supply lines in September 1914.[58] Ahmad al-Sharif echoed the Ottoman call to jihad in all territories under Allied control at the end of 1914, and Italy's decision to join the war on the side of the Allies a few months later crystallized the opposition between the Sanusi figurehead and Italian state presence in Cyrenaica. Assaults against Italian garrisons and supply lines escalated in April 1915, when allies of Italy based on the *politica dei capi* system joined Sanusi forces led by al-Sharif's brother, Sayf al-Din, defeated Miani's column in the Battle of Bu Hadi (also known as Gardibiyyah). In what was Italy's most dramatic military disaster in the colonies since the Battle of

Adwa in 1896, Miani's forces lost five hundred soldiers and over five thousand arms.[59] From that point until the fascist administration initiated the series of military campaigns of the "reconquest" in the late 1920s, the colonial state presence remained confined to urban centers on the coast. It was, as Lisa Anderson judged it, a sign of the total failure of the Italian *politica dei capi*.[60]

Replacing the "Grand Senusso"

Facing the loss of control of key areas in Cyrenaica and the certainty of Ahmad al-Sharif's enmity, the Italian administration took steps to identify a more amenable Sanusi authority during World War I. In a last effort to strike a deal with al-Sharif (and hoping to avoid the total expulsion of Italians from the Libyan territories in case Italy landed on the losing side of the broader European war), the Italian ambassador in Cairo proposed a joint Italian-British accord with the Sanusiyya.[61] The British initially refused; they were concerned that cooperating with the Italians in the Libyan territories would turn Sanusi adherents among the Bedouin tribes of Western Egypt against them. The British also expressed a fear that negotiating a power-sharing relationship between al-Sharif and the Italian colonial administration would set a dangerous precedent for other religious figures in Egypt and the Sudan to claim positions of political authority within a colonial system.[62] But the Italian entry into the European war as an ally in May 1915 placed the British in a delicate position. The negotiation of some sort of peace between Italian colonial officials and the Sanusiyya offered the best means to avoid accusations of abandoning either their ally in Europe or the Sanusi *ṭarīqa*.[63]

Despite Ahmad al-Sharif's explicit support of Ottoman war aims, British officials in Egypt still believed they could find a way to work with him. As late as July 1915 officials presented al-Sharif with an offer of British and Italian recognition of his position of religious authority and the payment of a small subsidy in exchange for an end to hostilities.[64] Two factors convinced the British Foreign Office to end its pursuit of negotiations with al-Sharif. First, British officials reacted against references to a Sanusi government in the discussions. Sanusi elites had taken to marking their correspondence with "*al-Hukuma al-Sanusiyya*," or the Sanusi government, since early 1913, but the British feared that official recognition of Sanusi claims to formal political authority would set a dangerous precedent for religious-based challenges to state control throughout the colonial world.

Second, indications that al-Sharif intended to accept an Ottoman proposal for him to lead an attack in Egypt's Western Desert convinced British agents of the futility of continued negotiations.[65]

When British and Italian officials abandoned the hope of negotiating with Ahmad al-Sharif, they turned to Idris al-Sanusi (see figure 3.2). The identification of Idris as an alternative intermediary followed the basic logic of the *politica dei capi*. Italian officials in the Ministry of Foreign Affairs began to discuss the possibility of dealing with Idris as a potentially more compliant Sanusi figure as early as 1914 when, after a failed attempt to negotiate with al-Sharif on Italy's behalf, the Egyptian khedive connected Italian representatives to Idris. The khedive first floated the idea of naming him as the official religious representative of the sultan-caliph in the Libyan territories.[66] Though the suggestion was not implemented, the idea that some factions of the Sanusi family could be more easily persuaded to form an alliance with the Italian colonial state gained

FIGURE 3.2 Idris al-Sanusi (date unknown).
Source: Il Laboratorio di Ricerca e Documentazione Storico Iconografica, Università degli Studi Roma Tre.

momentum. From his post in Istanbul, where he was sent to attempt to counter negative images of Italy in the Ottoman capitol, Insabato threw his support behind the idea of negotiating with Idris by providing a report explaining the latter's position to the colonial administration. He even offered to take the lead in negotiations—this time without the dubious assistance of Muhammad ʿAli ʿAlawi. Considering Insabato to be a bit too enamored of his own ideals to act as an effective emissary to Idris, the governor of Cyrenaica declined the offer.[67]

The concept of negotiating with Idris al-Sanusi inspired the production of more information about his role in the Sanusi *ṭarīqa*. To calculate the possible benefits of forming an alliance with Idris, Italian officials expanded on charts that the occupying forces had previously made of tribal alliances in the region when they were implementing the *politica dei capi*, this time marking divisions within the Sanusi *ikhwān* and tying them to particular tribal factions in the Libyan interior. The charts connected specific members of the Sanusi family to particular *zawāyā* in order to identify points of division within the Sanusi *ṭarīqa*. The Political Office of the Italian governor of Cyrenaica postulated the formation of such a division after the death of Muhammad al-Mahdi in 1902, between those *zawāyā* that followed Ahmad al-Sharif and his brothers and those that followed Idris and his brother, Muhammad al-Rida. Out of a total of forty-four Sanusi *zawāyā* in Cyrenaica, the Italian administration calculated that nineteen fell under the influence of al-Sharif and his brothers and nineteen were in the camp of Idris and al-Rida; the remaining six fell within the territories under Italian control and therefore posed little interest in terms of gauging Sanusi influence in the region.[68]

It was a seductive theory that generated hope for a Sanusi alliance despite Ahmad al-Sharif's continued support for Ottoman interests. In the hubris of the colonial setting, Italian officials imagined they could achieve a restructuring of the Sanusi *ṭarīqa* by sowing internal discord and recognizing Idris al-Sanusi as the rightful leader of the Sanusiyya. To that end, the governor's office in Benghazi found evidence to support theories of a decline in influence of al-Sharif as a religious and political figure in the region. In the summer of 1915 Italian officials began to note indications of discontent among Sanusi adherents in Cyrenaica due to the strain on local resources caused by involvement in the Ottoman and German war effort.[69] Italian analysts even began to question the validity of recognizing al-Sharif as the spiritual head of the Sanusi *ṭarīqa* from a technical standpoint; though al-Sharif had the advantage of age, Idris could claim legitimacy based on his direct descent from a popular figure in the Sanusiyya, Muhammad al-Mahdi.[70] Furthermore, since the properties going to al-Sharif's branch of the family had to be divided among more members than that of al-Mahdi's branch of the family, Italian informants concluded that the sons of al-Mahdi had more wealth at their disposal than al-Sharif and his family, "which seems to be not a small preoccupation for the actual "Senusso" [al-Sharif] because wealth is an element of greater influence, and the aspiration seems not entirely dormant in Said Idris of having the title and the position that passed, perhaps without absolute legitimacy, to Ahmad al-Sharif."[71] After al-Sharif led attacks in the Western Desert, British officials produced similar reports suggesting that a large number of the adherents of the Sanusiyya did not consider al-Sharif the true leader of the Sufi *ṭarīqa*, and that many, including Idris, would prefer alternate leadership.

Idris al-Sanusi seemed to confirm these theories when he contacted British and Italian officials in Cairo in the summer of 1916 and offered to resume the relationship they had first established through the mediation of the Egyptian khedive two years earlier.[72] For months they danced around the alternatives of Idris declaring his formal submission to Italian sovereignty or plans for a general disarmament of the tribal populations in the interior. In the spring of 1917 they finally agreed on a temporary treaty. Named after the town of Akrama, where the modus vivendi was signed, the agreement led to an immediate end of hostilities between Italian and Sanusi-Ottoman forces. In the years that followed, Italian and British officials made a concerted effort to support Idris's authority within the Sufi *ṭarīqa* and to promote the authority of the Sanusiyya as a political force in the region.

This is not to say that Idris al-Sanusi's claims to authority in Cyrenaica derived solely from his ties with the British and Italian governments; he also obtained the crucial backing of the Sanusi *ikhwan* and tribal leaders in regions where the Sanusiyya had the most influence. Italian observations of discontent with Ahmad al-Sharif among Sanusi adherents were not without foundation. Al-Sharif's insistence on pursuing Ottoman war objectives by leading attacks on the western border of Egypt created a dire situation for Sanusi forces and the wider population of Cyrenaica. Famine caused by a drought in 1915 was made worse by lack of access to Egyptian markets. Facing Italian enemies along the coast and British enemies to the east, many people in the region considered continued warfare untenable. The effects of war were devastating. As Muhammad Fuʿad Shukri noted, in the city of Ajdabiya, just 150 kilometers south of Benghazi, the "streets were filled with the remains of the dead."[73]

Known for his vocal opposition to Ahmad al-Sharif's support of Ottoman war efforts, Idris al-Sanusi's willingness to negotiate with European imperialists offered a solution to those inhabitants of the region eager to see an end to hostilities. After the British definitively routed Sanusi forces on the Egyptian border and al-Sharif beat a hasty retreat to the south in February 1916, Sanusi *ikhwan* began to distinguish between al-Sharif as a purely religious figure and Idris as a political leader. They continued to see al-Sharif as responsible for the spiritual guidance of the Sanusi *ṭarīqa*, but Sanusi affiliates increasingly turned to Idris for decisions on how to cultivate political alliances with foreign powers. Idris established an administrative center in the city of Ajdabiya (see figure 3.3), a city Hisham Matar described as "a cluster of buildings in a vast emptiness."[74] Before long Sanusi *ikhwan* pushed for Idris to claim both the religious and political leadership of the Sanusi *ṭarīqa* to give him sufficient authority to negotiate with Italian and British officials.[75] The transformation of the Sanusi *ṭarīqa* from a pro-Ottoman armed force to a colonial intermediary therefore occurred as an external and internal process simultaneously; pressure from European forces coincided

FIGURE 3.3 Sanusi administrative center in Ajdabiya.
Source: ASMAI II 181/70/362, Ministero dell'Africa Italiana, "La Senussia," 1949.

with pressure from within the Sanusi *ṭarīqa* for Idris to put an end to al-Sharif's disastrous war against Britain.

However, support for the shift in leadership was far from universal among Sanusi adherents. In the year between the beginning of negotiations in April 1916 and the conclusion of the Akrama Accord in April 1917, Sanusi armed forces and Ottoman officers committed to the opposition to Italian colonialism defected and joined the government of Ramadan al-Suwayhli in Misrata, recognizing in him a new leader of anti-Italian resistance during the years of negotiations between the Italian administration and Idris al-Sanusi.[76] Among those who remained in Cyrenaica, discontent over the turn away from a pro-Ottoman position emerged with force in the months after the conclusion of the modus vivendi in Akrama. Italian officials were relying on Idris to meet with tribal leaders in the interior to convince them to submit to Italian rule and hand over their weapons to fulfill his obligations under the Akrama Accord, and they expressed constant discontent with his slow rate of progress. At the same time, persistent rumors of the proximate return of Ahmad al-Sharif to the position as head of the Sanusi *ṭarīqa* told of widespread unease with Idris's leadership.[77] And when Idris began his campaign in favor of submission to Italian sovereignty in November 1917, he met with more resistance to the concept than Italian officials had expected. Notables of the ʿAwāqir tribe who met with the famous Sanusi military leader, Omar al-Mukhtar, as Idris's representative refused under any circumstances to surrender their arms to either the Italian government or a Sanusi authority. They even opposed the notion of recognizing Idris as a political authority or the Sanusiyya as a political entity. Hoping to forestall the ability of the Sanusi *ikhwan* to collect taxes, take possession of tribal territory, or dictate ʿAwāqir relations with outside powers (including the Ottomans), they made their loyalty to the Sanusiyya contingent on the Sufi *ṭarīqa* maintaining a purely religious identity.[78]

Given signs of discontent with the expansion of Sanusi political authority under Idris al-Sanusi's leadership, Italian officials saw an immediate need to take measures to secure his authority. Recognition of his relative weakness in the Sanusi *ṭarīqa* informed Idris's approach to negotiating the agreement in Akrama. In some of his initial discussions with Italian and British officials, Idris called for a position of almost total independence in which the Italian state would provide him with the resources to cement his control over a Sanusi administration and expand the Sanusi trade network through Italian-funded infrastructure projects. Idris asked that the Italian state provide him with arms, money, and officers for military training so that he could have the armed forces to back up his claims to political power. Initially, the prospect of supplying Idris with military forces clashed with Italian objectives of procuring his formal submission to the Italian colonial state. The logic of colonial submission seemed to require the total disarmament of the Sanusi *zawāyā* and affiliated tribes in Cyrenaica.[79]

British involvement in the negotiations compelled compromise on both sides, but due to concern about the weakness of Idris al-Sanusi's position, the final agreement corresponded more closely to his stipulations than to an Italian desire for full submission. British agents pushed Idris to compromise in his agreement with the Italian state by threatening to confiscate Sanusi properties in Egypt's Western Desert and by making the conclusion of a treaty a prerequisite for the application of a separate British-Sanusi agreement, which had always been one of Idris's primary objectives as a means of reopening access to Egyptian markets, which had been closed off during World War I. But the British delegate to the negotiations, Colonel Milo Talbot, pushed harder for the Italians to attenuate their demands, with the understanding that both Italian and British officials needed to promote Idris's authority as a younger member of the Sanusi family[80] with relatively weak claims to a position of power. Talbot warned the Italians against asking Idris to perform the formal submission to Italian rule or to attempt full disarmament, as measures that would damage his greatest resource: the ability to influence inhabitants of the region through a claim to moral authority. As Talbot pointed out in his reports to the British Foreign Office, that moral authority stemmed from Sanusi-led resistance to European colonialism. Negotiating with the Italians, Talbot predicted, would make him less popular in the short term, though he would gain some support by opening markets. In the absence of a common enemy, Talbot argued, Idris would also face the possibility of regional rivals challenging his position.[81] The British were eager to have a friendly and strong Sanusi authority to secure Egypt's western border, but in their written communications with Italian representatives they were quite clear that this would involve the *creation* of Idris as a political figure through state sponsorship. That meant supplying Idris with arms and supplies to offset the damage done to his "religious prestige" through his negotiations with European powers.[82] There was a tipping point; Idris required enough state support to overcome possible enemies who opposed his involvement with Italian colonial authorities, but overreliance on British and Italian support would detract from his appeal by making him seem to be a colonial collaborator.

To protect against this possibility, the European officials considered it important for inhabitants of the region to perceive Idris al-Sanusi as a political figure whose authority was independent of his relationship to the British and Italian states. With that objective in mind, the final Akrama Accord recognized Idris's right to maintain armed camps and allowed the tribes of the Cyrenaican interior to maintain sufficient arms for self-defense, though with the understanding that Idris would promote a gradual program of disarmament and prevent any opposition to Italian disarmament programs in the regions along the coast under direct Italian control. The agreement included a clause requiring Idris to eject all Ottoman agents from the region. This was a provision British officials supported in order to eliminate the threat of Ottoman military action along the western border of Egypt, but the measure also promised to eliminate elements of the Sanusiyya who supported continued aggression alongside Ottoman officers in opposition to Idris's leadership. Most significantly, the agreement established the principle of a Sanusi sphere of influence in the Cyrenaican interior, attributing to Idris the responsibility of maintaining security in all of the regions not under direct Italian occupation. The territorial demarcation followed the process of submission; the Italian colonial government only claimed direct control over those tribes who had officially submitted to Italian rule. The distinction left ample room for Idris to expand the territorial reach of Sanusi religious and political authority among a diverse population not living in the limited regions under the Italian colonial administration.[83]

In the circular logic of colonial rule through intermediaries, the prospect of strengthening Idris al-Sanusi's influence in the region led European officials to wring their hands over the possible implications for European hegemony. In the interests of preventing an overinflation of Sanusi authority, British officials also made an effort to bolster the relative strength of the Italian colonial state. British representatives offered to provide Idris with the military supplies necessary to construct a strong Sanusi authority, but they insisted on channeling the resources through the Italian colonial administration in Benghazi to ensure the illusion, at least, that Idris depended on Italian patronage. The British were eager to ensure that he had access to adequate supplies to counteract the continued influx of arms and ammunition from Istanbul to Ahmad al-Sharif's pro-Ottoman forces in the autumn of 1917, but they also hoped to extricate themselves from a delicate situation with an Islamic *ṭarīqa* whose adherents stretched across the indistinct border between Cyrenaica and Egypt.[84]

Though the construction of a Sanusi military and political power under Italian supervision answered their strategic interests, British authorities in Egypt feared the possible implications for claims to political authority among Muslim elites in other British territories. As a result, British representatives constantly pulled back from any formal recognition of Idris al-Sanusi's political power or regional autonomy, focusing instead on his (questionable) position as a purely religious figure.[85] This ambivalence caused some confusion in the British approach to dealing with Sanusi properties in Egypt, many of which had been seized during Ahmad al-Sharif's military campaign against the western border. Eager to promote their relationship with Idris, the British tried to distinguish between the *zawāyā* that Idris could claim as personal property—which they agreed to return to him and his family—and those that belonged to the Sanusi *ṭarīqa* more broadly. British officials in Cairo and the Frontier Districts Administration decided to destroy the Sanusi *zawāyā* in the Western Desert that did not belong directly to Idris as "the outward symbols of the Senussist [*sic*] temporal power," though they promised not to damage mosques connected to the Sanusi territories, as evidence of their respect for Islam and for the strictly religious authority of the Sanusi family.[86] The destruction of Sanusi properties was an effort to limit Idris's influence, despite his relatively friendly attitude toward the British, for fear that outward support of his authority could encourage other challengers to European colonial rule among the religious leadership in Egypt, if not further abroad.

If British representatives in the negotiations worried about the implications of recognizing a Sanusi political authority, Italian representatives were doubly afraid that their material support of Idris al-Sanusi and his armed forces might undermine the already tenuous claims to Italian sovereignty in the Libyan territories. The governor of Cyrenaica, Giovanni Ameglio, was a particularly outspoken critic of the agreement signed in Akrama as a challenge to Italian sovereignty. He considered the modus vivendi a concession to British interests that did little to advance Italian "pacification and domination" of the Libyan territories. Most egregiously for Ameglio, the Akrama Accord recognized Idris's political authority over the tribes of the Cyrenaican interior. This, Ameglio noted, went well beyond the principle that had guided Italian intentions for the Sanusiyya since the beginning of the occupation of the Libyan territories: to use the religious authority of the Sufi *ṭarīqa* to facilitate Italian economic and political penetration of the interior.

Instead, the agreement supplanted Italian sovereignty with that of a semiautonomous Sanusi state.[87]

In the short term, however, the negotiations with Idris al-Sanusi seemed to serve both British and Italian interests, especially when Idris effectively blocked a renewal of Ahmad al-Sharif's assaults on the Egyptian border in March 1917. Idris also turned his attention to rooting out pro-Ottoman elements in the Sanusiyya. In the summer of 1917 the governor of Tripolitania reported that Idris had two Sanusi officers shot and several tribal leaders arrested for being in communication with Nuri Bey, the Ottoman officer who had trained and managed al-Sharif's armed forces during the attacks on western Egypt.[88] His willingness to take a firm stance against his cousin's pro-Ottoman position confirmed the utility of Idris as an alternate leader of the Sanusi *ṭarīqa* and encouraged the European powers to increase their supplies of provisions to Idris's Sanusi forces in Cyrenaica.[89] Idris leveraged his position to pressure British and Italian officials to expedite a resumption of trade to the region. Beyond the humanitarian concerns of dealing effectively with famine, Idris's European allies understood an increase in trade as a step that would help to affirm the legitimacy of the Italo-Sanusi agreements among merchant tribes and Sanusi elites, who stood to benefit from the influx of revenue into Cyrenaican *zawāyā*.[90]

An increase in supplies of arms and ammunitions accompanied the focus on resuming normal trade routes, and a relationship of mutual military dependence between Idris al-Sanusi and the Italian colonial administration was formalized when Rome issued a royal decree in the spring of 1918 to establish Sanusi armed garrisons with government funding. The stated purpose of this measure was to bolster Idris's nascent authority both within Cyrenaica and against possible incursions from Tripolitania, where Ottoman officers continued to operate. The directive called for two distinct categories of armed garrisons. The "gruppi Idrissiti" were intended to defend against possible attacks from Tripolitania and consisted of two garrisons of about one thousand men each. The "Campi armati senussiti" consisted of a force of over two thousand men organized specifically to support Idris's hold on regional authority against both internal and external threats and to help him maintain the security of trade routes—the key to preventing effective challenges to his position as the head of the Sanusi *ṭarīqa*.[91] A series of maps issued by the governor of Cyrenaica provided a visual representation of the integration of the Sanusi armed camps into spatial representations of Italy's effective control. Starting in January 1918, these maps tracked the location and strength of both Italian garrisons and the forces of Idris al-Sanusi, including Sanusi outposts as Idris expanded his authority in the region. These maps demonstrated a heightened ability and desire to maintain a close watch on the Sanusi forces; monthly maps traced the number and movement of weapons throughout the region. But the structure of the maps suggested the status of the Sanusi armed camps as an extension of Italian control in the imagination of the colonial administration and the utility of the Sanusiyya as Italy's "tool of penetration," as Minister of Colonies Gaspare Colosimo put it.[92]

Perversely, in the course of developing a military system of mutual dependence following the Akrama Accord, the minister of colonies also hoped to curtail Idris al-Sanusi's political authority. Colosimo did not imagine this would be a difficult task. The deepening of relations between Idris and the Italian colonial administration, he argued, would naturally raise doubts among tribal leaders of the interior about the benefits of the political authority of the Sanusiyya and would eventually inspire dissension among tribal leaders. Italy's reinforcement of Idris's military power, in Colosimo's estimation, would only be a temporary measure, which would lead to "the reduction of the Confraternity to religious confines" in order to make it a more effective "instrument" of Italian expansion without challenging the sovereignty of the state.[93] In the long term, Colosimo hoped that the benefits Idris accrued from his negotiations with Italian colonial authorities would convince tribal leaders in the Libyan interior of the utility of circumventing Idris to establish direct relationships with the Italian administration.

Idris al-Sanusi's position as the head of the Sanusi *ṭarīqa* gained additional validation with the departure of Ahmad al-Sharif for exile in 1918. Leaving first for Istanbul, al-Sharif would never set foot again in Libya before his death in 1933.[94] In Tripolitania al-Sharif's departure and the Ottoman settlement after World War I sparked competition for resources and political influence in the region that was so fierce, some historians have characterized it as civil war.[95] But for the Italian administration in Cyrenaica, al-Sharif's departure seemed to confirm the successful development of Idris as the new representative of the Sanusiyya. The actual relationship between Idris and al-Sharif during this period of transition remains something of a mystery. British intelligence reported indications that al-Sharif had preserved his position as the spiritual leader of the Sanusi *ṭarīqa*. Idris himself indicated to his British contacts that he and al-Sharif had remained on friendly terms and that they had essentially divided responsibilities within the *ṭarīqa*: Idris claimed a civil administrative position, while al-Sharif remained a spiritual leader.[96] The Italian administration posited its support of Idris on a supposed division of loyalties among the Sanusiyya, but it is possible to see the maneuverings of the Sanusi family as a savvy political move to hedge their bets between the two sides of the European alliance system in a tumultuous era of interimperial conflict in World War I.

Limiting Religious Authority in the Era of Negotiations

Despite some fear that Ahmad al-Sharif might continue to wield influence in the region, the idea that the two cousins were dividing their roles within the Sanusi *ṭarīqa* actually seemed to provide some relief to Italian officials. They worried that Idris al-Sanusi's ability to negotiate a power-sharing relationship would provide him with a potent mixture of political and religious authority that could ultimately challenge state sovereignty, and the continued popularity of al-Sharif suggested reassuring limits to Idris's ability to unite the inhabitants of the Cyrenaican interior. In the contradictory nature of power-sharing systems under colonial rule, Italian officials constantly sought out ways restrict Idris's authority even while they contributed to the material needs of his political presence; one strategy was to undermine his claims to religious leadership. The Ottoman defeat in World War I opened up new possibilities in this regard. The dissolution of the original Treaty of Lausanne meant the end of the sultan's position as caliph. In the context of the Libyan territories, this allowed Italian officials to claim direct control over an Islamic judicial system that had remained under the purview of a representative of the Ottoman sultan after the Italian invasion. Minister of Colonies Ferdinando Martini advocated direct state involvement in naming functionaries in the Islamic and civil courts in the Italian-controlled territories as a possible check on Sanusi influence in religious matters.[97] The process of establishing a new cadre of functionaries began in 1916 under the guidance of a commission of urban notables. The transition generated uncertainty in the colonial administration over how Italian state representatives were meant to behave toward this cadre of Arab functionaries. In an attempt to clarify the new order, avoid giving offense, and provide a "tangible sign of the consideration for their function, their office, and their social status," the governor established a system of identification based on color-coded cards issued to individuals recognized as notables, official functionaries, and ʿulamaʾ.[98]

The color-coded cards offered glaring proof of both the lack of experience among Italian colonial officials and the fragility of this constructed hierarchy. To provide conceptual support for the process, the Ministry of Colonies commissioned a series of studies defending the practice of nominating functionaries from the Commission for the Study of Islamic Issues, a group of scholars that the noted Italian orientalist Leone Caetani helped establish in 1914. The pet project of Giacomo Agnesa and Ferdinando Martini in the Ministry of Colonies, the commission's objective of correcting what they both considered the deplorable lack of knowledge in the Ministry of Colonies about the concerns of local populations found clear purpose in exploring the ramifications of Italy's new position in the Islamic judicial system after World War I. The Ministry of Colonies published two studies from members of the commission to help establish principles to guide the process of increasing Italian control over the judicial system. Both studies also pointed to the utility of the process in creating an opportunity to balance the influence of Idris al-Sanusi through the integration of urban qadi into the colonial system.

First, a study by the legal scholar David Santillana addressed the issue of property rights. With the end of the Ottoman caliphate, the Italian colonial administration claimed direct control over the administration of *awqāf,* or religious properties. This opened up the possibility of redefining the legal status of Sanusi *zawāyā,* which an article in the Akrama Accord required the Italian state to protect. But many of the Sanusi properties had been abandoned during World War I, and the Ministry of Colonies hoped to seize the opportunity to redefine their status. Santillana recommended using the expected increase in state influence over local qadi to have them generate detailed explanations of the terms of waqf ownership in the Libyan territories, suggesting that through their interpretation of the Akrama Accord, the state could retain ownership rights over those Sanusi *zawāyā* and their related properties that had been abandoned during the war.[99]

Less explicitly aimed at controlling the Sanusiyya was a study by Carlo Alfonso Nallino, another member of the Ministry of Colonies Commission for the Study of Islamic Issues and arguably Italy's foremost orientalist. Published in 1919, Nallino's study served as justification for Italian control over the Islamic judicial system in the Libyan territories by distancing the qadi from the religious authority of the Ottoman caliph. The main thrust of Nallino's study was his argument that the Italian administration had been mistaken in formalizing a distinction between the roles of the sultan and the caliph in the original stipulations of the Treaty of Lausanne, such that—much like the pope—the administration thought he could exercise religious authority in the Libyan territories without exerting political authority. The Treaty of Lausanne had formalized this theory, Nallino noted, by giving the caliph absolute authority over the religious hierarchy in the Libyan territories and by defining the qadi as local representatives of the sultan's religious authority. Nallino instead attributed a firmly civil role to the qadi, arguing that the Italian administration should understand its position as that of judicial magistrate. As such, Nallino's study suggested that the Italian administration could, and indeed should, take full control of naming and training the qadi as a balance to Sanusi authority.[100]

Though not part of the official advisory Commission for the Study of Islamic Issues, in 1920 Enrico Insabato also produced a study intended for an international audience, in which he echoed Nallino's criticism of the Ottoman caliphate as a political artifice. But while Nallino promoted the state's increased integration of the qadi as way of decreasing Sanusi moral authority, Insabato's interpretation continued his consistent support for the Sanusiyya. His work targeted the fear among European imperial powers of the potential for pan-Islamic unity through the continued influence of Istanbul (and broader Islamic networks) in local religious, civil, and political affairs. In opposition to the implications of Nallino's study, Insabato recommended that imperial powers in North Africa should be more concerned with the potential that qadi—as traditional Islamic elites in urban areas—might perpetuate their subordinate position relative to Istanbul. In keeping with his tendency to paint the Sanusiyya as fiercely independent of Ottoman control, Insabato recommended that imperial powers cultivate relationships with Sufi elites to counteract the risk.[101]

Occupation and the Catholic Missionaries

If officials in the Italian colonial administration were concerned with finding creative ways to constrict Sanusi authority, they also felt the need to maintain control over Catholic missionary activities as a threat that could derail their fragile negotiations with Idris al-Sanusi. The wars of the Italian occupation introduced a delicate transition for the Franciscan mission in Cyrenaica. The introduction of an Italian colonial administration brought with it material benefits and the promise of an eventual expansion of the congregation. In August 1913 the minister of colonies increased the regular state funding for the mission in recognition of its value as a source of education and medical services and as a representation of Italian culture abroad. The minister of colonies also cited examples of other imperial powers that provided subsidies to religious missions in the colonies as a model for his decision to increase state funding for the Frati Minore di Lombardia. "Other Nations, and especially Germany and France, spend considerable sums in subsidies of this kind in the certainty that doing so they benefit from expanding the influence of the motherland abroad."[102] Maintaining positive relations with the Franciscans, therefore, served as part of an arsenal for solidifying Italian dominance in the region and proving Italy's stature as one of Europe's imperial powers.

As a direct result of the increase in the size of the Catholic mission in the Libyan territories, the region was elevated from an apostolic prefecture to an apostolic vicariate in the summer of 1913. To fill the new role of titular bishop, Propaganda Fide nominated Ludovico Antomelli, a Milanese Franciscan who proved less eager than his predecessor, Buonaventura Rossetti,[103] to embrace an Italian nationalist message. Antomelli's tenure as bishop in Tripoli from 1913 to 1919 was marked by an increase in tension between the mission and the colonial administration. Apprehensions over the potential for conflict emerged even before his arrival in October 1913. Soon after his nomination to the position, a military chaplain wrote a letter of complaint to the Ministry of Colonies that painted a picture of Antomelli as an intransigent Catholic, pitted against the Italian state.[104] So when the mission developed a plan for an elaborate public festival to celebrate the arrival of the new bishop, the Ministry of Colonies was on high alert. In what would be a test of the willingness of the new church leadership to cooperate with the Italian colonial administration, the ministry expressed concern to members of the church hierarchy, complaining that the preparations for the festival alone had made the local Arab population "uneasy" as a sign of Italian disregard for local customs.

In their exchanges over the possibility of having a festival for Antomelli, both state and church officials appeared to be caught in a web defined by the conflicting requirements of the diplomacy of warming church-state relations in Rome, the perceived need to prevent offense to a Muslim population, and the desire to work for mutual advantage in state and church expansion. Not wanting to appear to force the bishop to genuflect to state authorities, the office of the minister of colonies did not issue a written official prohibition of the festival. The ministry preferred to inform members of the church hierarchy verbally and discreetly that state officials discouraged the plans as a risk to public health and—more important—as a risk to political stability.[105] Antomelli's response was ambivalent. On the one hand, he seemed eager to prove his willingness to do whatever he could to ensure "that the government and ecclesiastical authorities proceed in common accord," due to his perception that their collaboration would "heighten our prestige with these people." But when he at first misunderstood the request to be a dictate against any form of public festival outside the walls of the church, Antomelli agreed reluctantly, arguing that "the presence at religious festivals of the Vicario Apostolico of Libya, or Bishop of Libya as it is commonly called, elicits such patriotic enthusiasm in our populations, that it is difficult to imagine."[106] When Antomelli finally arrived in Tripoli on October 3, the governor of Tripolitania was happy to note that only a "discrete number" of Catholics participated in a simple processional from the port to the city's main church, a far cry from the original celebratory intentions.[107]

Despite this détente, Antomelli's presence in the colonies continued to trouble authorities in the Libyan colonies. At times his conflicts with the colonial administration took on a bitter personal overtone, especially in his tumultuous relationship with General Giovanni Ameglio, who served as governor of both Cyrenaica and Tripolitania during the bishop's tenure in Tripoli. In their conflicts, one can see the influence of domestic Italian issues regarding the role of the church in nationalism—especially during the heightened nationalism of World War I—combined with the particularities of the colonial setting in North Africa. In 1917, for example, tensions flared when Antomelli accused Italian state schools in the colonies of the unimaginable act of employing teachers who were professed atheists, a claim both the director of the Technical School of Tripoli and Ameglio denied vehemently. It is not coincidental that Antomelli attributed the accusation to an anonymous Muslim student who, he claimed, told him "we Muslims cannot hold in high regard certain professors when we hear them make an open profession of Atheism." In his rebuttal to the accusations, Ameglio made it clear that the teachers at the state schools were careful not to express any religious affiliation, reflecting his own support for a liberal principle of laicism in state institutions.[108]

Ameglio portrayed the conflict over state education as evidence of a lack of loyalty on the part of Antomelli that laid bare the conflicts of church and state in the process of national expansion abroad. In response, the governor called for the replacement of the prefect and even questioned the value of state support for the mission. The context of World War I made the challenges of dealing with the prefect seem particularly offensive to Ameglio, during a time when "in Italy, Archbishops and Cardinals kneel . . . to the glory of our Dynasty, to the entire Military in combat for the holy cause of independence and civilization in Europe," while Antomelli seemed intent on discrediting state enterprises in the colonial territories.[109] But Ameglio also cited issues that were specific to establishing a colonial administration in a Muslim territory as factors contributing to their conflict. In a stream of complaints to the Ministry of Colonies, Ameglio condemned Antomelli for "ceding nothing to those political necessities that a bishop called on to do his work in Muslim lands, in countries of colonial conquest of his Fatherland, should instead always take into consideration while carrying out his actions."[110]

Conclusion

Tensions between Antomelli and Ameglio came to a head when the qadi of Tripoli—one of the new cadre of judges appointed to the civil and religious courts by the Italian administration in consultation with a Libyan commission—wrote an open letter in *La Nuova Italia* to encourage local populations to accept Italian rule. He based his argument on parallels he traced between Islam and Christianity. The author, ʿAbd al-Rahman al-Busairi, equated the piety of Christians to that of Muslims and urged greater cooperation in the Libyan territories rooted in a shared sense of religiosity. In a letter to Governor Ameglio, Antomelli expressed discontent with the qadi's admonition that "Mohammed is equal to Jesus, in birth and in death," a statement that Antomelli found to be a blasphemous challenge to core principles of the Catholic Church. That it had been printed in Italian with the permission of government censors (and perhaps at the urging of local officials) Antomelli cited as evidence of preferential treatment in favor of Islam over Catholicism under Ameglio's administration.[111] Antomelli demanded an official denunciation of the article and greater protection of Christian values as part of Italy's heritage and legal framework. "And in asking for this, I ask that which justice and fairness require: both because the Catholic religion is the religion of our Italian statutes, and for that feeling that in any place, but especially in the colonies, must be used by everyone to avoid exasperating others and generating discord."[112]

Antomelli's complaints against the administration of Ameglio attracted little attention in the Ministry of Colonies. In the period between the

signing of the agreement at Akrama and the moment when the relationship between the Italian government and Idris al-Sanusi began to unravel
in 1921–1922, an economically minded "pro-Islamic" approach to colonial
rule seemed to be working in Cyrenaica for the mutual benefit of Italian
and Sanusi elites. There was little interest among colonial authorities in
appeasing the Franciscan mission at the risk of endangering the Italo-
Sanusi alliance. As we will see, this would be an era marked by a heightened courtship of Idris on the part of the Italian administration. Feted and
fussed over—as would befit a head of state—Idris was meant to become
an extension of the Italian power, but his engagement with the Italian
colonial system would end with the dissolution of popular support for his
position as a colonial intermediary.

4

Railways and Resistance

IDRIS AL-SANUSI'S FALL FROM POWER

IN JANUARY 1923 Idris al-Sanusi took one of the many cars in his posses-sion[1] and left for self-imposed exile in Egypt. He would not return to the Libyan territories until he was placed on the throne of the independent Kingdom of Libya in 1951. His departure was not a total surprise to Italian officials in the Ministry of Colonies; he had sent a number of requests to ministry officials for permission to travel to Egypt for medical attention since at least the beginning of 1922. But it did leave the Italian adminis-tration in Benghazi holding a series of worthless agreements with little pretense of any form of political control or military security in the inte-rior of Cyrenaica. A new government under Benito Mussolini seized on al-Sanusi's departure as an opportunity to turn away from power-sharing relationships and initiate a new phase of military campaigns to expand direct territorial control.

The fact that Idris al-Sanusi's departure coincided with the rise of fas-cism has provided historians with an easy explanation for the failure of the power-sharing arrangement; most accounts characterize his decision to leave as a reaction to the perceived threat posed by the political changes in Rome. One oral testimony from a former anti-Italian mujahid even cites a supposed plot to murder Idris by Italian agents as a deciding fac-tor in the latter's departure.[2] Although it is true that the formation of a government under Mussolini at the end of 1922 brought a leadership to the Ministry of Colonies that embraced an aggressive rhetoric of absolute state control in the Libyan territories, the emphasis on the rise of fascism in accounts of Idris's departure misses the impact of a regional context in the dissolution of the Italo-Sanusi arrangement. Idris had lost the support of his political base in Cyrenaica well before the political shift in Rome. The arrangements he had established with Italian and British representatives in Akrama in 1917 found initial acceptance among populations worn down by warfare and in need of the stability his position as an intermediary provided. In later iterations of the Italo-Sanusi negotiations held in al-Rajma, however, regional power brokers contested the extent to which his arrangements with Italian officials promised to consolidate political and economic power in his hands.

Given the troubled legacy of Idris al-Sanusi as a colonial collaborator during the Italian occupation and as a British/US ally after independence, I caution the reader against taking this as an attempt to "save" Idris. This is not the story of a missed opportunity, nor is it meant as a defense of the subsequent military action of the fascist administration in the 1920s. Examining the breakdown of Idris's political support in colonial Cyrenaica reveals the limits of Sanusi authority and pulls the curtain back on the network of relationships necessary for his ability to act as an intermediary. It offers an opportunity to understand how the connection between access to economic resources and the political-religious authority of the Sanusiyya changed during the Italian occupation and as a result of the series of Italian-Sanusi agreements. It also allows us to gain some perspective on what motivated Idris al-Sanusi to enter into a relationship with the Italian colonial state in the first place, enabling us to escape from the postcolonial imperative to focus on histories of resistance and turn instead to an inquiry into the logic of collaboration in a colonial setting. What did al-Sanusi expect to gain in return for his position as an intermediary, and where did he think the relationship would lead him and the Sanusi *ṭarīqa*?

With the political agenda shifting in Rome, the objectives for Italians at the negotiating table were just as murky. Domestic pressure to exert full control on territories that had been under formal Italian sovereignty for close to a decade made Italian representatives increasingly insistent on taking concrete actions to fulfill a long-term plan for territorial aggrandizement. Initial steps in that direction included stationing Italian soldiers at armed Sanusi camps and expanding transportation infrastructure into the Libyan interior. A railway construction project under joint Italian and Sanusi protection, however, met the stiff resistance of Idris al-Sanusi's regional support base. The response of the Italian colonial administration focused on bolstering Idris's military capabilities to prevent a full assault on his intermediary position. In the process, however, Italian officials encountered problems common to colonial intermediaries: How much political authority would al-Sanusi have without Italian support? Were they supporting a diminishing regional power? And at what point would the relationship become counterproductive for all concerned?

Railroads and Camels: Transportation and Sanusi Authority

The agreement signed by Italian and Sanusi representatives in Akrama was only meant to be a temporary settlement. In October 1920 they signed another agreement in the city of al-Rajma to establish a more permanent Sanusi administration in the Cyrenaican interior. The core provisions of the al-Rajma Accord echoed the agreements signed in Akrama in that they focused on a gradual consolidation of state power through a Sanusi intermediary. The primary objectives were to establish a Sanusi emirate in the region—thus solidifying Idris al-Sanusi's political authority—in exchange for the disarmament of tribes of the Cyrenaican interior. The issue of disarmament proved volatile and contributed to the ultimate failure of the al-Rajma Accord.

A secondary provision, however, called for infrastructure development, especially railway construction. The issue of railroad construction drove forward negotiations between Idris al-Sanusi and Italian officials as an abiding concern of both parties. But the prospect of an expansion of existing railway networks from the coast into the interior detracted from Idris's ability to rely on his political base in Cyrenaica. From the beginning of the occupation, access to safe travel routes for supply lines proved a constant concern for Italian officials in the Libyan colonies. During the 1910s the combination of a lack of state funds, the disapproval of local populations, legal restrictions on landownership, and technical difficulties with the geographical terrain of the Jabal al-Akhdar plateau near Benghazi restricted the construction of railroads in Cyrenaica.[3] The absence of railways presented challenges to the transportation of the people and supplies of the Italian military during the initial wars of occupation. After the establishment of the Italian Ministry of Colonies in 1912, the civil administration continued to focus on the issue of railway construction as a tool for pacification and further incorporation of the Libyan interior into the colonial administration.

Arguably, railway construction held a deeper significance for Italy than for other European powers engaged in infrastructure projects in overseas colonies. As a latecomer to both industrialization and imperial expansion,

Italy's railway construction lagged behind that of other European nations. In the late nineteenth and early twentieth centuries, a nascent nationalist movement seized on the discrepancy as symbolic of the weakness of the claims of the liberal Italian state to answer the needs of its citizens.[4] As Italian imperialists rushed to catch up with international competitors, statistics on the number of kilometers of railway in Italy and its colonies offered a potent symbol of Italy's shortcomings as an industrialized nation and one of Europe's great powers. Of course concerns over railway construction in the Libyan territories also focused on the practical issues facing an imperial power expanding in a marginal territory of the Ottoman Empire. Ottoman proposals to build railway lines into the Sahara as a means of confirming Istanbul's control in North Africa in the 1890s went unfulfilled.[5] As a result, supplies reached both Italian and Ottoman forces via camel during most of the Italo-Turkish War of 1911–1912.[6] The Italian military built a short line of railway around Tripoli for troop movements and supply lines, which was opened to public use in May 1913, but railway construction in the Libyan territories stalled after the formal establishment of Italian sovereignty. A lack of interest among Italian investors in the colonial enterprise and a shortage of state funds in the uncertain atmosphere of the initial occupation and World War I can account for the failure of the early colonial administration to extend the railway networks beyond a narrow region around Tripoli.

Railway construction moved at an even slower pace in Cyrenaica. By the end of June 1915 the Ministry of Colonies calculated that only 19 kilometers of railroad track had been laid in Cyrenaica, compared to 180 kilometers in Tripolitania. In explaining the disparity, Italian officials pointed to the greater technical difficulties in Cyrenaica involved in dealing with the mountainous terrain of the Jabal al-Akhdar plateau. But a report from the Ministry of Colonies on the shortcomings of railway construction also indicated a level of resistance to railway construction among local populations as well as legal restrictions on state land acquisitions as factors limiting construction in the eastern region of Cyrenaica. Revealing a measure of frustration within the ministry at the lack of progress in railway construction, the report identified two primary factors stemming from regional conditions that blocked the extension of existing railways. First was a shortage of labor. Native workers, according to the ministry's assessments, proved reluctant to join railway construction projects; when they did participate, they required the oversight of Italian officers for a level of workmanship that the ministry did not judge to be worth the effort and cost.

Second was the problem of access to water along the expanding railway lines, an issue that proved a major source of friction. One of the central goals for railway construction was the ability to send water supplies to Italian outposts deep in the region's interior. But paradoxically, the process of railway construction also required greater access to supplies of water for the workers constructing the lines. This proved difficult to achieve in the Cyrenaican interior. The proposed railway construction passed through regions in which access to water constituted a source of political and economic power. In the Libyan interior, people who had not officially submitted to Italian sovereignty tightly controlled wells in these strategic areas. Even in regions where populations had submitted to the Italian colonial state, access to water remained a politically potent issue. Therefore, the prospect of constructing railways raised both the short-term issue of access to water for workers and a long-term issue, in that the construction of railways would decrease the value of wells in the Libyan interior for regional trade.[7]

Resolving the labor and water problems with railway construction lay at the heart of negotiations between Idris al-Sanusi and representatives of Italian imperial interests in the years following the Akrama Accord. In fact, railway schemes were at the core of the earliest attempts by Italian colonial officials to single out Idris as an alternative intermediary to Ahmad al-Sharif. When the Italian Ministry of Foreign Affairs reached out to al-Sharif through the mediation of the Egyptian khedive in 1913, the arrangement was based on a goal of increasing Italian involvement in trade and infrastructure projects between Cyrenaica and Egypt at the expense of similar British development projects.[8] Starting in 1906, the Italian consulate in Cairo began to track the khedive's intentions to extend a railway to the western border of Cyrenaica. Concern that the project would secure British control over commerce in the Libyan territories spurred Italian officials to pursue an understanding with the khedive.[9] A semisecret agreement established between the khedive and Italian representatives also included provisions for the construction of Italian railways between Tripoli and Benghazi that would eventually extend all the way to Alexandria to facilitate regional trade.[10] The khedive's mission to al-Sharif failed to meet the objective of securing Sanusi support for the Italian occupation, and the British managed to put a stop to the backdoor dealings of the khedive and Italian representatives. But since it was during the course of these discussions and through the mediation of the khedive that Italian and British officials developed the strategy of building up the

authority of Idris al-Sanusi to circumvent the refusal of his cousin to bro-
ker a deal, it seems reasonable to assume that infrastructure development
projects played some role in their initial conversations.[11]

In the original list of demands Idris al-Sanusi issued prior to negotiating the terms of the Akrama Accord, he requested that the Italians construct railways into the interior from the coast, a project that fit with Italian
military objectives to facilitate transportation of colonial troops. In his
demands Idris included the stipulation that half of the revenue from the
railways would belong to him immediately and that the entire railway system would fall under his control after ten years.[12] The final agreements in
Akrama did not make infrastructure projects an explicit aim of the Sanusi-
Italian relationship, though the modus vivendi did establish provisions
for the Italian state to provide telephone and telegraph wires between the
coastal region under Italian control and the Sanusi armed camps in the
Cyrenaican interior as a way to improve communications between Italian
state officials and their Sanusi allies.[13] Clearly Idris was on a modernizing mission; his relationship with Italian colonial officials offered an avenue for increasing communications infrastructure that would facilitate
regional trade and consolidate power under Sanusi leadership.

The shared interest in railway construction informed the creation of a
secret "Italo-Arab Union" (Unione Italo-Araba) in August 1918. The project was initiated by a private individual, the engineer Tullio Benedetti,
but he had the assistance of Italy's primary negotiator in the Italo-Sanusi
accords, Luigi Pintor. The formation of the union also drew the support
of the governors of both Tripolitania and Cyrenaica, who celebrated the
opportunity to create a tool that "must be the principle means of our penetration among the populations of the interior."[14] Mediated by Idris al-
Sanusi and signed by twenty Sanusi *ikhwan* and tribal chiefs, the union
was to have its official seat in Ajdabiya, where Idris had maintained his
administrative headquarters since the signing of the Akrama Accord. The
agreement committed its signatories to joint action by Italian financiers
and Sanusi notables in a range of projects targeting economic development: support for agriculture, increasing the flow of goods from interior
oases to the coast, and financing storage facilities along trade routes. One
example of the kinds of development projects the union could address that
was detailed in the formal charter for the association was railway construction. The charter foresaw an agreement by which Italian financiers would
provide financial backing while the Sanusi shaykhs would provide access
to local labor forces and armed security to protect the project. Ultimately,

the goal was for both Italian and Cyrenaican signatories to benefit financially based on a previously negotiated system of return on investments. Recognizing the unpopularity of Italian penetration of the Cyrenaican interior through infrastructure development, the proponents of the association made an effort to conceal Italian involvement. Italian officials saw the union as a means of establishing "joint interest in the work of economic penetration" such that the shaykhs of Ajdabiya could give the illusion of working for their own self-interests while secretly working to extend Italy's effective control into the interior.[15]

For Idris al-Sanusi and the shaykhs of Ajdabiya, the union meant an increase in Italian funding for Sanusi armed camps and an unequivocal claim to the right to maintain armed forces. The fact that the union was kept secret—only those directly involved knew of the project—points to the unpopularity of the kinds of economic development projects the union promoted and the associated risk of violent protest. Indeed, some opponents publicly accused Idris of having "sold the country"; he met such criticism with harsh retribution.[16] As evidence of Idris's interest in railway construction, the armed camps under his control began to offer security to employees working on railroad construction in the region of al-Abyar in September 1919. On monthly maps tracking the strength and position of Sanusi armed camps (as seen in Map 3), the Italian administration marked the relatively small camp at Bu Maryum as a defensive force for the workers of the Ferrovie dello Stato.[17] The designation of Sanusi camps as protection for railway construction offered a clear indication of the mutual interest in infrastructure development that would shape future negotiations for a final settlement of a power-sharing relationship.

Railway Construction under the al-Rajma Accord

The moment to determine the final settlement arrived in 1920, when Idris al-Sanusi and Italian representatives returned to the negotiating table in al-Rajma. Compared to the negotiations at Akrama in 1917, Italian representatives found themselves in a greatly weakened position relative to Idris. The devastating effects of the initial wars of occupation and the conflicts of World War I—especially Ahmad al-Sharif's failed attacks on the western border of Egypt—had given the Italian colonial administration a higher degree of leverage in 1917, though as we have seen, this leverage was tempered by the perceived need to bolster the tenuous position of Idris as the figurehead of the Sanusi *ṭarīqa*. In 1920 relative economic

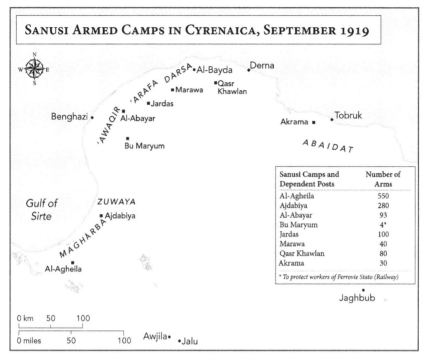

MAP 3 Sanusi Armed Camps in Cyrenaica, September 1919

and political stability in Cyrenaica evened the scales to a greater degree. This new round of negotiations also occurred in an international atmosphere of opposition to wars of imperial aggression. It was a context in which Egyptian nationalists had embraced Wilsonian rhetoric of self-determination, and the great powers at the Paris Peace Conference were gingerly moving toward a mandate system based on British ideals of "trusteeship" and imperial rule through Arab mediation.[18]

The turn away from imperial conflicts after World War I informed a general program of liberalization in the Italian approach to colonial rule. Supported by the efforts of the Italian orientalist Carlo Alfonso Nallino, this approach took its most concrete form in the Libyan Statutes (*Legge Fondamentale*) of 1919.[19] Considered by some historians to represent the "high point" of Italy's "pro-Islamic" approach to colonial rule, the Libyan Statutes established a goal of limited local autonomy through the election of representative assemblies, recognized Arabic as the official language of the state, and accorded the inhabitants of the region the possibility of attaining a modified form of Italian citizenship.[20] For Italian colonial administrators, the primary objective in establishing the Libyan Statutes was to answer the demands of Tripolitanian notables who, along with the Egyptian anti-imperial activist ʿAbd al-Rahman ʿAzzam, declared the establishment of a Tripolitanian republic (al-Jumhuriyya al-Tarablusiyya) in the city of Misrata in November 1918. Rather than fight the declaration of self-government, Italian lawmakers hoped to defuse the anti-Italian sentiment that had inspired the Tripolitanian republic and incorporate its proponents in an expansion of Italian state control through the extension of the statutes.[21]

In al-Rajma, Italian officials hoped to gain the cooperation of Idris al-Sanusi in the application of the Libyan Statutes in the Cyrenaica interior as a means of expanding Italian sovereignty by proxy. The al-Rajma Accord established an autonomous administration under Idris (who took the title of "Emir") centered in Ajdabiya and extending into the Cyrenaican interior. The primary purpose of the new round of negotiations, as the governor of Cyrenaica Giacomo De Martino understood it, was to define the relationship between the political authority of Idris and the Italian colonial state. The Akrama Accord, De Martino complained, had left the nature of that relationship ambiguous by allowing Idris to recognize Italian sovereignty nominally without requiring him to take steps to ensure effective state control. By publicly declaring his commitment to upholding the Libyan Statutes, Idris would bring the tribes of the interior—the leadership of which had officially recognized his political authority—into the orbit of state sovereignty.[22]

Colonial officials saw no ambiguity in the fact that the establishment of a Sanusi emirate in Cyrenaica constituted a relinquishment of Italian power in the Libyan territories. Symbolically, the al-Rajma Accord recognized Idris al-Sanusi as an official representative of the Italian state, therefore laying claim to his authority as a proxy for the Italian state. In the hierarchy of colonial authorities, Idris was second only to the governor of Cyrenaica and was owed official salutes from members of the Italian military as greeting, as pictured in figures 4.1 and 4.2. Not everyone was pleased with this arrangement. Some officers, for example, refused to salute him in protest against his rank, but such refusal met with swift disciplinary action.[23] For De Martino, the government's sanction of Idris al-Sanusi's de facto autonomy meant avoiding a potentially disastrous armed conflict. The central government also seemed happy to take the opportunity to reduce spending on armed forces in the Libyan territories; the Italian troop presence of about thirty thousand was reduced by a third after the conclusion of the al-Rajma Accord.[24] De Martino chose

FIGURE 4.1 Italian forces saluting Idris al-Sanusi, ca. 1919.
Source: Il Laboratorio di Ricerca e Documentazione Storico Iconografica, Università degli Studi Roma Tre.

FIGURE 4.2 Official greeting of Idris al-Sanusi in the Sanusi *zawāyā*.
Source: ASMAI II 181/70/362, Ministero dell'Africa Italiana, "La Senussia," 1949.

to interpret the official recognition of limited Italian authority as a potential economic benefit, confining Italian presence to the truly "useful and productive" areas along the coast.[25]

The utility of the arrangement, however, depended entirely on the expansion of roads, railroads, and telegraph lines into the Cyrenaican interior to promote an opening of markets and to more fully integrate the interior with the zones of Italian control along the coast. The nineteenth article of the al-Rajma Accord explicitly linked the application of the Libyan Statutes with the completion of infrastructure projects. After noting the importance of Idris al-Sanusi's willingness and ability to assure the application of the Libyan Statutes in Cyrenaica as a precondition for his position in the Italian state system and for his receipt of a regular salary, this crucial article charged Idris with promoting private industry and the development of communications and transportation infrastructure: "The Emir for his part will undertake a project of persuasion by means of his high influence so that there should be no obstacle on the part of those who oppose the creation of roads and railroads, of postal, bus, telegraph and telephone lines, all works required for the progress of the country and the interest and prosperity of commerce."[26] This article reveals a central thrust of the treaty for the Italian officials and their regional allies involved in the negotiations: the establishment of conditions for investment in and construction of transportation infrastructure. It was a measure that made the private, secret relationship established in the Italo-Arab Union a core component of Idris's official position in relationship to the Italian colonial state.

Giacomo De Martino had long been an advocate of combined state and private activities in Italian colonial expansion. As a senator and the founding president of the Istituto Coloniale Italiano, De Martino counted as one of the more vocal proponents of imperialism in early twentieth-century Italy. In 1907 De Martino took a well-publicized trip through Libya and Tunisia during which he calculated the worth of Cyrenaica based on the possibility of establishing railroads between the Bay of Ṭubruq and Alexandria. He estimated that the trip could be cut down to be as short as twenty hours, thus incorporating Cyrenaica into far-flung markets.[27] The promise of railway construction for the commercial development of eastern Libya informed an agreement between De Martino and the Banco di Roma in May 1910 to conduct preliminary studies on the feasibility of a new railway line extending between the Egyptian border and Tripolitania.[28] De Martino's interest in connecting the region using the railroad continued when he was involved in the failed scheme in 1913 to establish a secret agreement with the khedive of Egypt to extend railway networks from Benghazi to Alexandria in exchange for the khedive's assistance in forming an alliance with the Sanusiyya.[29]

In 1920 De Martino expressed reservations about allowing Idris al-Sanusi to confine direct Italian control to the coast, but he also celebrated the negotiations in al-Rajma as an opportunity to encourage private and state investments in the Libyan territories. In a memorandum on the economic benefits of the accord, De Martino explained a broader theory of colonial development as a process comprising two stages that clearly demonstrated his commitment to the goal of private and state investments working in tandem. In the first phase, the state limited its functions to political and military operations. In the second phase, ushered in by the al-Rajma Accord, a heightened level of security allowed for greater private enterprise and a limitation of state functions to "guiding and collaborating" with private projects: "Following the accords with the Sanusiyya and the application of the liberal Statutes, Cyrenaica has doubtlessly entered into the second period: it follows that development will follow from private initiative, strongly supported by the State."[30] De Martino identified the construction of roads and railroads as a first step in the agricultural development of Cyrenaica and its eventual colonization by Italian immigrants, a step that would, he claimed, help transform the region into its proper state as "a piece of Sicily nestled in the African continent."

The push for the development of infrastructure in Cyrenaica represented the combined interests of political elites and entrepreneurs in Italy who, like De Martino, expected immediate financial benefits in the Libyan territories, as well as the more distant promise of its future transformation into a destination for Italian emigrants. The prospect of infrastructure development in the interior inspired a renewed interest in agricultural development schemes and spurred colonial institutions in Italy to encourage Italian officials to finalize a settlement with Idris al-Sanusi. In October 1920 a commission from the Syndicate of Studies for the Improvement of Cyrenaica (Sindacato di studi per la valorizzazione della Cirenaica), an organization founded in Milan by Senator Angelo Valvassori Peroni, arrived in Benghazi just a few days before the conclusion of the al-Rajma Accord. The commission supported a plan for joint sovereignty under Italian and Sanusi authority with the understanding that it would allow for the development of roads and railways in the region between Benghazi and Derna, an area deemed to have the best agricultural land in Cyrenaica.[31]

The commission's recommendations and the conclusion of the al-Rajma Accord inspired the colonial administration to focus construction of roads and rail in the area between Derna and al-Marj. The construction contributed to the dramatic transformation of al-Marj from a small village into a major town during the 1920s, not least due to the appeal of a new well dug to provide water to the railway station.[32]

Highlighting the centrality of infrastructure development as an objective in the al-Rajma Accord tells us a couple of things. First, it demonstrates the ways in which a liberal model of imperial expansion based on power-sharing structures and development projects overlapped with the objective of agricultural settlement, a long-standing interest of Italian imperialists that would become a pet project of the fascist administration. The continuity belies attempts to identify a sharp break from the liberal to the fascist period of colonial rule, by fascist contemporaries and historians alike. The emphasis on the role of infrastructure development in the al-Rajma Accord also hints at the ambitions that drove Idris al-Sanusi's collaboration with the Italian colonial state beyond simply reacting to the initiatives of imperialists; he seized on the prospect of an influx of Italian state and private capital to launch a program of infrastructure development that promised to achieve greater economic integration of the region under the control of the Sanusi *ṭarīqa* and his leadership. In his dealings with Italian officials during the period of their negotiations, Idris demonstrated an interest in gaining access to modern technologies of transportation. While the formal negotiation emphasized the construction of railways for mutual benefit, Idris also requested trucks and cars from Fiat through personal communication with colonial officials. The ability to move efficiently conferred power, especially in a semidesert terrain with the immense scale of distances that defines the Cyrenaican interior. The stylish Torpedo with the specialized gold insignia that Idris ordered from Fiat in the spring of 1919, however, suggests that he valued the Italian automobiles for their style as much as their efficiency.[33]

Losing Consensus in the Sanusiyya

The provision for infrastructure development in the al-Rajma Accord also helps to explain the dissolution of Idris al-Sanusi's political support in Cyrenaica. His cooperation with the Italian officials on railway construction projects threatened to derail the economic strength of tribes whose control over access to wells and camel supplies gave them an advantage in

Saharan caravans. The fact that the negotiations with al-Sanusi occurred on the heels of the passage of the Libyan Statutes in 1919 suggests that the infrastructure projects represented both an economic and a political threat to tribes in the Cyrenaican interior; as the colonial state expanded access to citizenship and representation, it also proposed to expand its physical reach through communications infrastructure.

Just as they had in the formation of the Italo-Arab Union, Italian colonial officials anticipated a certain measure of resistance to the introduction of railway construction schemes. The stipulation in the al-Rajma Accord requiring Idris al-Sanusi to provide security for infrastructure projects suggests as much. When a group of approximately one hundred ʿAwāqir and Maghārba notables convened in the town of Antelat (outside of Ajdabiya) to express opposition to the Libyan Statutes in February 1920, railway construction proved a key sticking point. De Martino sent his director of civil and political affairs with a group of officials to the meeting to provide reassurances about the government's intentions. They found a group of tribal leaders who were not entirely satisfied with Sanusi leadership and seemed eager to use the Libyan Statutes as an opportunity to initiate a period of direct contact with the Italian colonial administration, despite having signed a declaration of their intentions to recognize the Sanusi flag—and only the Sanusi flag—as a symbol of state authority in the region. ʿAbd al-Salam al-Kiza, whom Italian officials considered to be the most important Sanusi intermediary of the ʿAwāqir tribes, requested the suspension of railway construction as a sign of friendship, "because this was not acceptable to the ʿAwāqir, who feared being greatly damaged in caravan traffic." Beyond simply opposing railway construction, al-Kiza's opposition constituted a challenge to Idris al-Sanusi's authority, in that he rejected the right of the Sanusi leader to negotiate with the Italian government concerning tribal lands, especially in the area between al-Rajma and al-Marj immediately under threat by the expansion of railway lines. [34]

De Martino offered two possible explanations for al-Kiza's complaints, both of which were dismissive of any real concerns over the effects of railway construction. First, he saw a possible insurrection against Idris al-Sanusi within the Sanusi *ṭarīqa*. Objections to his authority to negotiate with the Italian government on behalf of tribal interests, De Martino imagined, constituted an attempt to wrest control of the Sanusiyya away from Idris by "more orthodox and less conciliatory" factions.[35] Second, De Martino thought al-Kiza's complaints masked an attempt by Idris to engineer a façade of regional opposition to the Libyan Statutes in order to gain leverage in upcoming renegotiations of the al-Rajma Accord. De Martino further suspected that Idris welcomed the signs of discontent with the centralization of the statutes as an excuse to ask for an increase in state funding for his armed forces.[36]

Despite De Martino's attempts to downplay the risk of opposition, the Italian Ministry of Colonies wrote directly to leading members of the tribes in Ajdabiya and the Jabal al-Akhdar regions to reassure them that the statutes did not represent a threat. Italian authorities focused on the issue of political autonomy. They assured the assembly of shaykhs that the state would keep out of tribal politics and leave them to choose their own representatives to a future Cyrenaican Parliament, which they intended to establish in Benghazi to fulfill the promises of the Libyan Statutes. The Ministry of Colonies also told the Maghārba and ʿAwāqir notables that they could even choose to abstain from engaging in the Italian state system entirely if they so wished. "Those Tribes who do not wish to accept the Law will remain in peace in their country, but they will not be represented either in the House of Deputies or in the Council of Administration, nor will their Shaykhs be granted any privileges by the Government."[37] The notables assembled in Antelat had every reason to doubt the sincerity of Italian intentions to allow them to absent themselves from the Libyan Statutes; full incorporation of the Cyrenaican interior was the clear goal of Italo-Sanusi negotiations. But more immediately concerning was the failure of Italian authorities to address the economic threat posed by the expansion of Italian- and Sanusi-controlled infrastructure.

The tribal leaders of Cyrenaica responded to the reassurances of the Ministry of Colonies with an absolute refusal to recognize the validity of any negotiations Idris al-Sanusi had concluded with the Italian government that went beyond the original agreement in Akrama from 1917. Their opposition focused on the centralization of authority in the Italian state center of Benghazi through the formation of a Cyrenaican Parliament as a move that would undermine the dominance of the city of Ajdabiya, a key center of trade among the more influential tribes of the Sanusi ṭarīqa. But they also voiced explicit concern over Italian plans to extend the railroad and roads, "as this would cause a loss to us in the trade of hiring camels."[38] De Martino's proposed railway construction and the concentration of political power in Benghazi threatened to shift regional influence away from Ajdabiya and the nearby region of Sirtica, where Maghārba notables dominated trading patterns in their region based on their access to camels and their ties to merchants in the interior oases. Besides detracting from camel-based trade, the new wells that would be required to supply water to the workers building the lines further threatened to diminish the value of the control of wells in a network from Sirte to the oases of Kufra that fell under the ownership of Maghārba tribes.[39] The Maghārba and ʿAwāqir shaykhs did not object to Italian involvement in regional commercial activities. On the contrary, they noted their approval of the Akrama Accord because they understood it to limit Italian presence in Cyrenaica to commercial influence, but they drew a line at the construction of railways.[40] The al-Rajma Accord represented a step too far in the centralization of trade through the development of infrastructure.

The refusal of the collected Maghārba and ʿAwāqir shaykhs to accept the validity of the al-Rajma Accord precipitated a crisis of leadership in the Sanusiyya that would ultimately inform a shift toward defining the *ṭarīqa* as an anticolonial movement. The Cyrenaican shaykhs referred to "our Senussi Black Flag, the flag of our Prophet" as a symbol of freedom from Italian state control, thus claiming collective ownership over one of Idris al-Sanusi's symbols of political power and redefining it as an anti-Italian symbol. They also asserted their independence of action and Idris's reliance on their approval by noting that "any peace made between the Italian Government and Said Idris without our consent will be valueless." The objection of the Cyrenaican tribal leaders revealed the symbolic value of the Sanusi *ṭarīqa* as a political movement for anticolonial independence that could be entirely divorced from the figure of Idris and, increasingly, from the entire Sanusi family. An uneasy coalition of Sanusi notables—military leaders and tribal elites with prominent positions in the Sanusi *ṭarīqa*—took up the Sanusi flag against the extension of Italian development projects into the interior.

The signing of the finalized accord at al-Rajma in October 1920 was followed quickly by a celebratory tour by Idris al-Sanusi and his entourage through Italy, during which he was feted in his official capacity as emir, but the inability of the colonial administration to answer the concerns of the tribal shaykhs became evident after his return to Cyrenaica. Armed attacks against Italian road and rail construction projects began in May 1921 in the Jabal al-Akhdar region outside the coastal town of Susa.[41] To underscore his disapproval of the attacks and his continued interest in promoting railway construction in the region, Idris organized meetings with shaykhs from Maghārba and ʿAwāqir tribes twice between February and the end of October 1921 to try to convince them to agree to an extension of the

Italian administration—along with disarmament—to implement the full terms of the al-Rajma Accord.⁴² But the proposed construction of the railroad between al-Marj and Derna remained a point of contention, and an initial meeting in al-Abyar ended with the Cyrenaican shaykhs declaring their intention to oppose the application of the accord with force if necessary.⁴³ After another meeting in Ajdabiya in October, Idris managed to gain the Maghārba shaykhs' provisional acceptance of railway construction and a temporary halt in attacks on infrastructure projects. In exchange, however, he offered the concession that Sanusi-affiliated tribes would be allowed to maintain armed forces during the period of construction. Given the marked determination to block railway construction and the continued access to arms, this agreement could only secure a temporary halt in hostilities.⁴⁴

In response to the resistance to railway construction and the related delay in disarmament, De Martino instituted measures to reinforce Idris al-Sanusi's authority. During the conference of regional leaders at Antelat in February 1920, De Martino established as a guideline for action the importance of preventing anything that might cause Idris to appear "discredited at our own expense," while doing everything in their power to ensure the construction of the railway line.⁴⁵ The key, De Martino insisted, was to promote stability through continued government support of Idris. Putting aside suspicions that the entire opposition represented a ruse by Idris to prevent Italian state expansion (De Martino was forever second-guessing Idris's motives), De Martino's administration placed the Sanusi armed groups under the joint command of Italian officials and Idris in May 1920.⁴⁶ The measure provoked objections from officials within the colonial administration and nationalists in Rome, who saw it as a further loss of control for the Italian state and an admission of the failure of the Libyan Statutes to extend state presence into the Libyan interior; Italian nationalists did not like the potential that Italian troops might end up in positions subordinate to Sanusi commanders. The minister of colonies at the time, Giuseppe Giardini, voiced his concern that armed camps in Cyrenaica under joint Italian and Sanusi administration would breed confusion about whether the Italians or Idris could claim effective control.⁴⁷ But as long as powerful affiliates of the Sanusiyya remained opposed to railway construction—and managed to forestall disarmament—joint control of Sanusi armed camps seemed the best option to try to fulfill the spirit of regional autonomy in the Libyan Statutes while making progress on De Martino's main concern of infrastructure development.⁴⁸ In November 1921 the Italian agent primarily responsible for negotiating with the Sanusiyya,

Luigi Pintor, met with an Sanusi intermediary in the negotiations, ʿUmar al-Kikhiya, in the town of Bu Maryam, between Benghazi and al-Abyar. They agreed to the mixed Italian-Sanusi armed groups, but with a proportion meant to maintain a semblance of Italian control in the region by establishing a ratio of ten Italian soldiers to every eight provided by Idris.[49] It was an arrangement that demonstrated a concerted effort by the Italian Ministry of Colonies to buttress the shaky position of Idris al-Sanusi while attempting to project an image of Italian strength, thus emphasizing the intertwined nature of Sanusi and Italian authority in Cyrenaica.

Giacomo De Martino died in Benghazi in the same month that the Bu Maryam agreement was concluded, and Luigi Pintor was named regent governor to maintain a sense of continuity in discussions with Idris al-Sanusi and the tribal leaders of Cyrenaica. When Maghārba shaykhs escalated their opposition to Italian state expansion by reaching out to nationalist activists in Tripolitania at the beginning of 1922—even voicing an interest in the establishment of a unified Sanusi authority in both territories—Pintor became an outspoken critic of the very treaties he had negotiated with Idris. Pintor's repudiation of the value of the agreements he had secured represented a crisis of confidence in the nature of Italy's ally in the region. Unsure whether Idris's failure to gain compliance for the al-Rajma Accord reflected a lack of authority among the Sanusi *ikhwān* and their affiliated tribes or a Sanusi plot to undermine the Italian occupation, Pintor joined a growing chorus of voices among Italian nationalists who saw the reliance on a Sanusi intermediary as a symbol of Italian weakness and as a potential opening for pan-Islamic influences.

Ahmad al-Sharif in Pan-Islamic Networks

With opposition to Idris al-Sanusi mounting in 1920–1921 in reaction to the al-Rajma Accord, the possibility of establishing an agreement with Ahmad al-Sharif reemerged in the foreground of discussions among officials in the Italian Ministries of Colonies and Foreign Affairs. Al-Sharif actually made the first moves to resume contact with Italian officials several times after his departure from Cyrenaica in 1918. The Sanusi notable hoped to establish the possibility of returning to Cyrenaica to claim his properties in the Libyan territories, but colonial officials in the process of cultivating Idris as an alternative authority within the Sanusi *ṭarīqa* found the idea of simultaneous discussions with al-Sharif too risky to contemplate.[50] The opposition to the al-Rajma Accord, however, demonstrated the limitations of support for Idris as a political figure, and at the same time the potential for an alliance with al-Sharif promised tremendous benefits on an international stage. As an active supporter of the Kemalist government in Ankara, al-Sharif's value as a symbol of Islamic resistance against European imperialism increased during his exile.[51] The involvement of popular Islamic figures like al-Sharif in the Kemalist government, aligned against the pro-British sultan-caliph, allowed the Turkish nationalist movement to broaden its appeal by calling on anti-European Islamic unity. Rumors that the Kemalist government might recognize al-Sharif as an alternative caliph suggested the possibility that his influence would only increase.[52] News that he might even be given a position as the emir of Hejaz and Mesopotamia struck Italian officials as an indication of the level of popular support he had acquired in the process of fighting against Ottoman enemy powers during World War I. A temporary alignment of interests between the Soviets and pan-Islamic/Turkish nationalist movements in 1920–1921 based on their shared anti-Western rhetoric added to the threat of al-Sharif as a public figure with the potential to destabilize colonial territories of Western European powers.[53]

For the Italian minister of foreign affairs, intelligence on Ahmad al-Sharif's activities indicated that "the faces of the most intransigent representatives of Ottoman-Muslim nationalism had turned with intense attention on Sidi Ahmad [*sic.*] as a possible valid contrast to figures, especially British creatures, in Eastern Anatolia and Arabia."[54] As unlikely as it might have seemed based on the history of animosity between the Italian colonial administration and al-Sharif, this reasoning suggested the potential for Italy to forge a unique position—one aligned against British interests—in a broader Muslim world based on a common understanding with Idris al-Sanusi's cousin. The anxiety over al-Sharif's position in pan-Islamic networks embedded Italy's problems of colonial rule in an international framework that inspired a collaborative approach between the Ministry of Colonies and the Ministry of Foreign Affairs. Minister of Colonies Giuseppe Giardini underlined the confluence of international and colonial issues in a memo to the minister of foreign affairs as they debated the best approach to dealing with the possibility of al-Sharif's return to Cyrenaica: "The vision that this Minister has always had of the situation in Libya that becomes clearer every day is that the events in Libya are not for the most part anything but the *local* manifestations of factors and actions that are prepared or matured in other places. Thus, it is not possible to conceive of a Libya policy in itself. Instead, it is necessary to consider it as a function of domestic, intercolonial, and international factors that contribute to its formation."[55]

It was only with his involvement in the Kemalist government that the possibility of a relationship with Ahmad al-Sharif returned to the foreground of discussions within the Ministry of Colonies.[56] Officials in the ministry developed the idea of reaching out to al-Sharif because they calculated that the British might help him return to Cyrenaica anyway, if only to remove him from Anatolia, where his presence as a charismatic leader with a pan-Islamic message threatened stability. In proposing to reach out to the former Sanusi leader, Italian officials hoped that it would allow them to gain the upper hand to assure that if he did return, he might do so with a more favorable attitude to the Italian state than he had demonstrated in the past.[57] Luigi Pintor took up the cause in favor of establishing a relationship with al-Sharif as a means of controlling the ramifications of his possible return, "with pacts and guarantees through our means rather than enduring it unprepared, and without links on his part to the fraudulent help of others."[58]

The potential to negotiate directly with Ahmad al-Sharif spoke to broad anti-British sentiment among nationalist groups in Italy following World War I. Proponents of the plan recognized an alignment of interests with the Kemalist government in Ankara in opposition to British foreign policy that might convince al-Sharif of the benefits of a pro-Italian position.[59] The idea of establishing a relationship with al-Sharif fit with a range of Italian efforts to damage British standing in the broader Muslim world. The nationalist poet General Gabriele D'Annunzio, for example, developed relationships with influential Egyptian nationalists and helped establish pan-Islamic associations in Rome as a way to undermine British foreign policy.[60]

Ahmad al-Sharif's influence in the Kemalist government also added to his popularity in the Libyan territories—even in Tripolitania, where prominent political figures had long been wary of the Sanusiyya. Tripolitanian notables began calling for a return of al-Sharif to the Libyan territories because they hoped he could restore stability to a region devastated by a chaotic civil war between Ramadan al-Suwayhli, on the one hand, and an alliance of the Muntasir family and ʿAbd al-Nabi Belkhir, a leading figure in the Warfalla tribes, on the other. After Ramadan al-Suwayhli died in August 1920 during an attack on Warfalla forces, a group of Tripolitanian notables met in Gharyan in November 1920 to try to establish a consensus for unified political action. Including the Egyptian nationalist and proponent of pan-Arabism, ʿAbd al-Rahman ʿAzzam, this conference hoped to develop a system that would allow for relative autonomy from the Italian colonial state while promoting much-needed stability in the region.[61] Given his influence in Ankara, al-Sharif offered the possibility of integrating the interests of Tripolitanian notables into wider networks of Islamic activism. The ongoing negotiations between the Italian state and the Sanusi family suggested that the establishment of a Sanusi emirate in Tripolitania under his leadership could have the added benefit of preventing significant opposition from the Italian authorities, thus contributing to regional stability.[62]

The possibility of a Sanusi emirate being established in Tripolitania, however, detracted from the appeal of a return of Ahmad al-Sharif for Italian officials. The Ministry of Colonies was alarmed by the possibility that he could unify the resources of the two regions in opposition to the Italian colonial state with ties to international influence that could undermine Italian authority throughout the region. For most of the Italian occupation, rivalries between Tripolitanian notables—especially Ramadan al-Suwayhli—and Sanusi elites in Cyrenaica had reassured Italian officials, who hoped to maintain a strict division between the territories as a way to prevent any one regional figure from forming an anti-Italian coalition. In January 1922 the notables of Tripolitania met for a second time in Sirte, and as a signal of their intention to develop cross-regional ties, they invited Salah al-Atyush—a notable from Ajdabiya and one of the primary opponents to the implementation of the al-Rajma Accord—as a representative of Cyrenaican interests.[63] In April 1922 the Tripolitanian notables issued a proposal to the Italian Ministry of Colonies to form an emirate under the leadership of al-Sharif in Tripolitania that would answer to Idris al-Sanusi as a supreme leader of both territories. Not all of the Tripolitanian notables approved of a Sanusi emirate, but the proposal was an attempt to gain access to the considerable forces of the tribes of western Cyrenaica under the Italian sanction of a Sanusi intermediary.[64]

Local Officials in Revolt against Rome

The prospect of a Sanusi emirate uniting the two regions of Tripolitania and Cyrenaica under Ahmad al-Sharif and Idris al-Sanusi divided opinions in the Italian Ministry of Colonies. Some favored expanding reliance on the Italo-Sanusi arrangements as an entrée to connections with the broader Muslim world, while others began to advocate for expansion of direct state control in the Libyan territories at the expense of the power-sharing relationship with Idris. The divisions within the Italian colonial administration mirrored broader ruptures in Italian politics caused by the rising force of a nationalist platform after World War I. In the colony of Tripolitania, the moment that has generally come to be identified as marking the beginning of a shift toward more aggressive colonial policy in Italy occurred when Governor Giuseppe Volpi ordered the occupation of the city of Misrata in 1921. He initiated the military action with the objective of preventing ʿAbd al-Rahman ʿAzzam from establishing an independent administration in the coastal city.[65] An entrepreneur long interested in colonization schemes for the Libyan territories, Volpi saw his occupation of Misrata as an act of defiance against politicians in Rome who hoped to project an image of Italy as friendly to pan-Islamic or pan-Arab networks in alliance with ʿAbd al-Rahman ʿAzzam, Egyptian nationalists, and al-Sharif as part of an effort to diminish and supplant British and French influence in the Muslim world.[66] The occupation of Misrata generated a public debate in Rome and energized a growing movement calling for greater direct territorial control in the Libyan territories.

Volpi initiated the occupation without the permission or knowledge of the central government in Rome, but when he announced the success of the military campaign in February 1922, he gained the approval and support of the newly appointed minister of colonies, Giovanni Amendola. Following Volpi's lead, Amendola shifted away from his predecessor's willingness to negotiate with the Tripolitanian notables or consider the possibility of extending the Sanusi emirate to Tripolitania. The Amendola administration depicted those initiatives as concessions to international pressures to establish autonomous systems in colonial territories. In a speech before the Italian House of Deputies, Amendola signaled his discontent with directives from the Ministry of Foreign Affairs, which continued to promote the possibility of engaging pan-Islamic networks to achieve Italian anti-British foreign policy objectives:

> It is recommended to the government to meet the views and objectives of the pan-Islamic movement. But what good would it do for Italy? In that case, we would have to allow for the constitution in Libya of an Arab national state, an advanced sentinel of Islamic revolt against European occupation in North Africa for which we would be granted the honor of paying the expenses; we would have

to cover with our flag the reaffirmation in the Mediterranean of a principle of anti-Western and anti-Christian conquest.[67]

In keeping with the nationalist rhetoric that had begun to develop in Italy after World War I, Amendola argued that seeking alliances among pan-Islamic activists in the Muslim world would damage Italy's status on the international stage by tying the future of the nation to the Mediterranean and excluding it from the ranks of other European powers.

Despite his nationalist rhetoric, however, Amendola remained a staunch supporter of negotiating power-sharing systems with local notables in the Libyan territories. Amendola positioned himself in opposition to those who saw Volpi's success as initiating a dramatic shift toward a more aggressive approach to direct control, especially in Cyrenaica. In so doing, he drew a sharp distinction between the politics of Ahmad al-Sharif and his cousin. Calling for a "policy of absolute sincerity and loyalty," Amendola defended Idris al-Sanusi against suggestions that he might be connected to the pan-Islamic movements of his cousin. Amendola painted him instead as a firm ally protecting the Italian colonial administration against those influences.[68] In his steadfast defense of Idris, Amendola found himself in the unexpected position of opposing Luigi Pintor, who after years of negotiating with Idris al-Sanusi and pursuing measures designed to promote Sanusi political authority as an extension of the Italian colonial state, grew increasingly suspicious of Idris's motives in the spring and summer of 1922. Pintor's communications with the minister of colonies took on an alarmed quality as he reported a growing frequency of attacks on Italian supply lines, infrastructure projects, and tribes under Italian protection in the coastal regions. Concerned that Idris had either lost control of the Sanusi *ṭarīqa* and its allied tribes or intended to coordinate with Salah al-Atyush and nationalist leaders in Tripolitania to expand Sanusi influence in a unified anti-Italian front, Pintor's suspicions increased with the news that Idris had invited tribal leaders throughout Cyrenaica, including leaders from the tribes who had submitted to Italian authority, to a conference in Ajdabiya for the first week in June 1922. Pintor argued that in bringing together all of the Cyrenaican tribal leaders, Idris was either interested in securing their approval for the idea of a unified emirate with Tripolitania or in pushing for donations of money or arms—a move that would ultimately threaten to undermine his dependence on Italian support. Evidence that 'Umar al-Mukhtar and other Sanusi shaykhs had employed the personal bodyguards of Idris to intimidate tribal leaders into attending the meeting in Ajdabiya, Pintor claimed, revealed the true weakness of Idris al-Sanusi in the face of objections to the al-Rajma Accord, and he suggested that Idris lacked either the authority or the desire to disarm the tribal forces in Cyrenaica and enforce their acceptance of infrastructure development.[69]

Pintor's reservations about Idris al-Sanusi echoed the concerns over Sanusi political authority that occurred repeatedly over the course of Italian efforts to establish an alliance. But Volpi's aggressive stance in Tripolitania defined a context in which these concerns gained new resonance. As governor of Cyrenaica, Pintor initially opposed Volpi's occupation as a rash move undertaken without the support of Rome and in violation of the process of political negotiations. A large part of Pintor's opposition stemmed from a sense of competition with the governor of Tripolitania over resources and troops that had been diverted from Cyrenaica to Tripolitania to secure the occupation after Volpi's initial foray.[70] As the months went on, however, Pintor aligned himself with Volpi against the Ministry of Colonies as they both called for a more forceful state presence that would lessen their dependence on local notables. When complaints against a number of Italian functionaries in the Cyrenaican administration by ʿUmar al-Kikhiya induced the minister of colonies to dismiss the offending parties in the summer of 1922, Pintor expressed a sense of embattled isolation against the central office, and he grew increasingly vocal in his criticism of the process of negotiations with Idris al-Sanusi.[71]

The dispute between Pintor and Amendola escalated when Italian agents received confirmation that Idris intended to accept the proposal of the Tripolitanian notables for a united Sanusi emirate in conjunction with Ahmad al-Sharif in May 1922. Pintor argued that the reliance of the Italian state on the Sanusi intermediary had backfired, and he called for a dramatic change in the Italian approach to colonial rule. Pintor placed primary responsibility for the failure of the negotiations on the contradictory goals of the Italian Ministry of Colonies to simultaneously cultivate the political authority of the Sanusiyya while undermining it to prevent Idris al-Sanusi from becoming too powerful. He characterized the entire process of negotiations as a ruse on both sides, a relationship in which the Italians constantly sought to convince the Sanusi elite of their peaceful intentions and support for Sanusi authority. "But such veils and treatments and fatally insincere artifices could not hide the substance of a continuous attack against the Sanusi political structure, avoidance of which would require us not to follow al-Rajma or Bu Maryam, which are in fact essentially directed at dismantling the political structure of the confraternity, by now inextricably linked . . . to its organization as a *ṭarīqa*."[72] The Italian colonial administration, Pintor argued, had tied its fate to the diminishing power of a Sanusi *ṭarīqa* that looked to establish ties with notables in Tripolitania and British officials in Egypt in order to escape its reliance on the Italian state.

As Pintor turned against the relationship with Idris al-Sanusi he had helped to engineer, he began to advocate circumventing Idris as a local intermediary, in a process similar to the earlier tactic of turning away from Ahmad al-Sharif in the Akrama Accord. Apparent divisions in the responses to the al-Rajma Accord and the Bu Maryam agreement suggested the possibility of successfully further dividing the Sanusiyya. A meeting between Salah al-Atyush and an Italian agent in Zuwaytina in April 1922, for example, seemed to present an opportunity for the Italian administration to gain the direct support of tribal leaders without the mediation of Idris in exchange for regular payments.[73] But the tactic faced opposition in Amendola's continued defense of Idris as a colonial intermediary. Criticizing the idea as typical of what he called the "undisciplined spirit unfortunately not infrequent in the colonial administration" that prevented the full realization of Italian projects in the Libyan territories, Amendola rejected Pintor's recommendation to undermine Idris's authority.[74]

Over the following months Pintor persisted in his condemnation of the agreements, and both Idris al-Sunasi and ʿUmar al-Kikhiya complained to central authorities of the difficulty in dealing with him. Al-Kikhiya even traveled to Rome and threatened to relinquish his position as an intermediary between state officials and Idris—a position for which he had been paid a healthy sum of 600,000 lire.[75] As a sign of his commitment to negotiations with Idris, Amendola sent Edoardo Baccari, the former director of political affairs in the Ministry of Colonies, to replace Pintor as the governor of Cyrenaica. Amendola hoped the appointment of Baccari, who was known for having established a friendly relationship with ʿUmar al-Kikhiya, would improve relations with the Sanusi elite.[76] Idris's departure in 1923, however, put an end to the debate.

Conclusion

Idris al-Sanusi left the Libyan territories for Egypt in January 1923, three months after Mussolini staged his March on Rome to proclaim the beginning of a fascist revolution in the Italian state. Writing about the events several years later, official British historians characterized Idris's decision to leave Cyrenaica as recognition that the political transition in Rome spelled an inevitable rise of an aggressively nationalist colonial adminis-tration and an end to his relationship with the colonial administration.[77] Some within the Italian administration suspected that Idris had left for Egypt in order to break the accords and allow militant elements within the Sanusiyya to take control of the Sufi *ṭarīqa* without abandoning the pos-sibility of negotiating with European powers again at some future point. Idris's explanations recorded after independence did not offer much clarity on the matter. He cited both the replacement of Giacomo De Martino with "a much less liberal governor"—meaning Luigi Pintor—and the impor-tance of preserving his reputation as a religious authority by remaining distant from guerrilla warfare as his motivations for leaving.[78] It seems likely that the combined effects of dealing with the demanding attitude of Pintor and the awareness that stepping away from the mounting conflict with the Italian administration could open doors for action on an interna-tional level contributed to his decision to leave.

The fact that Idris al-Sanusi began to request permission to leave Cyrenaica for Egypt as early as March 1921 suggests another contributing factor: that he recognized his limitations as an authority within the Sanusi *ṭarīqa* as he lost the support of his political base for his position as an inter-mediary. Idris sent multiple requests to Italian officials over the course of 1921 and 1922 for permission to travel to Egypt for medical care. Nervous that a direct refusal might upset an already tense situation, the Italian consulate in Cairo asked the British authorities to deny Idris al-Sanusi's entry in order to keep him in Cyrenaica. The explanation Italian officials gave for their objection to Idris's journey was the fear that a trip to Egypt would completely derail the already beleaguered process of negotiations by exposing him to the atmosphere of anti-imperial discourse current in Egypt at the time.[79]

Idris al-Sanusi seized an opportunity in the confusion of administra-tive transition at the end of 1922 to leave without going through official channels.[80] After his departure, the Sanusiyya underwent another trans-formation, as the flag of the Sanusi *ṭarīqa* was taken up as a symbol of anticolonial armed resistance for an international audience, though rifts appeared in the Sanusiyya between those who refused to negotiate with the colonial administration and those who remained open to the possibil-ity. Likewise, Idris's departure did not lead to an immediate or total end of Italian attempts to establish a connection with some form of Sanusi power, despite the concurrent political changes in Rome in favor of an unapologetic nationalism. Railway construction became less important for colonial expansion as the age of automobiles transformed the possibilities for accessing the desert. Increasingly, automobiles became the primary tool of Italian penetration into the Libyan interior.[81] Until the "reconquest" began in earnest in the late 1920s, however, the concept of negotiating a power-sharing system through a Sanusi intermediary remained central to an Italian approach to colonial rule. Rhetorically, the fascist adminis- tration was eager to define a clean break with the practices of its liberal predecessors, yet colonial officials continued to debate the possibilities of negotiations with Idris al-Sanusi in exile or other Sanusi family members in Cyrenaica. The problem of governing a Muslim population remained close to the surface. The idea of negotiating authority through a Sanusi intermediary proved difficult to abandon as an organizing principle in the messy shift from a liberal to a fascist administration.

5

Religion and Power in
the Fascist Colonies

While elsewhere in more fertile colonies of other nations there is always present a discontent and the spirit of revolt, especially where secularism has separated from the civilizing activity the superb and Christian work of the missionary, in the Italian colonies, the
progress and strengthening of our advancement is accompanied by the progress and
strengthening of the missionary propaganda. The Cathedral of Tripoli consecrates our
secure colonial future, the civilization and faith of Italy being the civilization and faith of
Catholicism.[1]

THE CONSECRATION OF a new cathedral in Tripoli in 1928 highlighted a
new era in the Italian colonies. Painted in broad brushstrokes, the fascist
era of Italian colonial rule differed from the liberal era in an increased
willingness to resort to military action to achieve direct territorial control.
Celebrating the cathedral's construction in the fullness of the military
campaigns known as the "reconquest" of the Libyan interior, the colonial
publication *L'Oltremare* portrayed it as a sign of the fascist regime's commitment to a message of religious traditionalism. Embracing Catholicism
offered a means of appealing to a Muslim population, with the implication that such a message would provide stability for eventual mass Italian
settlement. The official paper of the Italian Nationalist Association (ANI),
L'Idea Nazionale, echoed the call for embracing religious identity in the
colonies when it praised the laying of the cathedral's first stone in 1923.
The construction of the cathedral was meant to be an opportunity to gain
the respect of the local population by demonstrating that Italians cared for
the Catholic Church rather than making the mistake, as *L'Idea Nazionale*
understood it, of thinking that "ignoring their own religion in the colonies" would make Italian rule acceptable to local populations.[2]

L'Oltremare's celebration of the cathedral also heralded the dominance
of a pro-Catholic, traditionalist form of fascist nationalism in the colonial

territories. Published by the Istituto Coloniale Fascista[3] starting in 1927, *L'Oltremare* had as its director Roberto Cantalupo. A former undersec-retary of state to the colonies (1924–1926) and author of the highly suc-cessful *L'Italia musulmana* (1927), Cantalupo made a career based on his colonial expertise during the fascist regime. Cantalupo was also a darling of Luigi Federzoni. Best known for bringing the conservative promon-archical worldview of the ANI into the Fascist Party, Federzoni was also the one person who more than anyone else dominated the transition to a fascist administration in the Libyan territories.[4] Mussolini appointed Federzoni as his first minister of colonies, a position the latter held for a first term in 1922–1924 and a second term in 1926–1928. When Federzoni took the helm, he initiated an effort to redefine the imperial project in fascist terms. But what it meant to transition from a liberal to a distinc-tively fascist style of imperial rule was open to interpretation, especially in the early years of the ill-defined fascist movement. Taking advantage of the ambiguity, Federzoni used his position at the head of the Ministry of Colonies as an opportunity to steer the fascist movement in a conservative direction, in both the colonies and the metropole. The colonial setting pro-vided a space positioned far enough on the edges of national awareness that Federzoni could use it as a dumping ground for radical elements of the early fascist movement—such as enthusiastic armed militias—to rid the Italian peninsula of those who did not fit his vision of a more conserv-ative Fascist Party.

Federzoni's efforts to transition colonial rule to a fascist system also betrayed an abiding concern with what was known as the "politics of prestige," a phrase with contested meaning.[5] For some, Italian prestige was best established through a show of force to prove Italian dominance. Federzoni's agenda partially fit with this definition of Italian prestige in the Libyan colonies because he embraced a sense of urgency to accelerate the process of catching up with Italy's imperial competitors. The violence of his agenda should not be underestimated. In the name of spreading *italianitá* in the Libyan territories, Federzoni oversaw the application of brutal military tactics, the internment of tens of thousands of civilians in grim concentration camps, and the massive divestment of both tribal and Sanusi property. The military campaign for direct territorial control, how-ever, conflicted with the genteel vision of *italianitá* Federzoni favored—a gentility that required training and cultural sensitivity. Unbridled violence ran the risk of showcasing Italy's lack of preparation for the task of gov-erning an overseas territory.

As a result, Federzoni's administration demonstrated contradictory impulses. On the one hand, he pushed for a speedy break with the past through the fascistization of the colonial administration. This involved a change in personnel to favor those loyal to the new political order and a focus on the message of direct action central to so many adherents of the fascist movement. On the other hand, Federzoni understood prestige to require a measure of expertise and experience to demonstrate Italian ability in the realm of colonial rule. To fill that need, Federzoni advocated the development of programs to train fascists to become good imperialists. He also ignored accusations of disloyalty to the regime against those colonial officials who proved capable of achieving results, leading to an incomplete process of fascistization. And though his administration portrayed its approach to imperial expansion as an immediate and total break with that of its liberal predecessors, he looked favorably on the idea of power-sharing structures when they promised stability. As a result, the transition from the liberal era to the fascist era was a messy process in which competing visions of fascism vied for dominance. Ultimately, however, a fascist approach to imperial rule came to be defined as a combination of land seizures and the embrace of a Catholic identity in colonial expansion, with the total elimination of the Sanusi *ṭarīqa* as a central goal.

Luigi Federzoni and the End of Italo-Sanusi Relations

Luigi Federzoni was a natural fit as the first fascist minister of colonies. In his early career as a journalist he reported from the front lines of the Italo-Turkish War, and as one of the luminaries of the ANI he had a long record of advocating for Italian imperialism and mass settlement programs. Federzoni also favored a promonarchical message, and his election to the Italian Chamber of Deputies in 1913 marked a distinctly conservative direction in Italian national politics. His leadership in the nationalist movement brought a measure of traditionalism and gravitas to fascism when the ANI officially fused with the Partito Nazionale Fascista (PNF) in 1923.[6] Federzoni's appointment as minister of colonies after the March on Rome in October 1922 signaled Mussolini's intention to usher in a new age for Italian imperial interests. The new regime promised to answer complaints about the previous administration's inability to maximize Italy's imperial potential.[7] In the nationalist publication *La rassegna italiana*, Federzoni characterized the political shift in Rome as a chance to give the imperial project and the colonial world added weight in Italian public opinion. He made it his mission as minister of colonies to eliminate apathy about African affairs in Italian public life, which he claimed had prevented the realization of expansionist designs. Federzoni intended to use his position in the Ministry of Colonies to promote greater awareness of colonial issues and greater respect for colonial expertise.[8]

As one of his first priorities, Federzoni oversaw an effort to define a clean break with the past. Both in personnel employed in the colonial administration and in the tenor of state policies, the rhetoric of the fascist political movement called for decisive action and dramatic change. As a leading figure in the decision to throw the weight of the conservative ANI behind Mussolini, however, Federzoni's penchant for traditionalism and a desire for stability tempered that impulse for change. The particular requirement of specialized expertise in colonial rule further suggested the benefits of maintaining some level of continuity within the colonial administration. One way to condemn liberal policies without alienating potentially useful functionaries was to target the deceased former governor of Cyrenaica, Giacomo De Martino. Well known for his defense of Idris al-Sanusi during the collapse of the al-Rajma Accord, the fascist press accused De Martino of instituting "policies of humiliation and degradation" and denounced him for valuing Arabic intermediaries above Italian officials. As evidence, it pointed to reports that De Martino's administration had paid a salary to ʿUmar Mansur al-Kikhiya, the Benghazi notable who served as the Sanusi representative in negotiations for the Italo-Sanusi accords, that was significantly higher than the stipends given to Italian officials.[9] Once De Martino was identified as a target, factions in the Italian parliament began to seek explanations for why De Martino's policies continued to shape the colonial administration after his death. Starting as early as the summer of 1922, officials in the Ministry of Colonies under Federzoni's predecessor, Giovanni Amendola, faced intensive investigation from a commission in the Chamber of Deputies that convened to investigate war spending. The commission followed a line of interrogation focused primarily on determining what had caused the failures of the al-Rajma Accord.

The commission went further, however, than simply looking for failures in the execution of the terms of the al-Rajma Accord; it sought to discredit the very concept of negotiating with colonial intermediaries. Amendola (perhaps inadvertently) added weight to arguments against a collaborative approach when he defended his tenure as the minister of colonies in terms

that pointed to the inherent weakness of relying on colonial intermediaries. Amendola saw negotiations as offering short-term gains for the Italian
administration, arguing that though the negotiations with the Sanusiyya
had only reached partial fulfillment, they "benefitted Italy much more
than the Sanusiyya . . . since for [Italy, the accords] assured the secure and
irresistible peaceful penetration in Cyrenaica, while for [Idris al-Sanusi]
they eliminated the most effective means of resistance, including the great
prestige that came to the Sanusi Confraternity due to the lack of all contact
with the hated infidel."[10] In the long term, Amendola's argument hinted at
the contradictions of a system that depended on the authority of a colonial
intermediary while recognizing that doing so damaged that authority. In
the calculations of liberal administrators like Amendola, Idris al-Sanusi's
weakness was his strength; the contingent nature of his authority represented an opportunity, albeit one with diminishing returns.[11]

As the Italian official primarily responsible for negotiating the terms
of the treaties with Idris al-Sanusi, Luigi Pintor also faced extensive
questioning before the parliamentary commission. Despite the doubts
he had expressed about the desirability of having a Sanusi intermediary during the gradual breakdown of the al-Rajma Accord—as explored
in chapter 4—Pintor followed Amendola's lead in defending the overall
value of the relationship with Idris. Pintor placed the blame for the failure
of the al-Rajma Accord squarely at the feet of ʿUmar Mansur al-Kikhiya.
Accusing al-Kikhiya of having pressured Idris to prevent the dissolution
of the armed camps under mixed Italian-Sanusi authority and of having
used the process of negotiations to increase his personal influence, Pintor
argued that al-Kikhiya had hindered rather than helped Italian attempts
to negotiate with Idris.[12] Based on Pintor's testimony, Italian authorities
arrested al-Kikhiya in January 1923 and condemned him to twelve years in
prison. The sentence was overturned on appeal in the Italian courts, but
state officials forced him to spend the majority of the remaining years of
Italian occupation in exile.[13]

Pintor's approach in his testimony before the parliamentary commission can be seen as highly strategic. By focusing on al-Kikhiya as primarily
responsible for the failure of the al-Rajma Accord, Pintor saved himself
from the commission's sweeping condemnation of the Amendola administration. Because Amendola had supported the selection of al-Kikhiya
as an intermediary in the Italo-Sanusi negotiations, Pintor's accusations
about the latter's duplicity further discredited Amendola. As Amendola's
political fate became clear, Pintor grew bolder in his criticism of the former

minister, even linking him to a local Freemason lodge that supported pan-Islamic ideals.[14] By distancing himself from the Amendola ministry, Pintor rebranded himself as an expert on native affairs for the fascist administration. It helped that he could point to a past record of doubt about Sanusi authority during the breakdown of the al-Rajma Accord and to his vocal opposition against al-Kikhiya as a mediator. As proof of his faith in Pintor's expertise, Federzoni appointed him vice director general in the Ministry of Colonies and assigned him the responsibility of taking the lead on investigations within the ministry to determine why the al-Rajma Accord failed.

The easy integration of Luigi Pintor into Federzoni's administration serves as an example of the continuities in personnel in the Libyan territories with the rise to power of Mussolini and his new political movement. There is plenty of evidence to suggest that Federzoni needed the expertise of Pintor in the first months of his administration. For one thing, Federzoni did not seem to understand some of the basic principles of the al-Rajma Accord, including how much money Idris al-Sanusi received from the state and for what purpose, and he looked to Pintor for answers.[15] Also, at the end of 1922 Federzoni began to collect evidence against Idris, creating a list of all the ways he had failed to fulfill the terms of the al-Rajma Accord. Again, Pintor's familiarity with the negotiations proved useful. Officials like Pintor, with extensive experience and specialized skills, proved too valuable to replace immediately with Fascist Party enthusiasts; Federzoni's Ministry of Colonies preferred to focus criticism for the power-sharing approach on the highest rungs of the liberal administration rather than condemn useful functionaries.

Pintor's accusation against al-Kikhiya was also strategic in that it allowed for the possibility of continuing discussions with members of the Sanusi family. By limiting the scope of censure to one individual and to the failure to fulfill the specific provisions of the agreement calling for disarmament, Pintor avoided denouncing the concept of negotiating with colonial intermediaries as a whole. Placing the responsibility for the failure of the accord on al-Kikhiya did signal a recognition on the part of the Italian administration of the limitations of Idris al-Sanusi's authority in the Libyan territories, insofar as it admitted that Idris should not be held responsible for all outcomes in the process of negotiations; this ran counter to the concept of the Sanusiyya as a tightly organized hierarchy. Nevertheless, the moral authority of Idris and his value as a colonial intermediary remained alive to some in the fascist administration.

The possibility of continuing to focus on a Sanusi intermediary as the centerpiece of Italian colonial rule seemed unlikely in Federzoni's Ministry of Colonies. Well before he stepped into the position at the head of the colonial administration, Federzoni had voiced opposition to the negotiations with the Sanusi elites. When he served on the parliamentary commission on foreign and colonial policies in 1920–1921—the same commission that had initiated the investigation into the costs of doing business with al-Kikhiya by questioning Pintor—Federzoni condemned the establishment of the Sanusi emirate in the al-Rajma Accord as a relinquishment of Italian state sovereignty that threatened to undermine Italy's great power status. The problem, Federzoni insisted, stemmed from a fundamental connection between religious and political-military authority in Islam that precluded the possibility of a true understanding between Italian colonial officials and the Sanusi elites. In his opposition to the negotiations with the Sanusi family, Federzoni pitted himself against moderate socialists who opposed military action in the expansion of the Italian colonies, but it made him a champion of imperialist interests and gained him the support of fascist enthusiasts in the colonial territories.[16]

Once in office, however, Federzoni's administration did not outright reject the prospect of further negotiations; the development of a fascist style of colonial rule was more haphazard and contingent than the rhetoric of his administration would indicate. Italian officials made some effort to resuscitate an alliance, though with less material support for Sanusi military power than the previous administration had provided. During his first term as minister of colonies Federzoni objected to the specific provisions of the Italo-Sanusi agreements that allowed for Sanusi control over armed garrisons in the Libyan interior, but he did not preclude the possibility of using a (weaker) Sanusi intermediary. In the first year of the fascist administration, the new governor of Cyrenaica, Luigi Bongiovanni, dissolved the mixed Sanusi-Italian armed garrisons by force and occupied Ajdabiya, the center of the Sanusi administration. At the same time, however, Bongiovanni reached out to Idris al-Sanusi and offered to reinstate the al-Rajma Accord—contingent, however, on Idris's being able to regain his influence among the Maghārba tribes around Ajdabiya and rein in the anti-Italian contingents of the Sanusiyya.

Underscoring the limitations of his political authority without the Sanusi military forces, Idris made it known through indirect communication that he had no intention of returning to the Libyan territories as an Italian intermediary.[17] The Italian Ministry of Colonies declared an official

end to negotiations with the Sanusiyya in May 1923. But officials in the fascist administration repeatedly attempted to contact both Idris and Ahmad
al-Sharif during subsequent military operations in Cyrenaica with the
hope that the combination of harsh military occupation and conciliatory
gestures would secure the Libyan interior as a region under full Italian
control. They even called on Enrico Insabato to resume negotiations at
one point.[18] In the following eight years—until the capture of ʿUmar
al-Mukhtar in 1931 led the Italian government to declare the interior of
Cyrenaica fully pacified—Italian officials and Idris danced around the idea
of resuming some form of negotiations. Multiple reports from the Italian
legate in Cairo over the years conveyed a sense that Idris remained open
to the possibility of resuming a relationship.

Discussions during the fascist regime about the plausibility of a return
to the days of the accords reflected the full spectrum of earlier Italian
debates over Idris al-Sanusi's political and religious authority during the
liberal era. Pintor, for example, remained firmly in favor of the idea of
pursuing negotiations with Idris al-Sanusi based on his perception of
the latter as a political leader driven primarily by economic motivations.
For Pintor, Idris seemed the ideal colonial ally due to his malleability and
financial dependence on the Italian colonial state. Roberto Cantalupo projected a less pliable image of Idris. As late as July 1930, in his role as the
Italian legate in Cairo (where he kept a close eye on Idris al-Sanusi's activities), Cantalupo warned against returning to negotiations because doing
so would damage the armed campaign against a rebellion for which, he
claimed, "the Senusso [sic] is known as the principal if not the only one
responsible."[19] Painting Idris as solely responsible for armed conflict in
Cyrenaica recalled the inflated sense of centralized hierarchy and intransigency that had characterized early European studies of the Sanusiyya.

Of course Idris was not the only Sanusi family member in the region.
His absence suggested the possibility of yet again seeking out another
member of the Sanusi elite as an ally in the efforts to expand Italian state
control. At various points in the 1920s the leadership of the Sanusiyya,
control over access to Sanusi resources in the interior oases, and alliances between Sanusi elites and regional tribal leaders changed, often
in response to the contentious issue of resuming negotiations with the
Italians. With Idris al-Sanusi and Ahmad al-Sharif in exile, other Sanusi
family members—al-Sharif's brother Saf al-Din and Idris's brother
Mohammad al-Rida in particular—gained status as potential figureheads
for the Sanusiyya. In Mohammad al-Rida, seen as a less ambitious if less

capable member of the Sanusi family, Federzoni's colonial administration found a willing ally in the renewed effort to define the head of the Sanusi *ṭarīqa* as a partner in centralized authority. Italian efforts at cultivating a new Sanusi alliance, however, were tepid at best and lacked the level of engagement that had characterized the development of Idris as the new face of the Sanusiyya during the negotiations for the Akrama and al-Rajma Accords.[20]

Ultimately two Sanusi shaykhs, Ghejiya ibn Abdullah and, most famously, 'Umar al-Mukhtar, overshadowed Sanusi family members, as military leaders who led Sanusi armed forces against the attempts of Italian state extension into the interior in the 1920s. Their leadership divided loyalties in the Sufi *ṭarīqa* and challenged the meaning of Sanusi authority over Sanusi family members. When al-Mukhtar refused to accept funding from Italian colonial officials at a time when al-Rida was accepting a regular salary from the Italian administration, the armed forces under the Sanusi flag split into two opposing camps. As Federzoni's administration initiated increasingly aggressive incursions in the Cyrenaican interior, the anti-Italian message of al-Mukhtar prevailed in the battle for popular support in the region. He became an international hero and a lionized symbol, defining the Sanusiyya as an anticolonial force rather than a colonial intermediary.[21] Violence, not negotiation, shaped the road ahead.

The Violence of *Squadrismo* in the Libyan Territories

Despite desultory efforts at forming a new Sanusi alliance, the departure of Idris al-Sanusi and the divisions among Sanusi affiliates ushered in the beginning of a new era of Italian colonial rule, one marked by indiscriminate use of violence rather than negotiations to achieve the goal of direct Italian control over the Libyan interior. Just as the shift away from a period of negotiations was more complicated and messy than the narrative of the fascist administration indicated, however, so was the introduction of fascist styles of armed violence. The battle cry of a fascist revolution for direct action and the spilling of blood for the glory of Italy proved difficult to import into the colonial environment, even among fascist officials. Perhaps nothing exemplifies the struggle over the shape fascism would take in Italy's overseas territories better than the introduction of fascist militias to the Libyan territories in the autumn of 1923. When armed squads of blackshirted youths arrived in the coastal cities of the Libyan territories, they wreaked havoc in the streets. Acting under the auspices of the Milizia Volontaria per la Sicurezza Nazionale (Voluntary Militia for National Security; MVSN), the militias targeted Arab and Jewish inhabitants, looted mosques and shops, and in at least one instance fired into groups of Arab youths at an Italian-run school.[22] Facing immediate condemnation from the military command and colonial police, Federzoni decried the violence as acts that were "less tolerable in the colonies than anywhere else and all the more objectionable coming from those who had taken on a special obligation of patriotic discipline and loyal collaboration in the work of the National Government."[23] The fact that he was responsible for the original proposal to send fascist militias to the Libyan territories did not prevent Federzoni from insisting that the governor of Tripolitania take whatever measures were necessary to gain control of the armed squads.

The troubled arrival of the fascist militias in 1923 reflected wider questions about the contested future of militant squads in Italy as the fascist movement sought to foster political legitimacy in Rome. In 1922–1923 Mussolini and Fascist Party leaders faced the delicate task of creating a centralized organization out of an amorphous movement that had encompassed a wide variety of political, economic, and social goals. Though it was part of the initial appeal of the fascist movement, especially to young Italian men, the violence of *squadrismo* became increasingly problematic in this period of transition as Mussolini tried to establish his credentials as a capable political leader. The violence of the fascist squads was particularly troubling for Federzoni's brand of conservative nationalism. The colonial space offered a convenient dumping ground to rid the peninsula of elements he deemed unsuitable for the future of a legitimate political party.

When Federzoni introduced a proposal to employ squads in the Libyan territories in one of his first official acts as minister of colonies in December 1922, he sold the idea as a solution to several problems in both the colonies and the metropole. In terms of Italian imperial ambitions, the militias could answer complaints from colonial military and civil administrators about the lack of adequate troops as they sought to expand Italian state influence in the Libyan territories. The need for an increase in Italian armed forces seemed particularly urgent at the end of 1922, just a few months after the previous minister of colonies had formally initiated a "reconquest" of the Libyan interior in a series of military occupations, with the goal of extending direct state control from the narrow coastal region into the interior. In his role as governor of Cyrenaica,

for example, Pintor had complained in March 1922 to Federzoni's predecessor, Amendola, about the lack of colonial officials, especially at a subaltern level.[24] Although the "reconquest" would not begin in earnest until
Federzoni initiated a surge of military support in 1926, the immediate
introduction of militias made up of young, untrained volunteers seemed
to offer an inexpensive form of support for the colonial troops in an initial
push into the Libyan interior.

Federzoni also sold the presence of fascist militias as an opportunity to
increase the number of Italian nationals in the Libyan territories, a central
goal of Italian imperialists in general and of the ANI in particular. The
ANI took up the cause of mass settlement programs in the first decade of
Italian occupation of the Libyan territories. As one of the ANI's leading
figures, Federzoni had called for the settlement of at least 300,000 Italian
nationals in the colonies over the following quarter century.[25] Proposals
to transplant Italian agriculturalists and industrial workers with their
families proved prohibitively expensive and unfeasible given the limited
nature of Italian control in the Libyan territories, but the young men who
typically volunteered for fascist squads provided a relatively inexpensive
source of potential settlers who could help fulfill the objective of trans-
forming the Libyan territories into an Italian cultural space in preparation
for further settlement.

Federzoni made no secret of the fact that sending militias to the colonies also fit within his domestic objective of reducing the dominance of
militant squads and their leaders during the transition of the early fascist movement into a political party. In his original proposal, Federzoni
noted that the exportation of squad violence to the Libyan territories would
answer a need he identified within the Fascist Party to "find an opportune
and convenient use of the generosity and exuberance of its militias,"[26]
projecting a clear message that sending fascist squads to the Libyan territories would eliminate their troublesome presence in Italy as Mussolini
and party officials established a legitimate parliamentary government.
Exporting militias to the colonies contributed to a larger effort to curb
their power that included placing them under a centralized administration. In December 1922 the newly formed Fascist Grand Council created
the MVSN to provide a formal structure for the loose coalition of fascist
squads and incorporate them into the party framework.[27] The formaliza-
tion of the national fascist militias inspired Federzoni to renew his call for
their deployment in the colonies in January 1923. The formal structure of
the MVSN offered a measure of assurance to the colonial administration

that the militias would operate under some level of control that might prevent the worst excesses of squad violence in the colonies. Later that year
the MVSN deployed the first units of fascist militias to the Libyan colonies
under an eight-month agreement, and a permanent unit of fifteen hundred men was established in Cyrenaica in the summer of 1924.[28]

The sudden influx of unruly bands of young men, most with little in the
way of personal resources, demonstrated the shortcomings of Federzoni's
ad hoc attempt to supplement colonial forces on the cheap. Reactions
against their presence also revealed resistance within the wider military-
administrative complex of the colonial system to the introduction of new
fascist elements that threatened to upset the balance of relative peace
achieved in the liberal era of negotiations. In the relatively small town of
al-Khums near the ruins of Leptis Magna to the northwest of Tripoli, for
example, regional military commanders reported the arrival of over one
thousand young men in black shirts, completely overwhelming an Italian
garrison that lacked adequate space or resources. The fascist militias looted
indiscriminately to supplement their meager supplies. Their violent activities brought them into direct conflict with commanders of the colonial
armed forces, who saw the arrival of the MVSN units as a direct threat
to their control over public order. Even worse, in a colonial army heavily
manned by Eritrean and Arab troops and with few recognizably Italian
commanders, members of the Italian armed forces were themselves targets of militia violence. In their zeal to assert an ideology of racial and
cultural superiority, the blackshirted militias upset what had been delicate
distinctions between friend and foe in the Italian colonial system.[29]

Tensions over the arrival of the militias offer a window into contradictions inherent in the fascist approach to colonial rule. In his initiative to
send fascist militias into the colonies, Federzoni relied on the position of
the Libyan territories as a marginal space on the borders of Italian identity, to which he could export a potential threat to his conservative brand of
fascism. Safely across the Mediterranean, the militias could expend their
enthusiasm for the call to militant revolution, which attracted so many
young men to the early fascist movement, without disturbing the balancing act of party formation in Rome. At the same time, Federzoni and other
nationalist proponents of the fascist movement called for a full incorporation of the Libyan colonies into an Italian national identity and insisted on
an increase in attention to colonial issues in Rome. On a more immediate
level, the introduction of indiscriminate violence inspired criticism from
long-term career officials in the colonial administration. Luigi Pintor, for

example, complained at the beginning of 1924 of a broader lack of organization in the fascist colonial administration; subaltern officials were even making decisions, with no directives from above, to disarm regions with populations that had already submitted to Italian rule. Pintor suggested that the arrival of the fascist squads fit a broader pattern of a breakdown in the chain of command in the colonial administration.[30]

The development of local branches of Fascist Party supporters among Italian settlers also raised concerns about disintegration of central control in the transition to a fascist regime in Italy's overseas territories. Although the number of Italian citizens living in the Libyan territories at the time of the formation of the first government under Mussolini was relatively small—especially compared with the influx of settler families in the late 1930s under state-directed programs—Italian communities in the Libyan territories became vocal proponents of the early fascist movement. Some Fascist Party enthusiasts within the Italian settler community saw the period of transition after the March on Rome as an opportunity to take an active hand in steering the future of the colonial administration. As early as December 1922, local Fascist Party headquarters were formed under the leadership of party captains in the city centers along the coast of the Libyan territories. Regular reports from local party branches to central party leaders served as a venue for *fasci* to make specific recommendations on policies and personnel in the Libyan territories as they began to assert their role as interpreters of the colonial setting for the Fascist Party. Soon after the March on Rome, for example, a small but vocal branch of the PNF in Derna latched onto the shift in the balance of power to formalize a series of complaints against the liberal colonial government. Party representatives from Derna accused Italian officials of favoring the interests of the indigenous population over those of Italian settler communities with the result of "numbing the national sentiments of Italian residents" and thus preventing the rapid spread of fascist ideals in the region.[31] Members of a branch of the Fascist Party that developed in Cyrenaica, in particular, considered themselves a vanguard of the movement in the colonies, and they seized on the transition to the fascist regime as an opportunity to abandon power sharing and assimilationist tactics in favor of what they referred to as a "strong government capable of administering with dignity."[32]

Accusing local colonial officials of associating with Freemasonry—the bogeyman of both the Catholic Church and the Fascist Party—local Fascist Party branches expressed frustration with the slow rate of turnover in personnel from the liberal era.[33] More often than not the accusations of local *fasci* proved more of an irritant than a welcome sign of growing party influence for party officials in Rome, and ultimately the PNF favored stability over the fervor of the local party enthusiasts. One of the greatest sources of irritation from local party members was a protracted campaign against the governor of Cyrenaica, Ernesto Mombelli. A veteran of World War I—and from all indications a clear supporter of the nationalist message and an aggressive imperial program—Mombelli had to defend himself against accusations of having an "antifascist attitude" and of keeping personnel in his offices from the liberal era who lacked adequate fervor for the fascist cause. Mombelli defended himself by noting the delicacy of his position in trying to weigh the benefits of experienced officers against the desire to introduce fascist supporters to the region in an atmosphere, he claimed, that "manifests the repercussions of national political battles, but instead of bursting forth in a field of noble competition, they often come out in questions of personal character often inspired by ulterior motives."[34]

The campaign against Mombelli's administration ended with a clear recognition on the part of the Fascist Party of the value of Mombelli's approach. Party leadership in Rome then moved to take direct control of the activities of local Fascist Party enthusiasts. The head of the Fascist Party branch in Benghazi was pressured to step down, and the PNF absorbed the *fasci* of the Italian colonies, previously organized under the separate offices of the Fasci Italiani all'estero e nelle Colonie. In part, the incorporation of the Fascist Party organizations in the Libyan territories into the centralized party in Rome furthered efforts to draw the Libyan territories fully into an Italian national identity. Party leaders called for the measure as a chance to enjoy "more direct contact, through this new hierarchy of dependency, between the Fascist Party and the lands that have been returned to the dominion of Rome thanks to the valor and sacrifice of the grey-green Military and of the Blackshirts."[35]

More important for PNF leadership, however, the inclusion of the Libyan *fasci* in a central hierarchy allowed for control over the definition of fascism and fascist activities in the sphere of colonial politics. The issue came to an end with a broader directive from the Ministry of Foreign Affairs that explicitly forbade the involvement of all *fasci* abroad in attacks against state representatives, a measure meant to prevent Fascist Party organizations in Italian communities throughout the world from meddling in Italian international affairs.[36] Following the absorption of the *fasci* of the Libyan territories into the centralized party structure, the secretary general of the PNF sent an inspector to report on the conditions of the party in the colonies in order to understand how PNF officials could encourage the fascistization of the settler population. His report echoed Mombelli's characterizations of the insular nature of fascist enthusiasts in the colonies, and he called for the elimination of those who had claimed leadership of local party organs during the transitional period of 1922–1926. "Real fascists," he claimed, felt uncomfortable with the distorted fascism of colonial *fasci*, and they welcomed the control of the central party.[37] The introduction of militias and the incorporation of local Fascist Party branches into a centralized system made up part of a broader effort by the fascist regime—and Federzoni in particular—to make Libya a fully Italian space.[38]

Negotiating Power in the "Reconquest"

The absorption of local Fascist Party organizations into a national structure contributed to a broader political and military effort to expand central state control into the Libyan interior. The centerpiece of that process was the military campaign that the colonial administration referred to as a "reconquest," a misnomer given that the majority of the territories in question were brought under Italian control for the first time in the 1920s. The "reconquest" symbolized the realization of a particular kind of fascist ideal of extreme and indiscriminate violence in the service of state expansion. From 1926 until the declaration of the successful pacification of the Libyan interior in 1931, colonial forces burned down entire villages and forced Bedouin populations into internment camps to prepare the region for the eventual settlement of Italian agriculturalists on state-organized family farms. Fascist enthusiasts celebrated the assertion of Italian military and cultural superiority in an era of unapologetic colonial dominance. For supporters of the fascist regime, the capture of the Sanusi military commander ʿUmar al-Mukhtar in 1931 in al-Kufra and the subsequent declaration of the pacification of the Libyan interior proved the effectiveness of this wave of military actions. Yet even in the midst of extreme armed violence, continued attempts to identify negotiating partners betrayed the limits of the fascist ideal in the colonial setting.[39] In 1926 Mussolini marked his interest in intensifying state energies in the colonial project with his first visit to the region. He also chose to appoint Luigi Federzoni for a second time to the position of minister of colonies, after the latter had spent two years as the minister of the interior. Mussolini had reassigned Federzoni, considered a moderate influence in the Fascist Party, from the Ministry of Colonies to the Ministry of the Interior in an attempt to counterbalance more radical strains within the Fascist Party that were calling for increased squad violence in the Italian peninsula. In his position as minister of the interior, Federzoni had continued the process of bringing the fascist squads under centralized control that he had begun in the Ministry of Colonies, but he faced fierce resistance to his attempts to curb *squadrismo* on the Italian peninsula. After failing to stem a wave of violence in 1925, Federzoni returned to the Ministry of Colonies with much to prove in terms of his ability to define the fascist agenda. Finding his particular vision of Italian nationalism marginalized in Rome, he instituted a vigorous program in the Ministry of Colonies focused on military expansion and centralized authority, all while championing the fascistization of the Libyan territories.[40]

The military operations initiated by Federzoni's administration targeted the territories under the control of tribes that were directly involved in redefining the Sanusiyya from an intermediary colonial power to a force of armed resistance after Idris al-Sanusi's departure from Cyrenaica. On his return to the Ministry of Colonies, Federzoni established a military agenda to expand the Italian presence to the 29th parallel, to bring the oases of Jalu, Awjila, and Marada under Italian control. Expanding to this extent was meant to block a caravan route from Egypt's western border into eastern Tripolitania and the Fezzan. The objective was to replicate the deprivations of World War I by cutting off the region from supplies and weakening the armed forces of the Sanusi resistance and the associated Maghārba-ʿAwāqir tribes. To take charge of the operations, Federzoni appointed as the new governor of Cyrenaica Attilio Teruzzi, a Fascist Party strongman who had fought in the initial occupation of the Libyan territories. Both Teruzzi and Federzoni identified the hostility of the Maghārba tribes of western Cyrenaica as the primary impediment to Italian expansion into the interior. They established their objective as the "total conquest and the definitive occupation of the entire Libyan territory up to its most remote Saharan borders."[41] They foresaw the removal of all remaining opposition to Italian state expansion into the Saharan oases of Kufra.

Despite the assertive rhetoric, the possibility of trying to pair military operations with a more conciliatory approach remained attractive to the Ministry of Colonies, if for no other reason than to limit the resources required for full-scale armed conflict. Fractures among former supporters of Idris al-Sanusi after the failure of the al-Rajma Accord offered an opportunity to divide the populations of the Cyrenaican interior between those committed to the cause of a Sanusi resistance and those potentially more willing to perform the act of official submission to Italian rule. In the regions closer to the coast, near the cities of Benghazi and Derna, the colonial military attempted to achieve this division through the establishment of settlement camps. Infamous for their repressive conditions and lack of hygiene, these internment camps imprisoned up to 100,000 nomadic and seminomadic people to prevent their participation in or support for anti-Italian armed activity. Without the resources to achieve a similar physical separation between armed rebels and unarmed civilians deeper in the Libyan interior, Federzoni attempted a more conciliatory approach. He sought to entice Maghārba populations of western Cyrenaica away from the influence of the emerging Sanusi resistance through an opening of markets, with the hope that doing so would reassure merchants of the economic viability of Italian rule.[42]

A division among factions of the Maghārba tribes facilitated Italian negotiations for the submission of some parts of the tribe to Italian authority during the "reconquest." The division was precipitated by disagreements between Sanusi shaykhs and the Maghārba notable Salah al-Atyush, the son of Kaylani al-Atyush, who was the kaimacon of Kufra when Ahmad al-Sharif agreed to the establishment of an Ottoman garrison there in 1910. Throughout the Italian occupation, Salah al-Atyush had been a constant ally of Idris al-Sanusi and a frequent representative of Sanusi interest in meetings with Tripolitanian notables.[43] Al-Atyush was also a vocal opponent of the application of the al-Rajma Accord, and after Idris's departure, he was one of many Sanusi-affiliated tribal leaders with an armed force (*dor*) at his disposal. At the end of June 1925 the 'Awāqir notable and commander of Sanusi forces, Ghejiya ibn Abdullah, attempted to seize control of Maghārba tribes under the leadership of al-Atyush. Ibn Abdullah's objective was to incorporate them into an anti-Italian army that would act in parallel to the armed forces under the command of 'Umar al-Mukhtar. One portion of the Maghārba forces followed al-Atyush into Sirte, while others remained in western Cyrenaica and accepted a new version of Sanusi leadership under ibn Abdullah.[44]

Facing a constant shortage of funds and troops, Federzoni embraced the possibility of a political approach to winning the support of the Maghārba population of western Cyrenaica. But first he considered military operations a prerequisite to gaining an upper hand in the negotiations.[45] By the end of September 1927 Teruzzi and officials from the colonial administration were using a combination of negotiations and force—including taking hostages from among family members of Maghārba and ʿAwāqir notables—to induce the Maghārba populations of western Cyrenaica to submit to Italian authority.[46] The Maghārba performance of the act of submission allowed Italian troops to use the entire territory of Sirte as a base for occupying the southern oases along the 29th parallel.[47]

For Federzoni and Teruzzi, the submission to Italian authority of the Maghārba population of western Cyrenaica seemed to prove their success in adapting to the dramatic shift in the political landscape of the Libyan territories after the departure of Idris al-Sanusi and the subsequent fracturing of the Sanusiyya. With the submission of the Maghārba, Federzoni rejected any future role of Sanusi intermediaries as an unnecessary detriment to Italian national prestige. From that point forward his administration favored a combination of aggressive military campaigns and direct outreach to tribal leaders. The clearest signal of Federzoni's intention to reject any further negotiations with Sanusi intermediaries was the decision to order Muhammad al-Rida's imprisonment on the Italian island of Ustica, where Italy kept many of the political prisoners from the Libyan territories.[48] In his memoirs Teruzzi celebrated the refusal to negotiate with Sanusi family members as an effort to replace their authority with that of the Italian state, to "detach, bit by bit, the populations from their Sanusi patrons."[49]

The decision to reject further negotiations with Sanusi intermediaries informed a renewed debate among Italian orientalists over the nature of the political and religious authority of the Sanusiyya and the capacity of the Sanusi family to act as state agents. The contest over defining the Sanusiyya took shape in two consecutive issues of the *Rassegna italiana* in 1928, which published a debate between Bruno Ducati, a former student of C. A. Nallino[50] and a prominent scholar on Islamic law, and Filippo Lo Bello, a frequent author on colonial subjects. In their articles the men disputed the value of negotiations with Sanusi intermediaries based on a valuation of the qualities of the Sanusi *ṭarīqa* as a state-like organization. Following in the spirit of Nallino, who in his role as part of Agnesa's Commission for the Study of Islamic Issues was a constant advocate for indirect systems of rule and the Libyan Statutes, Ducati defended the negotiations with Idris al-Sanusi as a colonial system that took advantage of competition between Idris and Ahmad al-Sharif to promote a friendly Islamic power with the authority of a regional state. "This brotherhood," he wrote, "in addition to its importance, has a special characteristic that differentiates it from all others; besides its religious program, it also has a political program, and it has entered into politics not as a simple force conforming to or subordinate to parties or trends, but acting as an independent unit, such that it is situated in Islam almost as a state within another State."[51]

The rebuttal by Lo Bello in the following issue of the *Rassegna italiana* reflected the official view of Federzoni's Ministry of Colonies in its repudiation of Sanusi elites as effective colonial intermediaries. Lo Bello disputed the characterization of the Sanusiyya as an independent political authority and argued that the process of negotiations had created a political authority where one did not exist. Contradicting the characterization of the relationship between the Ottoman central authorities and Sanusi notables as constituting a "state within a state," Lo Bello argued that the Ottoman authorities only dealt with the Sanusiyya to control them and prevent them from becoming overly powerful in regional politics. According to Lo Bello, the Sanusi family represented a purely spiritual authority that the Italian colonial administration had mistakenly endowed with state-like functions. After years of negotiations with centralized authorities, he argued, Sanusi elites had lost their legitimacy as religious leaders, "after many lies and due to the ruin and loss of human lives for a cause of which the majority, though ignorant, understand its exact scope, the Sanusiyya are blamed and condemned."[52]

Another fascist era critique of the Italo-Sanusi accords, by Giuseppe Macaluso Aleo, a functionary in the Agricultural Office in Benghazi, took a slightly different tack. While Lo Bello ridiculed officials of the liberal era for misunderstanding the extent of Sanusi political authority, Macaluso Aleo painted the establishment of an emirate under Idris al-Sanusi's leadership in the al-Rajma Accord as a total renunciation of sovereignty to a fanatical Islamic power. In a book dedicated to General Graziani, *Turchi, Senussi e Italiani in Libia*, Macaluso Aleo provided what he intended to be a reinterpretation of the Sanusiyya for a broad, nonspecialist audience in the new fascist era. His understanding of the Sanusiyya, based on twenty years of experience living in Benghazi, replicated the exaggerated view of Sanusi authority and fanaticism from the French literature on the Sufi *ṭarīqa* from the late nineteenth century, especially the alarmist position of Henri Duveyrier. For Macaluso Aleo, the Italo-Sanusi accords were a ruse by an Islamic power incapable of reaching a true understanding with the Italian government. He believed "that the Sanusiyya can never live in peace, without having first been defeated or perhaps destroyed; there are no half measures." And he deemed the establishment of an emirate under Idris "the worst and most damaging error" Italy could have committed because it constituted sanctioning full Sanusi sovereignty in the region.[53]

Macaluso Aleo's perspective on the Sanusiyya and the Italo-Sanusi accords faced fierce criticism from none other than C. A. Nallino. In a scathing review of Macaluso Aleo's book, Nallino rejected the characterization of the emirate under Idris al-Sanusi as a relinquishment of Italian sovereignty in Cyrenaica. Quoting the royal decree of October 25, 1920, that established the emirate, Nallino pointed to language that made it clear Idris al-Sanusi had served as a delegate of the Italian colonial administration. Nallino further bemoaned Macaluso Aleo's book as indicative of a trend among a new generation of Italian imperialists to write "pseudo-colonial literature" that demonstrated widespread ignorance of local culture.[54] But Nallino's criticism had little impact in an era defined by decreased interest in colonial compromise and indirect rule. The discord between the doyen of Italian orientalism and the newcomer highlighted the dramatic shift in attitudes toward Italian rule in a predominantly Muslim territory in the fascist era.

In Federzoni's administration, the turn away from power-sharing systems extended beyond the immediate members of the Sanusi family. Federzoni argued that the Italian colonial state should avoid negotiating with any Libyan notables because of the risk that it would feed expectations among local populations that the Italian state would entertain the possibility of a return to the Italo-Sanusi relationship. In discussions in the Italian Chamber of Deputies about the development of a new legal order to replace the 1919 Libyan Statutes, Federzoni advocated an alternative approach to eliminating anti-Italian unrest in the Libyan territories. He proposed overwhelming local populations with mass colonization from the Italian peninsula, based on the premise that creating a sizable Italian population would lessen the potential force of local dissent. Falling back on the long-standing goal of the ANI to have the Libyan territories act as a safety valve for excess populations, especially from the restive Italian South, Federzoni called for state-directed settlement of at least 300,000 Italians within a quarter century with the goal of balancing the racial demographics of the Libyan territories. Federzoni's interest in mass colonization thus went beyond the domestic objective of offering a solution to land distribution; he understood it as a political necessity that would promote stability by bringing in Italian nationals, "who would make a part of the Mediterranean coast of Africa Italian *in fact* and not just in law."[55] Mass colonization, Federzoni argued, would facilitate the ability of the colonial administration to claim full sovereignty over the Libyan territories.

The brutal military campaigns of the "reconquest," as well as the forced confinement of entire tribes in internment camps, did allow Italian settlements to spread significantly beyond the region around the coastal center of Benghazi after 1927. The completion of a railway line from Benghazi to al-Marj also contributed to an expansion of Italian settlements into the Cyrenaican interior.[56] The full implementation of a state-sponsored mass settlement scheme, however, would not occur until the declaration of the total pacification of the Libyan interior in 1931 following the occupation of the oases of Kufra and the arrest of ʿUmar al-Mukhtar. The subsequent organization of small family farms was a particularly Italian version of an imperial dream. Settlement programs promised the solution to Southern Italian economic development problems as well as a means of forcing stability in the Libyan territories by means of demographic dominance.[57]

The prospect of mass settlement programs as an end goal of the military "reconquest" fed into Federzoni's aspirations to bring greater public attention to Italy's imperial efforts. As the military campaigns of the reconquest took form, Federzoni sought to attract greater popular support for colonialism on two fronts: training within the colonial administration and increasing the involvement of the Catholic Church in the colonies. His efforts focused on bolstering the prestige of colonial functionaries—both in the colonies and at home—while promoting the spread of a conservative Catholic version of Italian identity in the expansion of the fascist regime. Rather than seeing these two objects as working at cross-purposes, Federzoni's concept of a fascist style of colonial rule embraced the apparent dichotomy between attempts to foster colonial personnel knowledgeable about local cultures and aggressively asserting Catholicism through Italian expansion.

Italian Prestige and the Culture of Colonialism

In the second half of the 1920s Federzoni's Ministry of Colonies initiated a series of measures designed to educate officials working in Italian overseas territories. The training program was meant to answer the problem of a shortage of Fascist Party enthusiasts with the skills and expertise considered necessary for colonial rule in Muslim North Africa. At the beginning of the Italian occupation of the Libyan territories, concern over a lack of training among Italian colonial officials originated primarily from critics of the annexation of the Libyan territories, like Leone Caetani and the other advocates of indirect imperial systems on the Ministry of Colonies' Commission for the Study of Islamic Issues. The idea that Italy lagged behind other European powers in the rigor of colonial expertise did not disappear with the transition to a fascist administration after 1922. If anything, a shared desire to direct resources to imperial projects in order to catch up with European competitors informed the support of nationalists for the fascist movement, and efforts to both expand a national awareness of colonial issues in the metropole and educate officials within the colonial administration about the history and culture of the region straddled the liberal and fascist eras. Federzoni, in particular, demonstrated a clear concern that Italy's relative lack of preparation for colonial rule would be exposed to an international audience as a sign of national weakness.

The fear of national inferiority in the colonial world was often expressed in terms of the need to demonstrate Italian prestige. As Barbara Spadaro has argued, the concept of prestige linked the system of colonial rule to a racial hierarchy that demanded Italians prove they were upholding a "certain kind of whiteness."[58] Italy's ability to claim a position as a full member of the European club of great powers was at stake. In the rhetoric of Italian imperialism, however, it was never clear what sort of approach to colonial rule would connote prestige; it was a term that imperialists of various stripes could deploy to argue in favor of their own particular agendas. State support of cultural programs, the ability to impose force at will, the administrative abilities of colonial functionaries—all were cited in various contexts as evidence of national prestige in the colonial setting. In the months immediately following the fascist March on Rome, for example, the futurist poet turned politician Francesco Meriano complained that the liberal state had abdicated national prestige in the colonial world through a combination of "foolish humanitarian policies," attempts at "economic collaboration with the indigenous masses," and failed "war against the rebels." The fascist state, he claimed, would restore national prestige in the colonial world by asserting Italian dominance. He did not advocate brutality; Meriano called for the fascist state to take a position he called "generosity of the strong" that would allow the Italians to "guarantee the elevation and wellbeing for the subject populations."[59]

Federzoni focused his anxieties about prestige on the level of preparation and training of colonial officials. Attempts to educate colonial officials or integrate expert opinion during the colonial administration of the liberal era had focused on identifying regional power brokers to act as intermediaries in the extension of Italian influence. Federzoni had no interest in mimicking this approach. The culture of Italian colonialism under Federzoni's guidance was to be a fascist culture, with little room for the power-sharing policies of the previous administration, which he argued had fostered "an insidious false peace."[60] A restructuring of the colonial administration in 1927–1928 established a preference for metropolitan Italians to fill positions at all levels of the administration and a requirement for them to occupy positions at a regional level.[61] The turn away from fostering relationships with colonial intermediaries became a guiding principle for the entire hierarchy of the colonial administration. The increased demand for metropolitan functionaries, however, came up against a shortage of qualified personnel. Federzoni's approach to the issue revealed a tension between the desire to encourage the fascistization of the colonial administration and apprehension over the lack of sophistication or experience among colonial functionaries. The efforts of his administration to train officials in the colonies were far from consistent or comprehensive, but they did include the establishment of an official publication, *Rivista delle colonie italiane*, along with a series of monographs in 1927. A year later, Federzoni complained to the governors of the Libyan territories about a lack of interest in this rather desultory program of professional development, and he made subscribing to both series of publications mandatory for officials above a certain pay grade. Though it is possible that the lack of interest reflected a form of resistance to the fascist direction of Federzoni's ministry, he took it to indicate the absence of a professional attitude among colonial officials that revealed the absence of a strong colonial culture among Italians more broadly.[62]

In February 1928, in one of his final acts as the minister of colonies, Federzoni issued new guidelines for the promotion of colonial officials that promised to address both the possibility of resistance to his fascist administration and the lack of professionalism. The new policy rejected previous requirements for the advancement of officials through the colonial hierarchy based on length of service. Instead, Federzoni sought the flexibility to place individuals with the specialized skills needed in the colonial setting and to reward individuals proven to be "good fascists." The measure was also meant to address the problem of a high turnover rate among colonial personnel, which Federzoni complained prevented the formation of a solid colonial tradition based on long-term service of those dedicated to the colonial project, with a strong foundation in the

kind of military and cultural knowledge deemed necessary for ruling restive Muslim populations. The guidelines for promotion also reflected an
attempt by Federzoni to prove that he was a party player at a time when
he faced increasing isolation from Mussolini's inner circle; Federzoni's
complaints about what he considered the inadequate attention the fascist
regime paid to the issue of colonial expansion led Mussolini to exclude
him from any positions of real power after he ended his last stint as minister of colonies in November 1928.[63] The measure also wrestled with a
contradiction: the Ministry of Colonies wanted to have the flexibility to
promote officers of solid fascist pedigree above those with more experience while at the same time creating a sense of continuity within a profes-
sionalized administration.[64]

Federzoni's concerns about the lack of professionalization among
colonial officials extended to the colonial armed forces, revealing a deep
rift between his administration and the military command. Federzoni's
criticisms of colonial troop preparedness drew a sharp rebuke from
General Rodolfo Graziani, the infamous general given primary responsibility for the Italian "reconquest" of the Libyan interior. In 1928, the
same year that Federzoni revamped the system of professional advancement, Graziani undertook a public relations campaign to defend colonial
officers against Federzoni's accusations that they lacked the professional
skills necessary for colonial warfare. Graziani adamantly defended the
professional capacity of colonial officials, especially the many self-trained
officers who had learned through direct experience in North Africa.
Graziani's reaction to accusations of lack of professionalism among colonial troops extended to a defense against fears in the Ministry of War
that the training and experience of fighting wars in North Africa would
make colonial troops too narrowly specialized, leaving them incapable
of participating in European warfare. Though he cautioned against the
risk of colonial officials losing track of technological developments in
the metropole (and established a fully stocked library of publications
on advancements in military strategy to counteract that risk), Graziani
sought recognition of colonial warfare and colonial troops as equal participants in the Italian national military forces. That they required specialized knowledge, Graziani freely admitted, but his defense of colonial
forces constituted a defense of the self-made man and a rejection of
Federzoni's insistence on promoting a specific culture of colonialism,
one that would necessarily include an educational component on local
culture and customs.[65]

Fascism and Catholicism in the Libyan Territories

Federzoni's efforts to promote the colonial project as a centerpiece of Italian nationalism found a more receptive audience among church leaders, who saw him as an ally in the fascist movement.[66] Federzoni's nationalist politics included an emphasis on celebrating a Catholic identity and resolving the long-standing contention between the church and the unified Italian state. In his colonial administration, Federzoni's interest in reconciliation informed a concerted effort to root out the influence of Freemasonry. Distrust of internationalism united these two aspects of his agenda. He equated the influence of Freemasonry with what he considered an excessive tolerance for Muslim traditions and the political power of native populations (with associated limitations of Italian state authority). In their condemnation of De Martino, Amendola, and the al-Rajma Accord, Federzoni and Luigi Pintor declared a political battle against what they depicted as a Freemason plot to diminish the power of the Italian government in favor of the Sanusi elite.[67] Outcries against the influence of Freemasonry spread among colonial military personnel during the course of the Italian military expansion into the interior in the late 1920s. Officers and regular soldiers complained that the influence of Freemasons created an atmosphere that stifled their ability to use violence against indigenous populations out of fear of punishment from the colonial administration. One colonial soldier in particular argued that this fear of recrimination weakened Italian military control and left Italian officials at the mercy of a Sanusi-aligned native elite.[68] Federzoni's commitment to eliminating Freemasonry in the colonial administration and military forces harmonized with the fascist regime's rejection of the previous power-sharing structures in a turn away from liberal international alliances.

The campaign against Freemasonry also aligned with Federzoni's favorable attitude toward the Catholic Church. Accusations of Freemasonry targeted anticlerical elements among both liberals and other branches of the fascist movement that were less amenable to Catholic influence. As one of the Fascist Party's preeminent conservative forces, Federzoni saw the Libyan occupation as a key moment in superseding the Roman question and incorporating the Catholic Church into the Italian nation.[69] Federzoni's support of the Catholic Church in national politics translated into increased financial support for missionary work in the Libyan territories during his tenure as minister of colonies. He saw the missionaries as a centerpiece of efforts to expand *italianitá* in the colonies. The relationship between the Catholic mission in Libya and the colonial administration was already much improved from the bitter disputes between Governor Ameglio and the Franciscan bishop Antomelli during World War I. In the era of Italo-Sanusi negotiations, Antomelli had often bristled at the restrictions placed on public displays of Catholic festivals, while Ameglio had struggled to assure local populations that the colonial administration would support the free expression of the dominant Muslim culture. The Roman Curia replaced Antomelli in 1919 with Giancinto Tonizza. A bishop with experience working in Muslim societies, Tonizza promised to refrain from public displays of Catholic identity in the colonial territories.[70] The change in missionary leadership corresponded to a wider shift in the church's approach to missionary work that sought to avoid political issues of colonial administration, a move that eliminated much of the fuel for disagreement between missions and colonial state officials.[71]

The mission's attempts to distance itself from past criticism of the colonial administration laid the groundwork for improved relationships with state officials; Federzoni deepened the goodwill by increasing state funding for missionary construction projects as part of general development plans to improve colonial infrastructure. In 1923 the mission used the state funds to begin construction of the long-anticipated cathedral in Tripoli.[72] In a report to Mussolini explaining an extraordinary budget increase for the mission, Federzoni emphasized the necessity of expanding the Catholic Church's presence in Libya in support of Italy's imperial ambitions and in confirmation of Italian racial superiority. "The construction of buildings for the Catholic cult is indispensable to assure the spiritual assistance to our colonists and it further constitutes a necessary moral affirmation of the dominant race which, in North Africa, resumes the tradition of the church of St. Augustine."[73] Mussolini happily followed Federzoni's lead on the promotion of Catholic identity in Italian imperial expansion. He declared his support of the Franciscan missions during his visit to the Libyan colonies in April 1926, and he wrote soon thereafter to the governor of Tripolitania, Emilio De Bono, to insist that the colonial administration increase funding to assist the mission in its construction projects.[74] In 1928, during his second term as minister of colonies, Federzoni reaffirmed his commitment to Catholicism in the colonies by setting aside 6.5 million lire out of an extraordinary public works budget of 800 million toward the construction of a new cathedral in Benghazi and a variety of churches. This plan constituted a dramatic expansion of the Franciscans' field of action into Cyrenaica that was meant to correspond to the military occupation of the Libyan interior.[75] The missionaries under-stood the advantage they gained with a fascist regime at the helm of colo-nial affairs; in requests for funding, they made frequent reference to a shared opposition to Freemasonry and an interest in ensuring Catholic prestige in a Muslim context.[76]

The Franciscan mission completed construction of the cathedral in Tripoli shortly before Mussolini replaced Federzoni as the minister of colonies in 1928.[77] At the official consecration, Emilio De Bono, newly appointed governor of both Libyan colonies, gave a speech marking the occasion in which he affirmed an abiding connection between Italian colonial expansion and the Catholic mission: "Every new attestation of our faith *in partibus infidelium* [in the land of unbelievers] is an affirma-tion of possession, and a pledge of civilization."[78] After decades of tension between the Italian colonial state and missionary leaders in the Libyan territories as Italian officials tried to negotiate a position as a pro-Islamic colonial power, the consecration of the cathedral served as a symbol of a new commitment to a collaborative approach between the church and state in spreading Italian culture across the Mediterranean. The fascist government's generosity to the Catholic mission also fit into a broader strategy in Mussolini's foreign policy that sought to augment Italian cul-tural, economic, and political presence in the Mediterranean to counter British and French influence. Mussolini hoped that the improved rela-tionship with the Holy See in the 1920s would work to Italy's advantage in the Mediterranean by using missionary networks to extend Italian influ-ence throughout the Arab world.[79] The improved relationship between the Franciscan mission and the colonial administration contributed to the general warming of relations between the Holy See and the Italian gov-ernment in the 1920s. The alignment of church and state interests abroad facilitated the final resolution of the Roman question in the Lateran Accord in February 1929.[80]

Conclusion

Federzoni's pro-Catholic traditionalism earned him many critics within the Fascist Party. During his stint as minister of colonies, many consid-ered the military operations in the "reconquest" of the Libyan interior to be going too slowly, and they interpreted the lack of faster results in terri-torial gains as a sign of Federzoni's weakness. Mussolini answered these criticisms by replacing Federzoni as minister of colonies in December

1928. In the following year he named Pietro Badoglio, a war hero and consummate imperialist, as the governor of the two Libyan colonies, with the charge of accelerating Italian state expansion into the interior. Badoglio, along with Rodolfo Graziani, oversaw the conclusion of Federzoni's plan for the "reconquest" and the ultimate pacification of the Libyan territories. Initially, Badoglio deployed Graziani to Tripolitania to occupy the Fezzan and Sirte regions, where Salah al-Atyush led Maghārba forces in collaboration with powerful members of the Sayf al-Nasr family and Awlad Sulayman tribes. Italian troops chased the Maghārba and Awlad Sulayman troops to the east, and Graziani had families of the Maghārba interred and moved northward toward the coast. His tactics led to a new wave of submissions of more than two thousand Maghārba troops, but al-Atyush fled with members of the Sayf al-Nasr family and a core group of armed forces, first to Kufra and then into Egypt, while Graziani and his troops, assisted by heavy aerial bombardments, chased them through the desert.[81]

Declaring the threat of the Maghārba neutralized, Graziani used his position to occupy the rest of the Fezzan. Badoglio sent Graziani to Cyrenaica in July 1930 to oversee military operations in the last territories where anti-Italian forces were congregating: the oases of Kufra and the Jabal al-Akhdar region. After bombing Kufra and chasing the anti-Italian forces concentrated there into Egypt, Graziani focused his attention on isolating ʿUmar al-Mukhtar and his supporters. The occupation of the Fezzan had already cut off potential supply lines from the west, so the only potential sources of arms and food for al-Mukhtar's Sanusi forces would come either from the Egyptian border to the east or from populations living in Italian-controlled areas who had declared their official submission to Italian authority. Citing evidence that *sottomessi* populations had provided al-Mukhtar with information about Italian troop movements and supplies, at times under duress, Graziani initiated an aggressive resettlement program. His efforts expanded upon a forced resettlement program along the coast that had begun under Governor Mombelli in 1925–1926. Over the course of 1930–1931, the Italian military confined 90,000 to 100,000 people in heavily controlled camps near the coast.[82] By some accounts the internments affected approximately half of the total population of Cyrenaica by the end of the military operations, and it left the forces of al-Mukhtar almost completely isolated.[83] The forced resettlement programs and a wave of emigration in the face of Italian military advances created space for Italian settlers. Many Libyans who left the region to find work in Egypt or to fight in other anticolonial campaigns returned to find their land confiscated by Italians or by Libyans who had submitted to Italian authority.[84]

The Ministry of Colonies and the colonial forces used the confiscation of territory to strike a further blow to Sanusi authority by eliminating the *ṭarīqa's* network of properties. On May 29, 1930, Italian military police organized a simultaneous attack on almost all of the Sanusi *zawāyā* in Cyrenaica. The Italian government then deported all shaykhs of the *zawāyā* to the Italian island of Ustica, where thousands of Libyan political prisoners were already being held.[85] The minister of colonies recognized the seizure of properties as differing from previous political activities of the colonial administration of Cyrenaica in its "strictly anti-Sanusi character, in that the Sanusiyya are recognized as primarily if not uniquely responsible for the rebellion."[86] On the occasion of his departure from the colonies in 1934, Graziani underscored his conviction, shared by the colonial governor, that the Sanusi elite should never reclaim positions of authority in what could finally be considered a fully Italian territory after the military operations culminated in the occupation of Kufra in 1931.[87]

After Graziani declared Cyrenaica pacified, the widespread displacement of populations and the seizure of Sanusi properties freed up land for settlement in some of the regions of Cyrenaica that Italian agricultural experts considered best for cultivation.[88] Concerns with appeasing a Muslim majority now perceived as largely subdued disappeared from official discussions, to be replaced with a focus on Italian colonization as a means of establishing political and economic stability. The project of colonizing the Libyan territories with Italian peasants offered the double benefit of consolidating Italian state power over the interior and promoting a fascist program of economic autarky by decreasing Italian reliance on imports from the colonial territories of Italy's European competitors. The settlement program failed on both counts; though the Italian population in the Libyan colonies totaled about 110,000 in 1940, it never exceeded the number of Italians in Tunisia, and the Libyan territories failed to develop as a source of raw materials and imports for the Italian peninsula. After years of armed struggle, the Libyan territories fell short of achieving self-sufficiency and depended heavily on imports and continuous assistance from Rome.

The designation of the Libyan colonies as an official administrative district, making up Italy's "fourth shore" across the Mediterranean in 1939 signaled Mussolini's intentions for the full integration of this North African territory. Mussolini continued to extol the idea of religious tolerance for Muslim citizens, even going as far as to declare himself the "protector of Islam" in a carefully staged ceremony during his visit to the colonies in 1937. But it was clear that the fascist administration had no intention of adopting an assimilationist approach to integrating the Muslim population into the Italian nation. Graziani's brutal tactics in the Libyan territories invoked a storm of criticism in the Arabic press against the Italian government, making ʿUmar al-Mukhtar an international hero and the Sanusiyya a symbol of resistance against imperial aggression. Mussolini took measures to improve Italy's image in the Arab world and placed new emphasis on propaganda depicting Italy as a bridge between the Muslim Mediterranean and Europe. He achieved some success among Arab nationalists, who saw the fascist regime as a potential ally against British foreign policies and aggression in Palestine.[89] Fascist officials, however, were explicit in expressing the intention for programs of mass colonization to decrease the relative influence of the Muslim populations and Muslim elites in the Libyan territories as they increased the numbers of Italian settlers.[90] The antagonism toward Islam in the Libyan territories under the fascist administration also found expression in a total condemnation of the Sanusiyya, not just as a political authority—which many in the fascist administration considered a false projection of liberal desires—but also in its capacity as a religious organization. In April 1934 the Office of the Vice Governor of Cyrenaica issued a report on the state of the colony that argued against any indication that the government would allow the Sanusi elites back into the Libyan territories, even if only to operate as a religious institution. The argument was based on an idea that even as a "purely" religious movement, in teaching a return to the original teachings of Islam, the Sanusiyya would necessarily deny the validity of Italian rule.[91] The definition of the Sanusiyya as an inherently anti-Italian organization conveniently supported the seizure of Sanusi properties and cast into stark relief the thinly veiled instrumentalism of attempts to project a shared sense of religious traditionalism across the Mediterranean.

Conclusions

ITALY'S DEFEAT IN World War II made the political future of the Libyan territories a subject of international debate. Italy officially renounced its overseas empire in 1947, but the agreements ending war stipulated further negotiations to determine what would happen in Italy's prefascist colonies. Some Italian imperialists clung to the possibility of some sort of imperial presence, at least in Eritrea, Somalia, and Libya.[1] This hope inspired a new wave of publications intent on explaining the benefits of an Italian approach to interacting with the Muslim world. For his part, Enrico Insabato wrote a book calling for increased Italo-Arab cooperation in 1950, "a relationship of understanding between Christianity and Islam"[2] A series of conferences held in Florence, Rome, and Naples in 1946–1949 promoted a return to the former colonial territories to domestic and international audiences. At these conferences it was clear that the state-sponsored settler colonies of the fascist era were no longer viable; most Italian settlers and colonial forces from North and East Africa were "repatriated" during World War II, either voluntarily or by force, as British prisoners.[3] Shifting international norms also precluded the possibility of a return to settler colonialism. After World War II the French were trying to rebrand their empire as a "union," and the British were moving closer to a concept of "trusteeship" that had originally developed in the wake of World War I.[4]

The hope that Italy could similarly reinvent the imperial project inspired the Ministry of Italian Africa (formerly the Ministry of Colonies) to keep its doors open and its offices functional even in the dire financial situation of postwar Italy. During the British occupation of Italian East Africa and Libya, the ministry was transformed into an agency whose primary function was to repatriate and provide aid to former colonial settlers.

But throughout this process ministry officials were determined to prevent a total dissolution of their offices. The ministry's budget for 1948–1949 explicitly sought a way of salvaging a skeleton structure, "with the purpose of preparing for new and substantial colonial activity in the future."[5]

Those efforts included the production of yet another official study of the Sanusiyya by officials in the Ministry of Italian Africa. Among the pre-fascist colonies, the possibility of retaining Italian influence in Cyrenaica seemed the most remote. During World War II the British had promised Idris al-Sanusi independence in exchange for military assistance. Though not large in number, the "Libyan Arab Forces" Idris organized from Egypt in 1940 effectively demonstrated his commitment to a pro-British position and his value as an ally.[6] In a move that seemed designed to demonstrate his value to the British and an audience of Libyans in exile, Idris threatened to withdraw his support for the war in 1942. The British foreign secretary, Anthony Eden, won him back by specifying that British efforts for Libyan independence would promote a Sanusi leadership in the postcolonial state or at the very least secure independence from Italy for the region of Cyrenaica even if the remainder of the Libyan territories remained under Italian control. To that end, Eden declared in the House of Commons: "His Majesty's government is determined that at the end of the war the Sanussi [sic] of Cyrenaica will in no circumstances again fall under Italian domination," and Idris continued to throw his weight behind the Libyan forces.[7]

The prospect of a Sanusi monarchy on Egypt's western border was therefore highly desirable to the British government as a solution to the Libyan question. It was not surprising that the Ministry of Italian Africa would challenge this solution, given Italy's extreme repression of Sanusi forces during the military campaigns of the "reconquest." Both sides positioned themselves in the debate through their interpretations of the political and religious authority of Idris al-Sanusi. In *The Sanusi of Cyrenaica* (1949), E. E. Evans-Pritchard established the English image of Idris al-Sanusi: militarily and politically competent, palatable to Western powers, and capable of uniting a fractured society through a shared Islamic identity. The new study of the Sanusiyya by the Ministry of Italian Africa, issued in the same year, offered a rejoinder.

Perhaps no document so clearly demonstrates the ways in which Italian imperialists tried to manipulate what they perceived as the connection between the political and religious authority of the Sanusiyya. Intended as both a defense of Italian efforts to negotiate with Idris al-Sanusi from 1916 until his departure from Cyrenaica in 1923 and an attack on his character and leadership abilities, the report laid full blame for the failure of their negotiations at the feet of Idris and cast Italy as a maligned supporter of his weak political authority. The most damning attacks in the ministry report, however, focused on Idris's conduct in exile. Attracted by the "worldly life" and seen "frequenting golf courses and the most elegant gatherings in Cairo, impeccably dressed in a European style" (as evidenced in figures C.1 and C.2), Idris was depicted by the ministry as a colonial intermediary corrupted by European wealth and morally bankrupt as a result. Accusations of ideological promiscuity were accompanied by an accusation of sexual promiscuity. Divorced from his wife (Ahmad al-Sharif's sister), Idris was rumored to have become engaged to and then jilted a (much) younger lady in Cairo. Some even claimed that he had taken to drinking alcohol.[8] The report represented a last-ditch effort to gather evidence against mounting international support for the formation of a united Libyan kingdom under Idris's rule, which threatened to undermine Italian efforts to return to the colonies.

The report's condemnation of Idris al-Sanusi's political authority, based on supposed moral weakness, laid bare the contradictions at the core of European attitudes in efforts to negotiate power-sharing relationships with Muslim elites. Fears of the potency of political Islam required religious moderation as a prerequisite for Muslim engagement with a European political sphere, but an assumption that most Muslims in North Africa (apart from a small number of urban elites) favored stringent anti-Christian attitudes suggested limits to the potential political authority of moderates. Thus, a willingness to engage with the non-Muslim world made Idris appealing, but also morally weak. In a European understanding of power in Muslim North Africa, his participation in a cosmopolitan and multifaith international order diminished his religious—and by extension political—authority, even if his participation amounted to an assertion of a nationalist agenda. The implication was clear: resistance rather than accommodation was supposed to provide the foundation of Sanusi spiritual and political leadership. This narrow vision of power in the Muslim world precluded the possibility of imagining political engagement with international allies as a source of strength; only a strict anti-Christian, isolationist approach could garner the necessary moral authority for popular support, though it would also pose an untenable threat to European hegemony.

Even in presenting him as the reverse image of the Italian report, the British promotion of Idris al-Sanusi after World War II echoed this

FIGURES C.1 AND C.2 Idris al-Sanusi at the Sporting Club in Cairo, May 1918.
Source: ASMAI II 181/70/362, Ministero dell'Africa Italiana, "La Senussia," 1949.

narrow vision of authority in Muslim North Africa. For Evans-Pritchard, Idris's position as the spiritual leader of a resistance movement justified British support for his political leadership of postindependence Libya. Evans-Pritchard recognized Idris as weak—in physical strength and in personality—but depicted his moral authority as the head of a *ṭarīqa* as beyond reproach. Because Evans-Pritchard understood the Sanusiyya as an organization that had created a national identity out of armed resistance, it followed that Idris could generate a sense of Libyan unity through his moral authority.[9] A United Nations commission organized to investigate conditions in the former Italian colonies in 1949 concurred with Evans-Pritchard. F. E. Stafford, the British representative on the commission, based his support for Sanusi leadership for the future of Cyrenaica on the presumed necessity of religious authority as the foundation for a national identity. "It is not incorrect to regard the word 'Cyrenaican' as being synonymous with 'Senussi [*sic*],' but the tie is one of faith, not one of blood."[10] Great Britain's chief civil affairs officer for the Middle East, Duncan Cummings, also favored Sanusi leadership, though he expressed some reservations about the "extremism" and "reactionary influence" of the Sanusi *ṭarīqa*.[11] The implication is clear: the future leader on the other side of Egypt's western border needed to be able to call on the moral credentials of Islamic authority to promote a sense of anti-imperial solidarity, but without being too Muslim for a European palate.

There were undeniable weaknesses in Idris al-Sanusi's monarchy, but they were due more to the failures of the international community involved in creating an independent state to deal effectively with regional divisions and the serious social problems facing the region after World War II than to any moral failings on the part of Idris. After the war the United Nations set out to develop a path to independence that was supposed to reflect the desires of the majority of Libyans throughout the three regions of Tripolitania, Cyrenaica, and Fezzan in order to promote stability. To that end, the UN formed a commission under the leadership of Adrian Pelt to determine the will of the Libyan people.[12] The Pelt Commission spent two years in discussions about the future of the region, finally deciding to establish a Sanusi monarchy in a united Libyan kingdom just one week before a UN deadline on December 24, 1951.[13] As Lisa Anderson has argued, the conclusions of the Pelt Commission placed the strategic interests of its member states above the opinions of the Libyan people.[14] Thus, the Pelt Commission supported British and (to a lesser extent) American interests in establishing a unified and independent Libyan state under a

monarch whom Western allies could trust to enter into military agreements in the ensuing Cold War. In the context of the formation of the new
state of Libya, the final arrangements of the Pelt Commission have been
blamed for breeding instability and regionalism by favoring the elites of
the Sanusi *ṭarīqa* at the expense of other segments of the population, especially residents of Tripolitania.[15]

Acutely aware that the appearance of favoritism would exacerbate
regional divisions, Idris went to great lengths to distance himself from
the Sanusi *zawāyā* during his reign. He delayed restoration of the Sanusi
zawāyā that had closed during the Italian military campaigns. When
they finally reopened in 1963, he accorded them highly restricted access
to political power. Baldinetti argues that the concern with limiting the
involvement of Sanusi shaykhs and *zawāyā* in the Libyan kingdom made
up part of a larger plan to prevent the development of opposition groups
that could pose a substantial threat to Idris's hold on power.[16] Distancing
himself from the religious authority of the Sanusi *ṭarīqa* was also a means
of avoiding internal rivalries in the larger Sanusi family as Idris navigated
a new arena of national politics. The issue was particularly important for
the question of succession: Would the throne of the Kingdom of Libya
pass to the descendants of Muhammad ʿAli al-Sanusi, the recognized
founder of the Sanusi *ṭarīqa*? In other words, would political leadership
of the Libyan kingdom become linked to the succession of the spiritual
guidance of the Sufi *ṭarīqa*? This arrangement would open up succession
to descendants of Ahmad al-Sharif and his brother. In his response to this
issue, Idris confirmed a strict division between his role as leader of the
Sanusiyya and his role as monarch of the Kingdom of Libya. While any eligible male member of the Sanusi family could become head of the *ṭarīqa*,
only descendants of his branch of the family could take the throne.[17]

Despite Idris al-Sanusi's efforts to avoid the appearance of favoritism, however, there were signs that tribes with long-standing ties to the
Sanusiyya—the Zuwaya in particular—enjoyed economic advantages in
the Libyan kingdom.[18]As a result, symbols of the Sanusi *ṭarīqa* became
targets after the 1969 coup, suggesting that Idris's attempts to distance
his position as king from his leadership of the Sanusiyya failed to have
the intended effect. Muammar Qadhafi's government confiscated Sanusi
properties and razed Sanusi *zawāyā*. It also funded historical research to
reinterpret Libyan nationalism that obscured or denied the role of Sanusi
elites in anticolonial resistance—except for those Sanusi shaykhs, like
ʿUmar al-Mukhtar, whose popularity was undeniable and whose deaths

eliminated the risk that they might challenge Qadhafi's rule. As with any revolutionary overthrow, one of the first tasks of the Qadhafi regime was to purge the government bureaucracy of Sanusi supporters and curtail the power of potentially subversive elites. Given the dismal lack of education or administrative experience in postcolonial Libya, Qadhafi failed to expel people associated with the *tarīqa* entirely from state offices, but there was little room for political activity that referenced a Sanusi identity in Qadhafi's Libya. George Joffre has argued that the goal of eliminating Sanusi influence extended to a reinterpretation of the role of Islam in Libyan political authority. In integrating his own particular form of Islamic principles into the revolutionary state, Qadhafi undermined the ability of Sanusi adherents to challenge his claims to moral authority as a source of political legitimacy.[19]

Despite these efforts, there are signs of a lingering influence of the Sanusiyya after 1969. Lisa Anderson has identified the continuation of Sanusi influence by tracing the regional roots of anti-Qadhafi sentiment in the years after the coup; the fact that opposition appeared earlier and was more forceful in Cyrenaica than it was in the rest of Libya, Anderson argues, indicates "residual attachment to or nostalgia for the order."[20] In the late 1970s Qadhafi became more aggressive in his efforts to squelch that nostalgia by attacking properties associated with the Sanusi *tarīqa* and intensifying his efforts to lay claim to the rhetoric of political Islam.[21] As a result, the end of the Qadhafi era raised questions not only about the legacy of the Sanusi *tarīqa*, but also about the broader issue of the link between religious and political authority in a postcolonial state. The revolution in 2011 saw a reemergence of the Sanusiyya as a symbol of Libyan national identity, especially with the adoption of the flag that Idris al-Sanusi had adopted for the postindependence Kingdom of Libya as a symbol of opposition to the Qadhafi regime. What is the position of the Sanusi *tarīqa* in post-Qadhafi Libya? How will this new era in Libyan history transform memories of resistance and collaboration from the colonial past?

Given Italy's position as an entry point into Europe for thousands of refugees arriving from North Africa, untangling the history of the formation of Italian national identities in relationship to a population overtly defined through religious difference also has immediate relevance. It is an issue that can be seen in recent conflicts over the presence of crucifixes on the walls of public classrooms in Italy; protected until recently by a law left over from the fascist era, the crucifixes asserted an exclusively Catholic national identity. When an Italian Muslim father of two initiated a campaign to have the crucifixes removed by court order in the early 2000s, it provoked fierce condemnation from public figures across the political spectrum. The link between Catholicism and *italianità* had been naturalized to the extent that an effort to accommodate a broader understanding of who counts as Italian seemed to many to be a fundamental attack on the nation. Historicizing Italy's Catholic national identity in relation to a nationalist program of imperial expansion in Muslim North Africa has the potential to widen perceptions of who belongs in the Italian nation.

Essay on Sources

MEMORIES OF RESISTANCE IN LIBYAN
ORAL HISTORY

The Commanders were the ones who set the plan, and they had a big role in instilling confidence in their abilities within the dor and defensive camps. You did not find among them those who came to make money or in search of glory. . . they all came for defense of the nation (al-watan) and the expulsion of the Italians—so for those who wonder, did ʿUmar al-Mukhtar come for his food? Or did other commanders come for their food? No, they only came to fight the Italians and kick them out . . . and ʿUmar al-Mukhtar was a symbol and source of their power.[1]

STARTING IN 1978, the Markaz Dirāsāt Jihād al-Libīyīn Dhad al-Ghazū al-Ītālī,[2] or the Center for the Study of the Libyan Struggle Against the Italian Invasion (commonly referred to in English as the Libyan Studies Center), launched a project to record oral interviews with former mujahidin, the men (and some women) who participated in armed resistance against the Italian occupation.[3] Since then the collection of oral histories has expanded to become the most significant historical source for twentieth-century Libyan history. As of 2012 the Libyan Studies Center counted 8,263 tapes of recorded interviews, with plans to expand.[4] The collection of oral histories offers a remarkable opportunity to access memories of war and trauma in colonial Libya and a valuable alternative to Italian colonial sources. But the project to record the voices of the mujahidin also reflected the concerns of a revolutionary generation claiming the mantle of political legitimacy after Qadhafi's coup d'état in 1969. It was the explicit intention of the initial project to turn the historic lens away from Idris al-Sanusi and a narrow circle of elites. Recording the stories of mujahidin created a new lexicon of heroes for the Libyan nation. But as the quote above demonstrates, the stories also confirmed the status of ʿUmar al-Mukhtar as a leading figure of the resistance.

Idris al-Sanusi, Ahmad al-Sharif, and other Sanusi elites also figure prominently in the accounts of the mujahidin. The oral history collection displays the full complexities of tracing histories of collaboration and resistance in postcolonial Libya.

The oral history collection was the first major project of the Libyan Studies Center. Founded in Tripoli in 1977 by Mohammed Jerary, a Libyan scholar with a PhD from Northwestern University in the United States, the center's primary concern was to document the history of the colonial era and narratives of resistance. Jerary invited the eminent oral historian Jan Vansina to oversee the oral history project. Although he lacked experience in North Africa or familiarity with the Arabic language, Vansina spent about six months in Tripoli in early 1978. He trained fourteen Libyan researchers to conduct interviews and helped develop a list of questions to guide the conversations. Vansina and his team divided Libya into fourteen distinct research districts, and individual researchers traveled to each district to identify former mujahidin and then record a series of interviews with them. Identifying mujahidin was an inherently political act that required distinguishing among nationalist resistance fighters, colonial collaborators, and what was probably a majority of people who fell somewhere in between. For his part, Vansina recognized the potential for local intermediaries to mislead the researchers from Tripoli in the identification of former mujahidin. He had the researchers record notes on where they obtained their information, and the team caught at least two instances of blatant prejudice in the naming of mujahidin.[5]

After a second interview to ask follow-up questions, staff at the Libyan Studies Center began the arduous task of transcribing the interviews. The transcriptions would eventually be published in volumes stored in the center's library. As of 2011, the number of published volumes had reached forty-three. This number falls short of the one hundred volumes the center anticipated when publication first began in 1990, and budget shortfalls threaten to stall a continuation of the transcription process.[6] Most—though not all—of the transcriptions involve translating the interviews from highly localized dialects into standardized modern Arabic.[7] Reading the transcriptions instead of listening to the recordings places an extra interpretive layer between the researcher and the original source, but the use of local dialects makes the recordings inaccessible to all but a very small handful of historians.

The development of the oral history project occurred at the tail end of a wider trend of collecting oral testimonies as historical sources that gained popular momentum in the aftermath of World War II. In European his-toriography, oral testimonies offered a chance to record the lived expe-riences of the traumas of the early twentieth century. The oral history movement resonated among historians of Africa in the 1960s and 1970s. Using oral sources allowed historians to escape the colonial archives while foregrounding precolonial oral traditions.[8] A first wave of oral histori-ans focused on oral histories as a source "to provide evidence about past events which could not be retrieved from conventional historical sources, usually written ones, or to uncover the hidden histories of individuals or groups who had gone unremarked upon in mainstream accounts."[9] Thus, oral histories were intended to be both supplemental and subversive, with value equal to that of written documents.[10]

Subsequently, historians turned a critical lens on the accuracy of oral sources. In the late 1970s historians began to ask how the weight of collec-tive memory might shape the narratives that emerge in oral testimonies. In her groundbreaking work on oral histories of fascist Italy, Luisa Passerini called for historians to understand oral history as "an expression and rep-resentation of culture, [that] therefore includes not only literal narrations but also the dimensions of memory, ideology and subconscious desires."[11] The result of this kind of critique of oral history practices was not to reject oral histories as sources, but rather to see the process of recording mem-ory as a document so that the interview itself—and not just the collected stories—became the object of study.[12] Another aspect of oral history prac-tices that generated criticism in the 1970s focused on the transformative nature of the relationship between the interviewer and the interviewee, a relationship that threatened to undermine the subversive potential of oral history "by the unequal relationships between professional historians and other participants in oral history projects." This concern has led historians to adopt a more self-reflective approach to the process of conducting inter-views and recording oral testimonies.[13]

Jan Vansina's concept of the oral history project in Libya placed it firmly in the first wave of oral history practices in the 1960s and 1970s. He saw the collection as a new repository for alternative sources that could challenge dominant narratives of anti-Italian resistance in colonial Libya. Vansina wrote about his involvement in the project in his memoir, *Living with Africa*, and I had the opportunity to ask him for more details in a per-sonal interview in 2007. According to Vansina, the collection provided "a history of the people, for the people" as a divergence from previous narra-tives of resistance that focused on elite leaders as national heroes.[14] In this sense, the collection of oral histories followed Qadhafi's general message of populism and localized power as part of his revolutionary agenda to establish direct popular democracy. Along those same lines, Vansina saw the collection as a source with the potential to correct an overemphasis on the leadership of elite figures in the Sufi *ṭarīqa* of the Sanusiyya—the power base of King Idris al-Sanusi's reign—in the historiography of resistance in colonial Libya. Vansina claimed that the interviews contradicted accounts of the Sanusiyya as central leaders of a nationalist resistance movement by demonstrating that anticolonial resistance arose organically in highly localized manifestations, which the leaders of the Sanusiyya then usurped for personal gain.

To the extent that the oral history project gave voice to a wide range of individuals throughout Libya, the end result fulfilled Vansina's stated goals. The accounts are focused primarily on describing the conditions of warfare in resistance to the fascist "reconquest" of the 1920s; given the date of the interviews, few of the mujahidin living in the late 1970s had clear memories of earlier periods of the Italian era. The majority of the interviews in the collection are organized around memories of specific battles. The accounts provide rich details to fill in a picture of what it was like to live and fight during the colonial era. A number of aspects of life under the occupation that emerge in the collection are well documented in written records: the constant threat of hunger in famine years as a motivation for reconciliation with Italian authorities and the importance of tribal alliances as an organizing principle for anticolonial troop formations, even under a Sanusi command.

The influence of international networks in assisting the anti-Italian resistance during the years of the "reconquest," also well established in the historiography, permeates the collection. The remembrances of the mujahidin paint a picture of a porous region that connected to a wider world of international aid, both in the supply of Turkish and German arms and in the maintenance of trade networks to western Egypt, even after the Italians constructed a barbed wire fence to block the way.[15] The testimonies in the Oral History Project also reveal the integration of the Libyan territories into a network of anticolonial resistance that stretched beyond Libya. One mujahid noted, for example, that ʿUmar al-Mukhtar fought in the Sudan against the French prior to mounting his opposition to al-Rida's negotiations with Italian authorities,[16] and in general the mujahidin took note of the number of nonlocal participants in battles against the Italian expansion. The emphasis on international networks of resistance derives from the personal trajectories of the Libyan mujahidin, many of whom went into exile in the 1930s in response to the repressive tactics of the Italian "reconquest." The activities of Libyans abroad provided a foundation for the development of a Libyan national identity after World War II.[17] Most of those in exile remained in Egypt, but some, like Muhammad Bubakir al-Rifi, went to Palestine to join in the Arab Revolt. Born in 1913, al-Rifi left Libya in 1936 and returned at end of the World War II. In his account, al-Rifi recalled using tactics of surprise the mujahidin had developed in Libya in the Palestinian context:

> The attack would usually begin with a group of horsemen while the infantry on foot would take their positions in front in a prostrate position on the ground and the horsemen would mount the attack on the enemy first then return and pass the lines of foot soldiers. The enemy would think the infantry were escaping or fleeing and that the road was open, then the Italians would give chase to find themselves under attack by the foot soldiers, and the horsemen would return to join the battle. This was how we trapped and defeated the enemy however large their forces, and this is the style of fighting we implemented in battles against the Jews in Palestine when we fought side by side with the Palestinian Fadaʿiin.[18]

Al-Rifi did not claim widespread involvement of Libyans in the Arab Revolt of 1936; he only knew of "a few" other mujahidin from his *dor* who fought in Palestine. But his memory of applying tactics from the anti-Italian resistance to a new battlefield is significant in that it illuminates intercolonial networks of knowledge to counter the interimperial networks of orientalism.

There are, however, a number of problems in using the testimonies recorded in the Oral History Project as a historical source. For one, many of the interviews occurred in public settings, lending a performative quality that influenced the stories the mujahidin chose to tell and the ways in which they told them. The interviewers and redactors of the printed volumes did not comment on the performativity of the interviews, and it is not clear if all of the interviews or only a handful were conducted in public. Reading the transcriptions of the interviews, one only becomes aware of the existence of an audience in moments of interruption. Throughout the transcriptions, furthermore, interviews of multiple individuals conducted in succession and in public led to a repetitious quality, and details and personal accounts faded into the background in favor of a frustrating level of abstraction that—despite Vansina's intentions—often foregrounded Sanusi elites as historical agents. Due to the focus on anti-Italian resistance, the majority of the accounts in the collection revolved around the descriptions of particular battles or particular interactions between the Libyan leadership and Italian officials. This emphasis means that (a) reaction to the Italian presence as a causal factor looms large in the accounts at the expense of any other relevant aspect of the social or political landscape of the region and (b) many of the stories seem to rely on hearsay or the collective understanding of events rather than personal experience.

The public and performative quality of the interviews also carried with it the possibility of self-censorship of the stories that were told. Consider, for example, a moment during an interview with a mujahid from the el-Shaata' region in northern Fezzan. When asked to recount his memories of the Italians' arrival in the area, he told a story about a group of tribal leaders from his region who traveled to talk to Turkish officials soon after the Italians landed in Tripoli. When the group of representatives returned, the speaker said, "I was amazed at the return of Mohammed bin ʿAmir," one of the tribal leaders in the group, but he did not explain why this would have been surprising. Instead, we find a break in the dialogue, and the researcher conducting the interview later inserted a note that the presence of Mohammed bin ʿAmir's sons among the group of people gathered for the interview prevented the speaker from divulging more details about their father's return, for fear that "some of the young men were embarrassed by the remembrance or account."[19] Memories of resistance or collaboration in the tumultuous times of colonial expansion were fraught with peril.

The public performances of the interviews also open fissures in the narrative; not all of the stories went uncontested. At times, audience members interrupted to correct the speaker or provide alternative accounts of particular events. For example, people present at the interview of Hasan al-ʿAjili Amhamad interrupted his narrative to provide names of individuals he could not recall.[20] Some interviewers were careful to note dissent among the onlookers, but they gave clear preference to the narratives of those being interviewed, the official storytellers. The voices of the volume editors and interviewers broke the narrative in other ways. Footnotes throughout the transcribed texts provide additional explanation for the process of transliteration (and the rendering of local dialects into standard Arabic). But they also interrupt to offer judgments on the validity of

the narratives in the testimonies of the mujahidin. In one case an editor interrupted an account of preparing for battle with three thousand
Ethiopian soldiers with a footnote to inform the reader that throughout
the interviews, mujahidin talked about fighting Ethiopian forces (*ascari*)
when in fact the Italian colonial forces employed Eritrean soldiers. The
footnote interrupts the oral history and the collective memory of Libyan
resistance fighters battling Ethiopians with information directly from the
state archives of the Italian colonial system, in an intersection of memory,
misunderstanding, and oral history.

A more fundamental problem in the Oral History Project is the exclu-
sive focus on providing a voice for those who were identified as mujahidin in Qadhafi's Libya. The interviewer and editor of one of the volumes
of transcribed interviews recognized this focus as a potential issue. The
researchers chose not to include stories about people who had abandoned
the resistance forces, even if some of those working for the Italian colonial system (whether voluntarily or by force) can be identified as having
assisted the anticolonial movement in some way.[21] Some of the lines of
questioning in the interviews reflect an interest in identifying a division
between collaborator and mujahidin. The interviewers were interested in
finding out what kinds of "temptations the Italians provided to become
collaborators,"[22] and they asked for identities of those regions, tribes, and
shaykhs who submitted first to Italian authority.

The actual narratives of the stories the mujahidin told often complicated the neat binary between collaborator and resister. Whether it was
recruits in the Italian military who buried ammunition for the mujahidin
to find after a battle or inhabitants of cities that had submitted to Italian
rule who would take information on Italian troop movements to the Sanusi
dor on the outskirts of the city, the mujahidin recalled many examples of
people living in the Italian colonial system while making active contribu-
tions to anti-Italian armed combat. The fact that such collusion occurred
amid conditions tantamount to civil war—in which the forces of ʿUmar al-
Mukhtar battled Libyan conscripts fighting for the Italians—speaks to the
difficulty of establishing a clear distinction between resistance and collaboration.[23] The structure of the Oral History Project, however, superimposes
a sharp contrast between the types of questions put to the mujahidin and
the absence from consideration of those who did not fight consistently
against the Italian presence as part of an organized armed force.

The image of the Sanusi elites and the role of the Sanusi *ṭarīqa* appear
similarly nebulous in the interviews. In the accounts of the mujahidin,

Sanusi elites appear at times in recollections of personal experiences or in the sort of stories one can imagine might have calcified in collective memories of the events of the Italian occupation. The inclusion of stories about Sanusi elites—Ahmad al-Sharif, Idris al-Sanusi, and ʿUmar al-Mukhtar in particular—is not surprising considering the efforts to lionize them in the postindependence historiography. But if we want to uncover the extent to which the Sanusi elites shaped an anti-Italian resistance, it would be best to look at moments when the interviewers in the Oral History Project sought explanations of motivations for taking up arms and joining an anticolonial jihad. After all, the core of the contested legacy of the Sanusiyya—and Idris in particular—can be found in the ability to claim responsibility for inspiring action in the face of occupation as an essential ingredient in the development of a national origin story. The political legitimacy of the Sanusi kingdom after independence rested on the assertion that the Sanusiyya served a unique function in uniting a highly divided tribal society against a common enemy. If the collection of oral histories decenters the Sanusiyya from the development of an anticolonial nationalist consciousness, as Vansina suggested that it did, then what motivated people to take up arms, at times joining forces across regional and tribal lines?

The interview subjects cited a variety of motivations for resistance. On a basic level, the accounts of the mujahidin emphasize the daily struggle to survive in the Libyan interior during the Italian occupation, especially in the period of the initial invasion, during World War I, and during the Italian "reconquest"—periods when warfare restricted access to trade routes and diverted labor from agricultural and pastoral enterprises. The threat of hunger, however, seemed just as likely to inspire negotiations with state authorities to prevent the closure of trade routes as it did the original modus vivendi between Idris al-Sanusi and Italy in 1916. When asked to identify leaders of the resistance—individuals who could mobilize an armed force by calling the mujahidin to fight—the accounts of the oral history project name a variety of tribal leaders, many of whom commanded their own *dor* in the region. But they were just as likely to name al-Sharif, Idris, or, of course, al-Mukhtar as being responsible for "inciting the people to combat."[24]

On an ideological level, the mujahidin appear more uniform in their explanations of why they chose to fight against the Italian presence. When asked what their rationale was for joining the jihad, the mujahidin most frequently referenced some form of a religious calling. Ahmed Ibn Salah al-Shibana, for example, when asked directly why he joined the jihad, replied that it was to answer a calling from Allah. Asked to distinguish if the motivation to take up arms against the Italians reflected a religious or a national identity, Muhammad Bubakir al-Rifa also focused on the religious, mixed with a heavy dose of territorial identity. "The motivation was primarily religious, and we knew that the infidel had come to rape our land and that it was our duty to fight it with all force."[25] Al-Rifa's explanation emphasizes the variety of ways in which the mujahidin could lean on religious motivation as an explanatory tool. And though not named as such, the focus on religious motivations hints at the underlying moral authority of the Sanusi elites as a potential organizing principle for anticolonial activity. Ultimately, however, responses to questions about motivation and leadership in the testimonies of the mujahidin reveal a complex landscape of tribal, military, and religious authority; decisions to move from one part of the region to another based on access to food and movement of arms; and international circuits of people and information. The stories of the Oral History Project achieve the goal of decentering the Sanusiyya from the history of anti-Italian armed resistance, at least in comparison with the historiography of the postindependence era, but they do not eliminate the Sanusi elites as highly visible figures with the power to shape interactions with the Italian state, whether armed or not.

If read deliberately, the Oral History Project, like most oral histories, has the potential to act as a subversive tool that can undermine dominant narratives and lacuna in written documents. Writing about oral history in Palestine, Kobi Peled has argued that the position of oral history outside of written documents allows it to "disrupt the nationalist narrative," but not automatically; oral accounts require careful handling to act as a corrective to standard documentation. "The danger of glorifying the past threatens the oral testimony, which is often characterized by veneration of the forefathers or of oneself. However, the oral testimony itself is capable of objecting to the mythologization, the unification and the flattening of the past for political ends."[26] Finding the moments of objection in the Libyan collection of oral histories takes careful work. But they should not be ignored as valuable sources that provide a different kind of collective understanding of colonial rule and resistance than that obtained in the state archives. If nothing else, the Oral History Project drives home the urgency of revisiting the origin stories of the Libyan nation in the colonial era.

Notes

INTRODUCTION

1. The arrest of Omar al-Mukhtar was commemorated for an international audience most notably in the film *Lion of the Desert* (1980), starring Anthony Quinn.
On the transnational significance of Omar al-Mukhtar as an anti-imperial hero,
see Hala Khamis Nassar and Marco Boggero, "Omar al-Mukhtar: The Formation
of Cultural Memory and the Case of the Militant Group That Bears His Name,"
Journal of North African Studies 13, no. 2 (2008): 201–217.

2. Ali Abdullatif Ahmida, *The Making of Modern Libya: State Formation, Colonization,
and Resistance, 1830–1932* (Albany: State University of New York Press, 1994), 2.

3. As Mostafa Minawi has pointed out, the terminology for referring to the Sanusiyya
is highly contested, reflecting the politicization of the history of a movement that
has been characterized in turn as religious or political. Those who emphasize the
religious mission of the Sufi order tend to refer to it as a *ṭarīqa* (literally, way),
while those who emphasize the political aspect of the Sanusiyya refer to it as
a *harika* (movement). While I find Minawi's argument in favor of avoiding the
conflict by referring to the Sanusiyya by the English term "order" compelling,
this approach raises its own issues in that it echoes the ways in which Europeans
writing about the Sanusiyya in the nineteenth and twentieth centuries drew parallels between the Sufi organization and religious orders of the Catholic Church.
Likening the Sanusiyya to Catholic religious orders casts it as a manifestation of
premodern tendencies (since most Catholic orders emerged in medieval Europe).
In anti-Catholic circles of European intellectuals, the comparison connoted deep
suspicion of the Sanusiyya as a secretive organization spreading antistate attitudes. Though I recognize the shortcomings of the terminology, I choose to refer
to it as the Sanusi *ṭarīqa* or the Sanusiyya because that terminology helps to avoid
the ways in which nineteenth- and twentieth-century authors defined the organization through a European prism and sets it firmly in a broader context of the

Sufi *ṭuruq* that emerged in the nineteenth century throughout North Africa and the Middle East. Mostafa Minawi, *The Ottoman Scramble for Africa: Empire and Diplomacy in the Sahara and the Hijaz* (Stanford, CA: Stanford University Press, 2016), 159n54.

4. The Sanusi *ṭarīqa* was one of a number of Salafist Sufi *ṭuruq* that developed in the nineteenth century, a trend Kemal Karpat has characterized as "the greatest revolution in the entire history of Islam . . . which surged up from among the lower classes under the guise of reviving the faith, but actually sought to find an 'Islamic' accommodation to the new order of things." Kemal Karpat, *The Politicization of Islam: Reconstructing Identity, State, Faith, and Community in the Late Ottoman State* (New York: Oxford University Press, 2001), 7.

5. There is no obvious terminology for the area that makes up the current state of Libya during the colonial era. In the Ottoman Empire, the three regions of Tripolitania, Cyrenaica, and Fezzan made up the Ottoman vilayet or province of Trablusgarp, and the Italian government maintained separate colonial administrations in Tripolitania and Cyrenaica until it unified them as one colony in 1934. Referring to the separate administrative districts as "Libya" runs the risk of reading a false sense of unified nationalism into the late nineteenth and early twentieth centuries, when evidence suggests that local and transregional divisions informed cultural and political identities. The Italian colonial administration emphasized regional distinctions by establishing parallel governments in Benghazi and Tripoli. Nevertheless, I refer to the region as a whole as the "Libyan territories" in order to reflect an Italian sensibility that often conceptualized Cyrenaica and Tripolitania as the site of a single imperial project. Furthermore, I choose to refer to this unified object of Italian imperial desire as the Libyan *territories* rather than as the Libyan *colonies* because there was a lack of strong state or settler presence in the majority of the region under consideration. Some might insist on distinguishing between the two administrative districts for clarity and strict historical accuracy, but avoiding any reference to a *Libyan* geography would prove clumsy and shortsighted, in that it would ignore the real effects postcolonial unification has had on a contemporary understanding of a shared experience of the past.

6. Despite the official withdrawal of military forces, Ottoman support for anti-Italian resistance did not cease with the Treaty of Lausanne, but rather moved to covert attempts to support armed rebellion materially and ideologically. Rachel Simon, *Libya between Ottomanism and Nationalism: The Ottoman Involvement in Libya during the War with Italy (1911–1919)* (Berlin: Klaus Schwartz Verlag, 1987), 122.

7. Edward Said, *Orientalism* (New York: Vintage Books, 1979), 3.

8. Ministero della Guerra, Stato Maggiore del Regio Esercito, and Ufficio Storico, "Proclama del tenente generale Caneva alle popolazioni della Tripolitania, Cirenaica e regioni annesse—13 ottobre 1911," in *Campagna di Libia*, vol. 1 (Rome: Poligrafico per l'Amministrazione della Guerra, 1922), 357.

9. Caneva, "Agli Arabi della Tripolitania," January 15, 1912, AUSSME L8/154/1.

10. Hashim Matar, *The Return: Fathers, Sons and the Land in Between* (New York: Random House, 2016), 125.

11. His full name was Muhammad ibn ʿAli al-Sanusi al-Khattabi al-Hasani. On discrepancies regarding his date of birth, see Nicola Ziadeh, *Sanusiyah: A Study of a Revivalist Movement in Islam* (Leiden: Brill, 1983), 35.

12. Because of its focus on returning to the practices of the Prophet Muhammad, the Sanusiyya, along with other similar Sufi orders that developed in the late eighteenth and early nineteenth centuries, has been labeled "neo-Sufist." These movements have often been attributed with a reformist social-political agenda analogous to the Wahhabi movement that emerged in Arabia in the eighteenth century. However, it is not entirely clear to what extent the early leaders of these newly emerging Sufi practices in North Africa in the early nineteenth century considered their focus on Muhammad a critique of earlier religious practices or social mores. Some scholars have questioned the value of the idea of "neo-Sufism" as a category that stemmed from postcolonial interpretations that misread political intention into the early formation of religious practices. See Valerie J. Hoffman, "Annihilation in the Messenger of God: The Development of Sufi Practice," *International Journal of Middle East Studies* 31, no. 3 (1999): 364; and Alexander Knysh, "Sufism as an Explanatory Paradigm: The Issue of Motivations of Sufi Resistance Movements in Western and Russian Scholarship," *Die Welt des Islams* 42, no. 2 (2002): 142.

13. Jamil M. Abun-Nasr, *Muslim Communities of Grace: The Sufi Brotherhoods in Islamic Religious Life* (London: Hurst, 1988), 143–147; and R. S. O'Fahey, *Enigmatic Saint: Ahmad Ibn Idris and the Idrisi Tradition* (Evanston, IL: Northwestern University, 1990), 58–70, 125–129.

14. Ziadeh, *Sanusiyah*, 113.

15. Minawi, *Ottoman Scramble for Africa*, 35–36.

16. Angelo Del Boca, "The Myths, Suppressions, Denials, and Defaults of Italian Colonialism," in *A Place in the Sun: Africa in Italian Colonial Culture from Post-Unification to the Present*, ed. Patrizia Palumbo (Berkeley: University of California Press, 2003), 17–36.

CHAPTER 1

1. There was some indication of interest in overseas expansion within the Foreign Ministry of the Kingdom of Piedmont-Sardinia in the 1850s before the wars of unification. Angelo Del Boca, *Gli italiani in Africa Orientale*, Vol. 1, *Dall'Unità alla marcia su Roma* (Milan: Mondadori, 2001), 12.

2. Giuseppe Finaldi has challenged the consensus among historians that early Italian imperialism failed to garner widespread support. Examining depictions of Italian activities in school textbooks and school ceremonies commemorating such activities, Finaldi argues that the early years of Italian imperial expansion

played a crucial role in developing a sense of nationalism among a broader population, calling into question the methods by which historians measure participation in imperialism. Giuseppe Finaldi, "Culture and Imperialism in a 'Backward' Nation? The Prima Guerra d'Africa (1895–96) in Italian Primary Schools," *Journal of Modern Italian Studies* 8, no. 3 (2003): 374–390.

3. Romain Rainero, *L'anticolonialismo italiano da Assab ad Adua (1869–1896)* (Milan: Edizione di Comunità, 1971), 22.

4. Del Boca, *Gli italiani in Africa Orientale*, 42, 51.

5. The Italian press mimicked images of Garibaldi's thousand volunteers (*I Mille*) in the portrayal of Italian troops landing in Massawa. Alessandro Triulzi, "Adwa: From Monument to Document," *Modern Italy* 8, no. 1 (2003): 100.

6. Giuseppe Finaldi, *Italian National Identity in the Scramble for Africa* (Bern: Peter Lang, 2009), 30–31.

7. Raymond Jonas, *The Battle of Adwa: African Victory in the Age of Empire* (Cambridge, MA: Belknap Press of Harvard University Press, 2011), 30–38.

8. Nicola Labanca, *In marcia verso Adua* (Turin: Einaudi, 1993), 51–52.

9. "Italy in Egypt," *New York Times*, February 6, 1885, 4.

10. Rainero, *L'anticolonialismo italiano*, 58; Alfredo Canavero, "I cattolici di fronte al colonialismo," in *Adua: Le ragione di una sconfitta*, ed. Angelo Del Boca (Rome: Laterza, 1997), 92–93.

11. "Colonialismo italiano," *L'Osservatore Cattolico*, January 27–28, 1885, 1.

12. "L'Entusiasmo per le imprese africane," *L'Osservatore Cattolico*, January 11–12, 1885, 1.

13. Theodore M. Vestal, "Reflections on the Battle of Adwa and Its Significance for Today," in *The Battle of Adwa: Reflections on Ethiopia's Historic Victory Against European Colonialism*, ed. Paulos Milkias and Getachew Metaferia (New York: Algora Publishing, 2005), 23.

14. Canavero, "I cattolici di fronte al colonialismo," 98; Nicola Labanca, *Oltremare: Storia dell'espansione coloniale italiana* (Bologna: Il Mulino, 2002), 79.

15. Jonas, *Battle of Adwa*, 72–73.

16. Tekeste Nagesh, *Italian Colonialism in Eritrea, 1882–1941: Policies, Praxis and Impact* (Uppsala: Uppsala University Press, 1987), 121.

17. Jonas, *Battle of Adwa*, 87.

18. For an explanation of the political connections between emigration and Italian imperialism, see Mark Choate, *Emigrant Nation: The Making of Italy Abroad* (Cambridge, MA: Harvard University Press, 2008).

19. Labanca, *In marcia*, 308. For an analysis of Crispi's expansionist policies as an extension of the process of territorial unification in Southern Italy, see Pasquale Verdicchio, "The Preclusion of Postcolonial Discourse in Southern Italy," in *Revisioning Italy: National Identity and Global Culture*, ed. Beverly Allen and Mary Russo (Minneapolis: University of Minneapolis Press, 1997), 191–212. As Verdicchio points out, administrative restructuring marked the new link

between the expansionist foreign policy and Italian emigration with the creation of a new section in the Foreign Ministry in 1887 dedicated to dealing with the issues of Italian emigration, expatriate colonies, and Italian schools abroad.

20. Jonas, *Battle of Adwa*, 99.
21. Ibid., 100.
22. Del Boca, *Gli italiani in Africa Orientale*, 579–585; Nagesh, *Italian Colonialism in Eritrea*, 125.
23. Douglas J. Forsyth, *The Crisis of Liberal Italy: Monetary and Financial Policy, 1914–1922* (Cambridge, UK: Cambridge University Press, 1993), 23.
24. Triulzi, "Adwa," 105.
25. The practice of recruiting Eritrean soldiers for Italian colonial forces began after the Italian defeat at Dogali in 1887, but it escalated and became more systematic in the first decades of the twentieth century. See Jonas, *Battle of Adwa*, 58–63. On the later employment of *ascari* (Eritrean soldiers) in the Italian occupation of Ethiopia in 1935–1936, see Alessandro Volterra, ed., *Progetto Ascari* (Rome: Edizioni Efesto, 2014).
26. Nagesh, *Italian Colonialism in Eritrea*, 107.
27. By 1911 at least, salaries for local elites were the largest single expense of the Italian colonial government in Eritrea. Nagesh, *Italian Colonialism in Eritrea*, 102–104.
28. Iris Seri-Hersch, "Confronting a Christian Neighbor: Sudanese Representations of Ethiopia in the Early Mahdist Period," *International Journal of Middle East Studies* 41, no. 2 (2009): 249.
29. Ibid., 251; Nagesh, *Italian Colonialism in Eritrea*, 104.
30. J. Spencer Trimingham, *The Sufi Orders in Islam* (Oxford: Oxford University Press, 1971), 116–118.
31. Jonathan Miran, "A Historical Overview of Islam in Eritrea," *Die Welt des Islams* 45, no. 2 (2005): 197–198; Joseph Venosa, "Adapting to the New Path: Khatmiyya Sufi Authority, the al-Mirghani Family, and Eritrean Nationalism during the British Occupation, 1941–1949," *Journal of East African Studies* 7, no. 3 (2013): 416.
32. Silvia Bruzzi has demonstrated the ways in which her position as a female leader of the *ṭarīqa* served to spread Italian-influenced medical practices in Eritrea. "Saints' Bodies, Islamic and Colonial Medicine in Eritrea (1887–1940)," in *Themes in Modern African History and Culture*, ed. Lars Berge and Irma Taddia (Padova: Biblioteca Universitaria, 2013), 69–84.
33. Letter from ʿAlawiyya al-Mirghani [Morghani in Italian documents], December 11, 1911, ASMAI II 136/1/1.
34. Italian Ambassador to Britain to Secretary of State, February 12, 1887, BNA FO 101/94.
35. Luigi Robecchi Bricchetti, *Il commercio di Tripoli* (Rome: Società Geografica Italiana, 1896), 40.

36. Luigi Robecchi Bricchetti to Minister of Foreign Affairs, April 20 and 28, 1895, ASMAI III, B. 24, Fasc. 4.

37. Abun-Nasr, *Muslim Communities*, 160–161; E. E. Evans-Pritchard, *The Sanusi of Cyrenaica* (Oxford: Clarendon, 1949), 14–22.

38. Knut Vikør, *Sufi and Scholar on the Desert Edge: Muhammad b. Ali al-Sanūsi and His Brotherhood* (Evanston, IL: Northwestern University, 1995), 143. It is important to note that Shukri would disagree with any notion that this meant Muhammad ibn ʿAli al-Sanusi was not aware of establishing a religious order. He presents the life of al-Sanusi as one directed tirelessly toward spreading a religious calling that would lead "inevitably" to the development of a political emirate. Muhammad Fuʾad Shukri, *Al-Sanūsiyah, din wa dawla* (Oxford: Centre for Libyan Studies, 2005), 51.

39. Lisa Anderson, "Nineteenth-Century Reform in Ottoman Libya," *International Journal of Middle East Studies* 16 (1984): 338.

40. A number of scholars have written about the life of Muhammad ibn ʿAli al-Sanusi and the early years of the Sanusi *ṭarīqa*. For an excellent synopsis of this literature, see Minawi, *Ottoman Scramble for Africa*, 29–34.

41. Evans-Pritchard, *Sanusi of Cyrenaica*, 5.

42. Ibid., 7.

43. Ibid.

44. In the expansion of the *ṭarīqa* of the Nasiriyya in eighteenth- and nineteenth-century Morocco, donations determined the status of adherents within the Sufi *ṭarīqa* and their subsequent access to the resources managed by the *ṭarīqa*. See David P. V. Gutelius, "The Path Is Easy and the Benefits Large: The Nasiriyya, Social Networks, and Economic Change in Morocco, 1640–1830," *Journal of African History* 43, no. 1 (2002): 32.

45. Ghislaine Lydon, *On Trans-Saharan Trails: Islamic Law, Trade Networks, and Cross-Cultural Exchanges in Nineteenth-Century West Africa* (Cambridge, UK: Cambridge University Press, 2009), 12.

46. Glauco Ciammaichella, *Libyens et Français au Tchad (1897–1914): La Confrérie senoussie et le commerce transsaharien* (Paris: Editions du Centre National de la Recherche Scientifique, 1987), 36; Dennis D. Cordell, "The Awlad Sulayman of Libya and Chad: Power and Adaptation in the Sahara and the Sahel," *Canadian Journal of African Studies* 19, no. 2 (1985): 337; and Minawi, *Ottoman Scramble for Africa*, 25.

47. Ahmida, *Making of Modern Libya*, 83; Emyrs L. Peters, *The Bedouin of Cyrenaica*, ed. Jack Goody and Emanuel Marx (Cambridge, UK: Cambridge University Press, 1991), 40–41. British intelligence reported that Zuwaya groups moved into the oases of Kufra to escape punishment for the murder of Ottoman officers near Ajdabiya in 1890. British Consulate in Benghazi to the Secretary of Foreign Affairs, April 2, 1894, BNA FO 101/84. This suggests that there were two movements of the Zuwaya into the Kufra oases. The second influx could have

precipitated a wider crisis with the Tibbu inhabitants, leading to the intervention of the Sanusiyya.

48. John Davis, *Libyan Politics: Tribe and Revolution* (Berkeley: University of California Press, 1987), 110.

49. Henri Duveyrier, *Exploration du Sahara: les Touâreg du nord* (Paris: Challamel Ainé, 1864), 401. On Duveyrier's connection with Saint-Simonian circles and its romantic ideas of a European-African fusion through imperial expansion, see Dominique Casajus, "Le destin saharien d'un saint-simonien rebelle: Henri Duveyrier chez les Touaregs," *Gradhiva*, Musée du quai Branly, 33 (2003): 11–31; Dominique Casajus, "Henri Duveyrier face à Prosper Enfantin: ribelle ou rival?," *Ethnologies comparées* 8 (2005): 1–8; and Michael Heffernan, "The Limits of Utopia: Henri Duveyrier and the Exploration of the Sahara in the Nineteenth Century," *Geographical Journal* 155, no. 3 (1989): 342–352.

50. Jean-Louis Triaud, *La légende noire de la Sanûsiyya: Un conférie musulmane saharienne sous le regard français (1840–1930)* (Paris: Éditions de la Maison des sciences de l'homme, 1995), 111–112.

51. Ibid., 9.

52. Ibid., 331–346; Henri Duveyrier, *Le Confrérie musulmane de Sidi Mohammed Ben 'Ali Es-Senousi et son domaine géographique, en l'année 1300 de l'hégire (1883 de notre ère)* (Paris: Société de Géographie, 1884), 12.

53. Karpat, *Politicization of Islam*, 43.

54. Evans-Pritchard, *Sanusi of Cyrenaica*, 91–92.

55. Accounts of the governor-general's adherence to the Sanusiyya (based on an account from Ahmad al-Sharif) state that at first he saw the Sufi leader as a suspicious figure but subsequently became convinced of his good intentions toward the Ottoman administration and converted as a sign of good faith. Vikør, *Sufi and Scholar*, 145; Ali Muhammad Sallabi, *Tarikh al-harakah al-Sanusiyah fi Afriqiya* (Beirut: Dar al-Ma'rifah, 2005), 42–43.

56. Azmi Özcan, *Pan-Islamism: Indian Muslims, the Ottomans and Britain (1877–1924)* (Leiden: Brill, 1997), 24–25; See also Cemil Aydin, *The Politics of Anti-Westernism in Asia: Visions of World Order in Pan-Islamic and Pan-Asian Thought* (New York: Columbia University, 2007), 110.

57. Le Gall's reading of the Ottoman documents suggests Muhammad al-Mahdi al-Sanusi positioned himself against the Ottoman Empire in response to taxation policies that targeted the relative prosperity of tribes active along the Wadai-Benghazi trade route, in essence siding with regional support networks over the demands of central authorities. According to Le Gall, Istanbul pursued a series of armed campaigns in the 1880s and 1890s against tribes loyal to the Sanusiyya in retribution for their refusal to pay taxes and as a means of applying pressure to Sansui elites to support Ottoman centralization. Some scholars have understood the move as an attempt on the part of the Sanusiyya to defend the region against French encroachments from the Lake Chad region. Le Gall has

argued that Sanusi interest in Kufra had more to do with the desire to control the Zuwaya and the resources of the residual slave trade and large salt deposits in the region than with retaining territorial integrity. In light of this context, Le Gall interprets the decision of al-Mahdi to move his residence and the headquarters of the *ṭarīqa* from Jaghbub to Kufra as an attempt to defend the economic interests of the Zuwaya while moving farther away from the Ottoman garrison in Awjila and Jalo rather than exhibiting concern with the French movements in the Lake Chad region—a further sign of al-Mahdi's focus on regional alliances over the support of central authorities. Michel Le Gall, "The Ottoman Government and the Sanusiya: A Reappraisal," *International Journal of Middle Eastern Studies* 21 (1989): 99–100. Some contemporary accounts also depicted Ottoman-Sanusi relations as tense at the end of the nineteenth century. The British consulate in Tripoli, for example, reported signs of an attempt by the Ottomans to extend their authority to Kufra in 1900, which they saw as a sign of antagonism between the Ottoman Sultan and the Sanusiyya. Letters from British Consul in Tripoli, 1900, BNA FO 101/90.

58. Salim Husayn Kabti, *Idris al-Sanusi: al-amir wa-al-malik*, 3 vols. (Benghazi: Dar al-Kutub al-Wataniya, 2013), 15. For further examples, see Minawi, *Ottoman Scramble for Africa*, 52.

59. Minawi, *Ottoman Scramble for Africa*, 36.

60. Shukri, *Al-Sanūsiyah*, 139–140; and Minawi, *Ottoman Scramble for Africa*, 51.

61. Minawi, *Ottoman Scramble for Africa*, 49. Evidence from the British archives provides additional weight for Minawi's extensive exploration of the issue in Ottoman documents. The suggestion of an alliance between al-Mahdi and the Ottoman Sultan after the mid-1890s could explain reports from British intelligence that the Sanusiyya had initiated a program in Kufra of unifying tribes under their leadership, as well as the subsequent battles between troops fighting under Sanusi leadership and the French Senegalese troops in the Lake Chad region in 1901 and 1902. General Staff, War Office, "Military Report on Tripoli in North Africa (Tripoli, Barka, and Fezzan)," 1905, 83, BNA WO 33/354.

62. As Selim Deringil has argued, "Abdulhamid was attempting to do precisely what he feared the British and the French would do to him, that is to use Muslims of French or British allegiance as a political fifth column." *The Well-Protected Domains: Ideology and the Legitimation of Power in the Ottoman Empire 1876–1909* (London: I. B. Tauris, 1998), 66.

63. Selim Deringil, "'They Live in a State of Nomadism and Savagery': The Late Ottoman Empire and the Post-Colonial Debate," *Comparative Studies in Society and History* 45, no. 2 (2003): 312. In a plan for modernization and centralization from the 1890s, Abdulhamid II called for "winning the affection of the local people [in Cyrenaica and Tripolitania] so that in the event of external aggression, say from Italy, it will be possible to defend the province without recourse to the sending of troops from the centre [sic]." Quoted in Karpat, *Politicization of Islam*,

319. See also Hasan Kayali, *Arabs and Young Turks: Ottomanism, Arabism, and Islamism in the Ottoman Empire, 1908–1918* (Berkeley: University of California Press, 1997), 19; Özcan, *Pan-Islamism,* 34; Michael A. Reynolds, *Shattering Empires: The Clash and Collapse of the Ottoman and Russian Empires 1908–1919* (Cambridge, UK: Cambridge University Press, 2011), 89; Dirk Vandewalle, *A History of Modern Libya* (Cambridge, UK: Cambridge University Press, 2006), 17.

64. Shukri, *Al-Sanūsiyah,* 161. In 1910 Ahmad al-Sharif agreed to the establishment of an Ottoman garrison in Kufra with Kaylani al-Atyush, a shaykh from the Maghārba tribe, in charge.

65. Karpat, *Politicization of Islam,* 264.

66. General Staff, War Office, "Military Report on Tripoli in North Africa (Tripoli, Barka, and Fezzan)," 1905, 85, BNA WO 33/354. There was also some evidence to suggest that arms reached Sanusi *zawāyā* from other conflicts in the region, including the Mahdist rebellion in Sudan. M. Defrance, Plenipotentiary Minister of the French Republic to Cairo to the Ministry of Foreign Affairs, January 19, 1911, FR CAOM FM SG AFRIQUE VI 185.

67. Minawi, *Ottoman Scramble for Africa,* 67.

68. On the establishment of the Sanusi *zāwiya* in Bir Alali in 1898, see the collection of letters that first Muhammad al-Mahdi and then Ahmad al-Sharif exchanged with the Sanusi *ikhwān* in Bir Alali, in Jean-Louis Triaud, *Tchad 1900–1902: Une Guerre Franco-Libyenne oubliée?* (Paris: Editions l'Hartmattan, 1987). See also Triaud, *La légende noire de la Sanûsiyya,* 669.

69. British Consul in Benghazi to the Secretary of State for Foreign Affairs, January 23, 1902, BNA FO 101/92; British Consul in Benghazi to the Secretary of State for Foreign Affairs, February 20, 1902, BNA FO 101/92.

70. Ahmad al-Sharif to the French mission of Bonnel de Mezieres, February 11, 1911, FR CAOM, AEF GGAEF 5D/20. Ali Abdullatif Ahmida has pointed to the centrality of education in the Sanusiyya in the late nineteenth century. He estimates the number of students in Sanusi *zawāyā* in 1900 at about 15,000. Ahmida, *Making of Modern Libya,* 98.

71. The redactors of these letters, Jay Spaulding and Lidwien Kapteijns, characterized the relationship between ʿAli Dinar and Ahmad al-Sharif and the latter's local agents as a formal alliance based primarily on a shared religious identity and a commitment to anti-European action. Jean-Louis Triaud has argued convincingly that this characterization is probably an exaggeration derived from the alarmed interpretations of British observers. Though they both faced a common source of anxiety in the increased presence of French troops, their relationship was based more on mercantile concerns during a period of restricted possibilities for trade rather than on a sense of united Islamic resistance to Christian expansion. Jay Spaulding and Lidwien Kapteijns, *An Islamic Alliance: ʿAli Dinar and the Sanusiyya, 1906–1916* (Evanston, IL: Northwestern University Press, 1994), 19. See Jean-Louis Triaud's review in *International Journal of African Historical Studies*

29, no. 2 (1996): 349–353. On fears that the letters between ʿAli Dinar and the Sanusi proved the existence of an anti-Christian Islamic alliance, see the copy of a British report dated June 10, 1916, in FR CAOM FM SG AFRIQUE/XI/190.

72. After 1904 the new sultan of Wadai, Dudmurrah, blocked ʿAli Dinar's access to Mediterranean trade through central Saharan routes in response to his refusal to end protectionist practices of placing high tariffs on goods coming out of Wadai. At the same time, a young shaykh from the Kababish tribe on the north-eastern frontier of Darfur, with the full backing of the Anglo-Egyptian officials in Khartoum, blocked ʿAli Dinar's access to Mediterranean markets on the old Forty Days' Road. As a result, ʿAli Dinar relied increasingly on his Sanusi contacts for supplies of arms and ammunition in exchange for a steady stream of food supplies (an increasingly valuable commodity considering the drastic level of drought in the Central and Western Sudan between 1903 and 1915) and commercial goods from the south, such as ivory and ostrich feathers, that enjoyed heightened popularity in European markets at the end of the nineteenth century. The alliance between Ahmad al-Sharif and ʿAli Dinar soured after 1911 when the invasion of Italian troops on the coast of Libya redirected the focus of the Sanusi elite northward. In 1914 ʿAli Dinar complained about a shipment of arms that never reached him because the Sanusi leaders decided to divert them to Fezzan to help in the battle of Qasr Bu Hadi. Spaulding and Kapteijns, *An Islamic Alliance*, 46.

73. British Consul-General in Tripoli to Secretary of Foreign Affairs, Sir Edward Grey, June 30, 1910, BNA FO 881/9909. Ahmad al-Sharif later called on the French to abandon Wadai as a precondition for possible negotiations with the English and Italians, a sign of his continued recognition of the importance of the region for the Sanusi *ṭarīqa* and the trade routes of their affiliated tribes. Minister of War to Minister of Colonies, June 8, 1916, FR CAOM, FM SG AEF VI 6.

74. "Situation actuelle des senoussis," March 6, 1911, report from the Minister of Foreign Affairs, FR CAOM FM SG AFRIQUE/VI/191.

75. Colonel Largeau to the Lieutenant-Governor of Oubangui-Chari-Tchad, November 10, 1911, FR CAOM FM SG AFRIQUE/VI/185.

76. "The Senussi," I.D. 0997, Secret report compiled by the Admiral War Staff Intelligence Division, May 26, 1915, ASMAI II 136/1/3. The lengthy report offered a summary of British intelligence on the Sanusiyya collected in the years leading up to 1911, but it was communicated to the Italian Ministry of Colonies only in 1915, in the same month that the Italians entered World War I as an ally of the British. Facing the potential—and eventual—outbreak of hostilities with Ahmad al-Sharif along Egypt's ill-defined western border, the British had clear motivations for sharing information that might help the Italian government defend shared interests.

77. Ahmad al-Sharif to the French mission of M. Bonnel de Mezieres, November 2, 1911, FR CAOM AEF GGAEF 5D/20.

78. French Minister of Colonies to the Minister of Foreign Affairs, "Voyage du cheikh Ben Tekkouk chez les Senoussistes," August 18, 1913, FR CAOM AEF GGAEF 5D/20.

CHAPTER 2

1. Barbara Sòrgoni, "Italian Anthropology and the Africans: The Early Colonial Period," in *A Place in the Sun: Africa in Italian Colonial Culture from Post-Unification to the Present*, ed. Patrizia Palumbo (Berkeley: University of California Press, 2003), 63–64.

2. For the French and German travel narratives, see chapter 1. An example of an early Italian account of the Sanusiyya can be found in the book by Giuseppe Haimann, who attempted to visit Giaghbub in 1881 as part of a scientific and artistic expedition on behalf of the Società di Esportazione Commerciale in Africa based in Milan. Giuseppe Haimann, *Cirenaica (Tripolitania)*, 2nd ed. (Milan: Ulrico Hoepli, 1886).

3. Insabato's career has attracted lively attention among historians of Italian imperialism, though in a personal conversation, one doyen of the field suggested research into his opinions was a waste of time because of his supposed anarchist tendencies. See especially Anna Baldinetti, *Orientalismo e colonialismo: La ricerca di consenso in Egitto per l'impresa di Libia* (Rome: Istituto per l'Oriente C. A. Nallino, 1997); Daniel J. Grange, *L'Italia et la Méditerranée (1896–1911)* (Rome: École Française de Rome, 1994); Carlo Gotti Porcinari, *Rapporti Italo-Arabi (1902–1930): Dai documenti di Enrico Insabato* (Rome: E. S. P., 1965); Meir Hatina, "Where East Meets West: Sufism, Cultural Rapprochement, and Politics," *International Journal of Middle East Studies* 39 (2007): 389–409; and Angelo Scarabel, "Una rivista Italo-Araba d'inizio secolo: An-Nadi (Il Convito)," *Oriente Moderno* 58, nos. 1/3 (1978): 51–67.

4. "Verso la . . . greppia," *Il Libertario*, October 13, 1904, ASDMAE, Rappresentanza diplomatica Egitto—Il Cairo 1864–1940, B. 86. Insabato contributed to the anarchist paper in Cairo, *Il Domani*, under the pseudonym Damocle in 1903. ASDMAE, Rappresentanza diplomatica Egitto—Il Cairo 1864–1940, B. 87. Insabato himself vehemently denied anarchist connections when his activities came under greater scrutiny in Cairo. Insabato to Commander of State Police, February 3, 1912, ASMAI II 137/1. There has even been some evidence that Insabato operated as a spy infiltrating anarchist groups in Paris abroad under the codename "Dante." Considering Insabato's connection to Giolitti (to whom he pledged absolute loyalty) and Giolitti's interest in suppressing anarchist activities, this seems a plausible explanation for Insabato's association with anarchist groups. See Pietro Di Paola, "The Spies Who Came in from the Heat: The International Surveillance of the Anarchists in London," *European History Quarterly* 37, no. 2 (2007): 206–207; and Giampietro Berti, *Errico Malatesta e il*

movimento anarchico italiano e internazionale: 1872–1932 (Milan: Franco Angeli, 2003), 337–338. Ameglio noted that some anarchists suspected Insabato of being a spy even in his student days in Bologna. Governor of Cyrenaica to Italian Ambassador to Constantinople, August 30, 1914, ASMAI II 134/6/40.

5. Prefect of Vicenza to Minister of Interior, February 6, 1930, ACS CPC 2639.

6. "Rome-Moslem 'Front' Planned," *Washington Post and Times Herald*, February 9, 1956, http://search.proquest.com/docview/148830762?accountid=14270; and "World Catholics, Moslems to Join in Fight on Reds," *Daily Boston Globe*, February 9, 1956, http://search.proquest.com/docview/840603687?accountid=14270.

7. The Prefecture of Bologna started a file on Insabato as an anarchist in 1898 based on his frequent association with the editor of an anarchist newspaper, *La Libertà*. Prefecture of Bologna, "Insabato Enrico, fu Michele . . . ," February 9, 1898, ACS CPC 2639. On the initial suspicions of the Italian Consulate in Cairo, see Salvago Raggi to Minister of the Interior, July 8, 1903, ACS SPD 2639. On the instructions to halt surveillance, see Salvago Raggi to Minister of Foreign Affairs, March 26, 1906, ASMAI II 102/2/11.

8. Though the government did not officially fund the dormitory, it was generally understood that students were to receive financial benefits from the Italian government, if indirectly. Widespread awareness of the open secret that these students were receiving financial support from Italy would inspire threats against their lives during the Italo-Turkish War. At the time of the Italian invasion of the Libyan territories, Insabato counted 140 students in a special *ruwaq* of students from North Africa (54 of whom came from Cyrenaica and Tripolitania) at al-Azhar as potential inhabitants in the Italian *ruwaq*. Despite fears of the danger of anti-Italian recrimination against the students of the *ruwaq*, the Italian Ministry of Foreign Affairs approved funding for the construction of a *ruwaq* for students from Tripolitania in June 1912. Minister of Interior to Insabato, January 23, 1912, ASMAI II 137/1; Insabato to Vigliani, January 30, 1912, ASMAI II 137/1; Italian Consulate in Cairo to Minister of Foreign Affairs, "Studenti tripolini di Al-Azhar," February 7, 1912, ASDMAE, Rappresentanza diplomatica Egitto—Il Cairo 1864–1940, 131/6; Italian Consulate in Cairo to Minister of Foreign Affairs, June 5, 1912, ASDMAE, Rappresentanza diplomatica Egitto—Il Cairo 1864–1940, 131/6.

9. Vikør, *Sufi and Scholar*, 12; Baldinetti, *Orientalismo e colonialismo*, 34. Insabato's program for students at al-Azhar would be adopted as a general policy of colonial rule by the Italian administration. After the occupation of the Libyan territories, the Ministry of Colonies established a similar program to house and assist Somali and Eritrean students at al-Azhar. Miran, "Historical Overview of Islam in Eritrea," 201.

10. The French administration in Wadai, for example, made similar arrangements for students from the region at al-Azhar as a panacea for the tensions caused by

the French conquest of Dud Murra. Minister of Foreign Affairs to Minister of Colonies, January 31, 1911, FR CAOM FM SG AFRIQUE/VI/185.

11. *Il Convito* was also published in Turkish. For an introduction to the magazine and its history, see Scarabel, "Una rivista Italo-Araba d'inizio secolo," 56. The Italian minister of the interior tracked Insabato's journey to Paris in February 1901. "Insabato," February 20, 1901, ACS CPC 2639.

12. "Salviamo la Tripolitania!," *Il Convito*, March 26, 1905, 1. Since the Istituto italiano per l'Africa e l'Oriente (IsIAO) in Rome closed in 2012, it has been difficult to find copies of *Il Convito/al-Nadi*. I extend my heartfelt thanks to Alessandra Marchi for sharing photographs of the publication she took before the closure of the library. As of May 2017, the Biblioteca Nazionale in Rome has absorbed the collection of the IsIAO library, but much of the collection (including *Il Contiv/al-Nadi*) remains inaccessible pending indexing.

13. Quoted in Gotti Porcinari, *Rapporti Italo-Arabi*, 19.

14. Meir Hatina has pointed out that Insabato championed pan-Islamic sentiment in his publications, though with a different emphasis from that which Abdulhamid II promoted contemporaneously. "*Al-Nadi* preached a more federative unity presided over by the Ottoman dynasty, in contrast to ʿAbd al-Hamid's [*sic*] centralized concept of unity. Ultimately, *al-Nadi* and Insabato had a political agenda as well: a diffused Islamic system, rather than a centralized system, would better aid in establishing an Italian presence in the Mediterranean basin." Hatina, "Where East Meets West," 394.

15. "Al Azhar," *Il Convito*, March 26, 1905, 1.

16. Insabato to Vigliani, November 2, 1911, ASMAI II 137/1.

17. Mark Sedgwick, *Against the Modern World* (Oxford: Oxford University Press, 2004), 69.

18. Meir Hatina has pointed to an article in *il Convito/al-Nadi* calling for the elimination of missionary activity in areas under Italian influence as evidence of Insabato's strict anticlericalism, an attitude Hatina links to Insabato's supposed anarchist leanings. As we have seen, however, Insabato's views on these issues seemed fluid. It seems reasonable to assume that Insabato, as an acolyte of Giolitti, would have supported Giolitti's formulation of the church and state as "two parallels that must never meet." For Giolitti, however, this formulation left room for ample political collaboration with moderate or leftist Catholics. Alexander De Grand, *Hunchback's Tailor: Giovanni Giolitti and Liberal Italy from the Challenge of Mass Politics to the Rise of Fascism, 1882–1922* (Westport, CT: Praeger, 2001), 140; Hatina, "Where East Meets West," 395.

19. His name is also transliterated at times as ʿUlaysh. Jocelyn N. Hendrickson, "The Islamic Obligation to Emigrate: Al-Wansharīsī's *Asnā al-matājir* Reconsidered" (PhD diss., Emory University, 2009), 255.

20. Grange, *L'Italie e la Méditerranée*, 390.

21. "Uno sceicco egiziano italofilo," *Corriere della Sera* 31, no. 49 (February 18, 1906); "Una moschea are Umberto," *L'Illustrazione Italiana* 33, no. 6 (February 11, 1906): 30–31. Also quoted in Baldinetti, *Orientalismo e colonialismo*, 43.

22. The Italian Foreign Ministry referred to the language instruction at the mosque as part of the "Scuola Tahdirieh" or "Scuola Tahdaria." Italian Consulate to Ministero Affari Esteri, March 29, 1908, ASDMAE, Rappresentanza diplomatica Egitto—Il Cairo 1864–1940, B. 145; Consulate General in Cairo, De Martino to the Minister of Foreign Affairs, March 14, 1910, in Ministero degli Affari Esteri, *I documenti diplomatici italiani, Quarta serie, 1908–1914*, Vols. 5–6 (Rome: Istituto Poligrafico e Zecca dello Stato, 2001), 180–182.

23. Salvago Raggi to Minister of Foreign Affairs, March 26, 1906, ASMAI II 102/2/11.

24. Salvago Raggi to Minister of Foreign Affairs, April 10, 1906, ASMAI II 102/2/11.

25. British Ambassador in Rome to Minister of Foreign Affairs, January 1, 1902, BNA FO 101/94.

26. Unsurprisingly, Insabato wrote about the construction of the mosque as a sign of Italy's pro-Islamic status, but it induced writers for Rashid Rida's journal *Al-Manar* to portray Abd al-Rahman 'Illaysh as a handmaiden to Italian plans to take control of Libya and Somalia. Hatina, "Where East Meets West," 392–393.

27. Grange, *L'Italie et la Méditerranée*, 1498.

28. Baldinetti, *Orientalismo e colonialismo*, 58.

29. Italian Consulate in Cairo to Minister of Foreign Affairs, "Senussi," April 24, 1901, ASMAI II 102/1/2.

30. The visit occurred just two weeks before the Italian consulate received word of Mohammed al-Mahdi al-Sanusi's death. Consul General in Cairo to Minister of Foreign Affairs, August 6, 1902, ASMAI II 102/1/5.

31. Osea Felici, *L'Egitto e la guerra europea* (Milan: Fratelli Treves, 1916), 171–172. Osea Felici was a frequent commentator on Italian imperialism and emigrant communities overseas. In 1936 he founded the periodical *L'Italia d'Oltremare*. See Sara Kapelj, " 'L'Italia d'Oltremare': Razzismo e costruzione dell'alterità africana negli articoli etnografici e nel romanzo 'I prigionieri del sole' " (PhD diss., Università degli Studi di Trieste, 2011), 1–2, https://www.openstarts.units.it/dspace/bitstream/10077/7407/1/Kapelj_phd.pdf.

32. "Note degli oggetti consegnati dal Signor Mohamed Ali Elui Bey interprete di Consolato Generale d'Italia al Signor Mohamed Taher Abu Sfeita per consegnarli al S. Santità Sidi Ahmed Scerif del Senussi," March 31, 1903, ASMAI II 102/2/8.

33. ASMAI II 102/1/7. The document has no clear name or date, but Daniel Grange has argued that it can be dated to 1906, and later references to the report indicate that Insabato was most likely the author. See Grange, *L'Italie e la Méditerranée*, 1495.

34. For example, Italian Consulate in Bengasi to the Consulate General in Tripoli, August 8, 1905, ASMAI II 102/1/7.

35. Carlo Arrivabene Valenti-Gozanga, "La Senussia e la sua influenza nell'Africa settentrionale," January 1906, ASDMAE, Serie P, B. 5.

36. Ibid.

37. Minister of Foreign Affairs, Ufficio Coloniale, Recommendation of Citizen Status for Elui Bey, September 28, 1905, ASMAI II 102/2/10.

38. Arrivabene to the Minister of Foreign Affairs, November 7, 1905, ASMAI II 102/2/10.

39. Arrivabene in particular voiced his support for financial compensation for ʿAlawi: Arrivabene to Minister of Foreign Affairs, November 7, 1905, ASMAI II 102/2/10. For an explanation of Salvago Raggi's opposition to state decorations or titles for Arabs, see Minister of Foreign Affairs, Ufficio Coloniale, September 28, 1906, ASMAI II 102/2/10.

40. Gaetano Manzoni to Minister of Foreign Affairs, October 23, 1906, ASMAI II 102/2/11.

41. Giuseppe Salvago Raggi, Consulate General in Cairo, to Minister of Interior, March 16, 1906, ASMAI II 102/2/11.

42. G. Sola to Agnesa, Director of the Colonial Office in the Ministry of Foreign Affairs, n.d., ASMAI II 102/2/11.

43. Giulia Barrera, "The Construction of Racial Hierarchies in Colonial Eritrea: The Liberal and Early Fascist Period (1897–1934), in *A Place in the Sun: Africa in Italian Colonial Culture from Post-Unification to the Present*, ed. Patrizia Palumbo (Berkeley: University of California Press, 2003), 89–91.

44. Ministry of Foreign Affairs, "Progetto di una missione da inviarsi al Capo dei Senussi in Kufra," ASMAI II 102/2/10. The report has no clear date but was completed sometime in early 1905. Interestingly, the memo noted Meï's status as a medical doctor as a benefit of expanding Italian influence, although the Ministero degli Affari Esteri never noted the same kind of utility in Insabato's position: "Doctors, of which they have great need, are our real missionaries towards the Arabs, and they greatly esteem European ones."

45. Italian Consulate of Cairo to Minister of Foreign Affairs, June 24, 1908, ASDMAE, Rappresentanza diplomatica Egitto—Il Cairo 1864–1940, B. 145.

46. De Martino to Ministero degli Esteri, February 8, 1908, ASDMAE, Rappresentanza diplomatica Egitto—Il Cairo 1864–1940, B. 145.

47. Italian Consulate to Minister of Foreign Affairs, March 29, 1908, ASDMAE, Rappresentanza diplomatica Egitto—Il Cairo 1864–1940, B. 145.

48. Ugo Lusena would serve on the inaugural general council of the Egyptian University starting in December 1908. Andrew Heiss, "Manufacturing Consent: Italy, the *Mutamassirun*, Egypt, and the Invasion of Libya" (master's thesis, The American University in Cairo, 2010), 101, http://dar.aucegypt.edu/bitstream/handle/10526/689/2010mestandrewheiss.pdf?sequence=1.

49. Italian Consulate to Minister of Foreign Affairs, June 3, 1908, ASDMAE, Rappresentanza diplomatica Egitto—Il Cairo 1864–1940, B. 117.

50. Italian Consulate to Minister of Foreign Affairs, June 24, 1908, ASDMAE, Rappresentanza diplomatica Egitto—Il Cairo 1864–1940, B. 117.

51. Minister of Foreign Affairs to Italian Consualte in Cairo, December 22, 1908, ASDMAE, Rappresentanza diplomatica Egitto—Il Cairo 1864–1940, B. 117.

52. Muhammad ʿAli ʿAlawi to Minister of Foreign Affairs, April 9, 1908, ASMAI II 102/2/12.

53. Italian Consulate to Minister of Foreign Affairs, June 2, 1908, ASDMAE, Rappresentanza diplomatica Egitto—Il Cairo 1864–1940, B. 117.

54. Enrico Corradini, *L'ora di Tripoli* (Milan: Fratelli Treves, 1911).

55. Giuseppe Piazza, *La Nostra Terra Promessa: Lettera dalla Tripolitania, Marzo-Maggio 1911*, 2nd ed. (Rome: Bernardo Lux, 1911), 172.

56. Ibid., 178.

57. Ibid., 176.

58. Note that *La Tribuna* was owned by a friend of the prime minister, Giovanni Giolitti. Giuseppe Perlato, "The War in Libya and the Italian Nationalism," in *The Libyan War 1911–1912*, ed. Luca Micheletta and Andrea Ungari (Cambridge, UK: Cambridge Scholars Publishing, 2013), 47.

59. Fabrizio Bollettini, "Leone Caetani e la questione libica," *Studi Romani* 41, no.1 (1993): 30–40.

60. Legislatura XXII, *Atti Parlamentari, Camera dei Deputati* 343 (June 7, 1911): 15371.

61. Leone Caetani, *Studi di storia orientale*, Vol. 1, *L'Arabia dalla preistoria all'Islam* (Rome: Edizioni di Storia e Letteratura, [1911] 2012), 3.

62. "Islam e Cristianesimo," *La Civiltà Cattolica* 63 (1912): 725.

63. Nathan was a prominent member of the Masonic order based in Rome. Bollettini, "Leone Caetani e la questione libica," 30.

64. Bollettini has noted that Caetani found himself stuck between the "coolness of the atmosphere of the bloc on the one side and suffering the biting offensive of the nationalists on the other." Bollettini, "Leone Caetani e la questione libica," 40; Francesco Gabrielli, *Orientalisti del Novecento* (Rome: Istituto per l'oriente C.A. Nallino, 1993), 49.

65. "It is very easy to offend them in their religious ideas, difficult to persuade them of a distinction between the civil and the religious that all of their education, culture and religion leads them to negate or even to misunderstand." Ministry of Colonies, "Costituzione di una Commissione per lo studio di questioni islamiche d'interesse coloniale," December 1914, ASMAI 109/1/3. Other members of the commission included David Santillana, C. A. Nallino, Luigi Guidi, Carlo Conti Rossini, and Guglielmo Ciamarra. In the introduction to a comparative study of European colonial rule meant as the first of a series of books on colonial issues issued by the new Ministry of Colonies, Agnesa established a position in favor of creating a system of experts available for consultation on colonial issues. Giacomo Agnesa, preface to *I Corpi consultivi dell'amministrazione colonial negli stati d'Europa*, by Angiolo Mori (Rome: Tipografia della Camera dei Deputati, 1912).

66. Leone Caetani, preface to *Annali dell'Islam*, Vol. 5 (Milan: Ulrico Hoepli, 1912), xvii.

67. P. Costanzo Bergna, *La missione francescana in Libia* (Tripoli: Nuove arti grafiche, 1924), 169–170; "Cronaca Contemporanea," *La Civiltá Cattolica* 59, no. 2 (April 18, 1908): 238.

68. As Giuseppe Perlato has argued, most members of the ANI were too focused on the issue of irredentism to consider the prospect for overseas expansion until rather late in the game. The nationalist press only latched onto the pro-imperial message after Giolitti's government had already begun preparations for the occupation. Well after the fact, as Perlato notes, the nationalist press claimed responsibility for generating public pressure in favor of the colonial occupation, and historians have perpetuated a theory dear to the nationalists themselves, "that without them, the colonial enterprise would never have come about." Perlato, "The War in Libya and the Italian Nationalism," 39.

69. *L'Osservatore Romano* was started in 1861 and *La Civiltà Cattolica* in 1854; they came under direct church control in the 1880s. John Pollard, *Catholicism in Modern Italy: Religion, Society, and Politics since 1861* (London: Routledge, 2008), 35.

70. Habib al-Hesnawi, "Note sulla politica coloniale italiana verso gli arabi libici," in *Le guerre coloniale del fascismo*, ed. Angelo Del Boca (Roma: Laterza, 1991), 35.

71. "Cronaca Contemporanea," *La Civiltá Cattolica* 59, no. 2 (May 2, 1908): 377.

72. Ferdinando Cordova, *Agli ordini del serpente verde: La massoneria nella crisi del sistema giolittiano* (Rome: Bulzoni, 1990), 17–18.

73. "La massoneria a Roma per il XX settembre," *Corriere d'Italia*, September 10, 1911, 1.

74. "Cronaca Contemporanea," *La Civitá Cattolica* 62, no. 4 (October 27, 1911): 362. For Caneva's proclamation, see Caneva, "Agli Arabi della Tripolitania," January 15, 1912, AUSSME L8/154/1.

75. Alice A. Kelikian, "The Church and Catholicism," in *Liberal and Fascist Italy 1900–1945*, ed. Adrian Lyttelton (Oxford: Oxford University Press, 2002), 46; Pollard, *Catholicism in Modern Italy*, 29, 47.

76. John Pollard, *Money and the Rise of the Modern Papacy: Financing the Vatican, 1850–1950* (Cambridge, UK: Cambridge University Press, 2005), 30. In 1864 the Italian state took responsibility for two-thirds of the Vatican's debt in a secret agreement to compensate for the properties lost by the Holy See during Italian unification, further encouraging an integration of Vatican finances with Italian national interests.

77. Ibid., 64–65.

78. Ibid., 99; R. A. Webster, *Industrial Imperialism in Italy 1908–1915* (Berkeley: University of California Press, 1975), 152; Giorgio Candeloro, *Il movimento cattolico in Italia* (Rome: Riuniti, 1974), 343; and Habib al-Hesnawi, "Italian Imperial Policy towards Libya, 1870–1911," in *Modern and Contemporary Libya: Sources*

and Historiographies, ed. Anna Baldinetti (Rome: Istituto italiano per l'Africa e l'Oriente, 2003), 61.

79. Pollard, *Money and the Rise*, 105–106.

80. Italian emigration from 1880 to 1914 reached about thirteen million, the highest rate of emigration in recorded history. Choate, *Emigrant Nation*, 130.

81. Uoldelul Chilati Dirar, "Church-State Relations in Colonial Eritrea: Missionaries and the Development of Colonial Strategies (1869–1911)," *Journal of Modern Italian Studies* 8, no. 3 (2001): 400; and Horst Gründer, "Christian Missionary Activities in Africa in the Age of Imperialism and the Berlin Conference of 1884–1885," in *Bismarck, Europe, and Africa: The Berlin Africa Conference 1884–1885 and the Onset of Partition*, ed. Stig Förster, Wolfgang J. Mommsen, and Ronald Robinson (Oxford: Oxford University Press, 1988), 95.

82. Choate, *Emigrant Nation*, 35, 139; Chilati Dirar, "Church-State Relations," 401; Lucia Ceci, *Il vessillo e la croce: colonialismo, missioni cattoliche e islam in Somalia (1903–1924)* (Rome: Carocci, 2006), 13–14; Claudio M. Betti, *Missioni e colonie in Africa Orientale* (Rome: Edizioni Studium, 1999), 227; and Metodio da Nembro, *La missione dei Minori Cappuccini in Eritrea (1894–1952)* (Rome: Istitutum Historicum Ord Fr Min Cap, 1953), 103. Note that Dirar asserted that the National Association to Support Catholic Missionaries sought the support of the Italian state for the project to replace the French Lazarists with Italian missionaries in Eritrea. According to Choate's research, the impetus for the project came primarily from Governor General Baratieri, and Ceci characterizes the shift in control of the mission as a victory for Crispi's government.

83. Stephen Bruner, "Leopoldo Franchetti and Italian Settlement in Eritrea: Emigration, Welfare Colonialism and the Southern Question," *European History Quarterly* 39, no. 1 (2009): 71–94.

84. Ceci, *Il vessillo*, 13–14.

85. Lucia Ceci, "Missioni e colonialismo italiano in Somalia (1903–1906)," *Studi Storici* 43, no. 1 (2002): 42.

86. Ibid., 74.

87. Ibid., 93.

88. Adrian Hastings, *The Church in Africa 1450–1950* (Oxford: Clarendon Press, 1994), 430. On the French dominance in the field of Catholic missionary activity, see J. P. Daughton, *An Empire Divided: Religion, Republicanism, and the Making of French Colonialism, 1880–1914* (Oxford: Oxford University Press, 2006), 33–38.

89. Padre Giuseppe Bevilacqua in Tripoli to Card. Gotti at Propaganda Fide, January 31, 1901, Archivio Storico De Propaganda Fide, NS Vol. 214 Rubrica 141/1901.

90. Padre Giuseppe Bevilacqua in Tripoli to Card. Gotti at Propaganda Fide, Archivio Storico De Propaganda Fide, NS Vol. 237, Rubrica 141/1902.

91. Governor of Tripolitania Garioni to Minister of Colonies Ferdinando Martini, "Missione Francescana—Pagamento di Sussidio," August 19, 1914, ASMAI II 121/1/3.

92. Frati Minori, Busta 6, Annual Report from Bonaventura Rossetti to Card. Gotti at Propaganda Fide, December 19, 1908.

93. Cinzia Buccianti, "Le scuole cattoliche a Tripoli nel XIX secolo," *Oriente Moderno* 13, no. 7/12 (Luglio–Dicembre 1994): 181.

94. Julia Clancy-Smith, *Mediterraneans: North Africa and Europe in the Age of Migration, c. 1800–1900* (Berkeley: University of California Press, 2011), 250. In the years preceding the occupation, the Italian population of the Libyan territories was small. The only census data for the population for the years 1909 to 1911 distinguished by faith instead of nationality, but representatives of the Maltese community in Tripoli estimated that they made up about 3,500 out of a total Catholic population of 6,000. For the estimate of the Maltese population in 1909 see Petition signed by representatives of the Maltese community, November 6, 1909, Archivio Storico De Propaganda Fide, NS Vol. 490, Rubrica N. 141/1910. For the estimate of the Catholic population in general in 1910, see P. Bonaventura Rossetti to Card. Gotti at Propaganda Fide, November 1911, Archivio Storico De Propaganda Fide, NS Vol. 520, Rubrica N. 141/1912.

95. Cinzia Buccianti has traced tensions over Italian language instruction in the nineteenth century, including the challenge posed by the arrival of two French nuns intent on providing French instruction to girls in the Libyan territories. Buccianti, "Le scuole cattoliche a Tripoli nel XIX secolo."

96. Padre Giuseppe Bevilacqua in Tripoli to Card. Gotti at Propaganda Fide, December 31, 1899, Archivio Storico De Propaganda Fide, Nuova Seria (NS) Vol. 193, Rubrica 141/1900. See also Buccianti, "Le scuole cattoliche a Tripoli nel XIX secolo," 188–189. Buccianti points to the conflicts over the Italian wars of unification as a factor contributing to the decision to turn to the French order.

97. P. Giuseppe Bevilacqua to Card. Gotti at Propaganda Fide, May 18, 1906, Archivio Storico De Propaganda Fide, NS Vol. 406, Rubrica 141/1907.

98. Ibid.

99. Secretary General of the Frati Minori to Card. Gotti at Propaganda Fide, July 16, 1907, Archivio Storico De Propaganda Fide, NS Vol. 406, Rubrica 141/1907.

100. Vittorio Ianari, *Chiesa, coloni e Islam: Religione e politica nella Libia italiana* (Turin: Società Editrice Internazionale, 1995), 13.

101. In December 1909 Undersecretary of State Scalea recommended continuing the monthly stipend to the mission as a way to diminish the threat of French presence as a possible erosion of Italian influence despite questions within the Foreign Ministry about the utility of the state subsidies for church activities. Frati Minori, Busta 6, Undersecretary of State Scalea to Consul General of Tripoli, December 22, 1909.

102. "Regolamento per la missione francescana della Tripolitania 1908," approved by Dionisio Schuler, General Minister of the Frati Minori, Archivio Storico De Propaganda Fide, NS Vol. 478, Rubrica 141/1909.

103. Mons. Pietro Pace, Arc. Vescovo of Malta to Card. Gotti at Propaganda Fide, January 10, 1910, Archivio Storico De Propaganda Fide, Vol. 490, Rubrica N. 141/1910.

104. Padre Valerio Apreda to Card. Gotti at Propaganda Fide, March 13, 1910, Archivio Storico De Propaganda Fide, NS Vol. 490, Rubrica N. 141/1910. Emphasis in original.

105. Frati Minori di Lombardia, Busta 1, Bonaventura Rossetti to the Italian Ambassador to Constantinople Barone, May 8, 1910.

106. Frati Minori di Lombardia, Busta 1, Bonaventura Rossetti to Minister of Foreign Affairs San Giuliano, May 20, 1911.

107. In May 1910 Rossetti noted his efforts to prove the right of the mission's existence in the preparations for state expansion. Frati Minori di Lombardia, B. 6, Rossetti to Propaganda Fide, May 7, 1910.

108. "Lo spirito religioso nell'esercito," *Civiltá Cattolica* 61, no. 3 (1910): 38; and "Cose Italiane," *Civiltá Cattolica* 62, no. 4 (1911): 244. The decision to station chaplains with the colonial forces was fraught with tension. The Italian minister of war spoke against state provision of chaplains accompanying the occupying forces as a presence of church representatives that he argued would threaten to undermine national unity in the colonial war. *La Civiltá Cattolica* celebrated the final decision to send Catholic chaplains with the Libyan invasion as recognition of the prevalence of Catholic soldiers in the occupying forces and of the centrality of a Catholic identity in Italian imperialism.

109. Frati Minori di Lombardia, Busta 6, Bonaventura Rossetti to Card. Gotti at Propaganda Fide, October 17, 1911.

110. Data on status of the mission, December 16, 1912, Archivio Storico De Propaganda Fide, NS Vol. 520, Rubrica N. 141/1912.

111. Bonaventura Rossetti to Card. Gotti at Propaganda Fide, March 12, 1912, Archivio Storico De Propaganda Fide, NS Vol. 520, Rubrica N. 141/1912.

112. Rossetti's proposals after the initial occupation included ambitious plans to construct a new technical school to train native workers for future industrial enterprises and to establish a local Catholic newspaper for the Italian population. Bonaventura Rossetti to Card. Gotti at Propaganda Fide, May 9, 1912, Archivio Storico De Propaganda Fide, NS Vol. 520, Rubrica N. 141/1912.

113. Minister of Colonies to Governor of Cyrenaica, February 15, 1915, ASMAI 134/8/15.

CHAPTER 3

1. "Un araba battezzata," *La Tribuna*, January 7, 1912, 1.

2. The consulate's most pressing concern, however, was that the girl would no longer be able to find a man willing to marry her as a Catholic and a native. Italian Consulate to the Minister of Foreign Affairs, February 6, 1912, ASDMAE, Rappresentanza diplomatica Egitto—Il Cairo 1864–1940, 131/5.

3. Minister of Foreign Affairs to Italian Consulate in Cairo, February 6, 1912, ASDMAE, Rappresentanza diplomatica Egitto—Il Cairo 1864–1940, 131/2.

4. In an oral testimony, the former mujahid Muhammad Aisi expressed no doubt that Ahmad al-Sharif was firmly opposed to Italian presence from the beginning of the occupation. If this was the case, it was far from clear to Italian officials. *Mawsuʿat Riwāyāt al-Jihād*, Vol. 22 (Tripoli: Markaz al-Jihad, 1990), 105.

5. This time Insabato was assigned a position as a subordinate to the Italian consulate in Cairo in an attempt to prevent the confusion and acrimony of 1908, but the consulate general in Cairo, Giacomo De Martino, disputed the idea that he would be responsible for managing Insabato's behavior. De Martino to Minister of Foreign Affairs, March 14, 1910, in Ministero degli Affari Esteri, *I documenti diplomatici italiani, Quarta serie*, Vols. 5–6, 179–181.

6. Insabato to Giolitti, August 8, 1911, in Ministero degli Affari Esteri, *I documenti diplomatici italiani*, Vols. 7–8, 133–134.

7. Insabato to Commander of State Police, October 20, 1911, ASMAI II 137/1.

8. Insabato to Commander of State Police, October 21, 1911, ASMAI II 137/1. ʿAlawi wrote to Ahmad al-Sharif suggesting that the Italian flag could include the *shahada* particular to the Sanusiyya. Muhammad ʿAli ʿAlawi to Ahmad al-Sharif, October 24, 1911, ASMAI II 137/1.

9. De Martino to Minister of Foreign Affairs, March 14, 1910.

10. Muhammad ʿAli ʿAlawi to Ahmad al-Sharif, October 24, 1911, ASMAI II 137/1; and Insabato to Vigliani, February 19, 1912, ASMAI II 137/1.

11. The official interpreter at the Italian consulate also dismissed the pamphlet as poorly written. Insabato accused him of being afraid that the pamphlet would supplant the importance of propaganda produced directly by the consulate. Insabato to Commander of State Police, February 3, 1912, ASMAI II 137/1; and Insabato to Commander of State Police, February 11, 1912, ASMAI II 137/1. Even the minister of the interior, who originally requested the production of a piece of pro-Italian propaganda, recommended that Insabato not fight against the sequestration of the pamphlet because of its low quality. The minister complained that the production of the pamphlet had been rushed and that its effectiveness was compromised by its connection to *Il Convito/ al-Nadi*, "which as much as it was pro-Islamic, was always the newspaper of a Christian and an Italian." Minister of Interior to Insabato, February 19, 1912, ASMAI II 137/1.

12. Insabato to Italian Consulate in Cairo, February 11, 1912, ASMAI II 137/1/8.

13. Italian Consulate in Cairo to Minister of Foreign Affairs, February 7, 1912, ASDMAE, Rappresentanza diplomatica Egitto—Il Cairo 1864–1940, 131/6.

14. Italian Consulate in Cairo to Minister of Foreign Affairs, April 27, 1912, ASMAI II 137/1/3. See also Baldinetti, *Orientalismo e colonialismo*, 127–129, 151.

15. Mohammed Abed al-Sanusi to Mohammed Ali ʿAlawi, ASMAI II 137/1. The translated letter does not include a date, but it accompanies another letter from Mohammed Abed al-Sanusi to Insabato dated May 1912.

16. ASMAI II 137/1/8. The entire folder deals with the possible alliance with Ahmad al-Sharif. Italian Consulate in Cairo, Grimani, to the Minister of the Interior, Giolitti, August 21, 1912, in Ministero degli Affari Esteri, *I documenti diplomatici italiani*, Vols. 7–8, 1083–1084.

17. The trial never took place. Baldinetti, *Orientalismo e colonialismo*, 66–69. Note that Ahmad al-Sharif told the Egyptian khedive that he faced difficulties gaining the support of Sanusi shaykhs for the idea of acquiescing to Italian colonial rule. It is possible that the Italian confusion stemmed more from al-Sharif's inability to play the political game than from the duplicity of ʿAlawi. Ahmad al-Sharif to Khedive, September 10, 1913, ASMAI II 137/2/14.

18. Baldinetti, *Orientalismo e colonialismo*, 61.

19. Captain Bianco, "Relazione sulle confraternite in Cirenaica e specie su quella Senussita," March 15, 1912, 24, AUSSME L8/233/10. The same document can also be found in ASMAI II 147/1/2. Copies were sent to the Ministry of War, the commander in chief of the military, the prime minister, and the minister of foreign affairs. The commander of the occupying forces, General Caneva, attached a note of support.

20. Captain Bianco, "Relazione sulle confraternite in Cirenaica e specie su quella Senussita," March 15, 1912, 5, AUSSME L8/233/10.

21. Ibid., 18.

22. Ibid.

23. Ufficio Politico Militare, "Le società religiose in Tripolitania," March 1912, 62, AUSSME L8/232/5.

24. Giuseppe Bourbon del Monte Santa Maria, *L'Islamismo e la Confraternita dei Senussi: Notizie Raccolte* (Città di Castello: Tipografia dell'Unione Arti Grafiche, 1912), 190–191.

25. Ibid., 220.

26. "Questo governo desidera di arrivare ad una pacifica occupazione del paese, sulla base della pacificazione degli animi che sola può permettere lo svolgimento del programma politico-economico coloniale." Minister of Colonies Bertolini to General Briccola, January 2, 1913, ASMAI II 136/1/5.

27. Anna Baldinetti, "Italian Colonial Rule and Muslim Elites in Libya: A Relationship of Antagonism and Collaboration," in *Guardians of the Faith in Modern Times*, ed. Meir Hatina (Leiden: Brill, 2009), 94.

28. Ahmida, *Making of Modern Libya*, 107.

29. Payment for submission of local notables identified as tribal chiefs in 1913 was around 100 to 200 lire. Governor of Cyrenaica, "Capi tribù. Stipendi," June 6, 1913, ASMAI II 148/1/2.

30. ʿUmar Pasha Muntasir occupied Sirte in December 1912, taking it from the control of Enver Pasha's brother Nuri bey and expanding the Muntasir family domain in the name of the Italian colonial administration. Soon after the Muntasir family claimed control of Sirte, Italian forces defeated Sulayman al-Baruni, a

staunch supporter of Ottoman control and a notable from the Ibadiyya of the Nafusa Mountains of western Tripolitania, in the spring of 1913. Paolo Soave, *Fezzan: Il deserto contesto (1842–1921)* (Milan: Giuffrè Editore, 2001), 266.

31. Angelo Del Boca, *La disfatta di Gasr bu Hàdi, 1915: Il colonnello Miani e il più grande disastro dell'Italia coloniale* (Milan: Mondadori, 2004), 43. On using Sirte to pacify Cyrenaica, see General Garioni to Minister of Colonies, August 16, 1913, ASMAI II 126/1/10.

32. The Sayf al-Nasr family famously led opposition to Qaramanli taxation policies in the region in the 1820s, and they later played an important role in facilitating the expansion of the Sanusi *ṭarīqa* into the Lake Chad region. Dennis D. Cordell, "The Awlad Sulayman of Libya," 328; and Ahmida, *Making of Modern Libya*, 46.

33. Ahmida, *Making of Modern Libya*, 53–60.

34. Grimaldi to Presidente del Consiglio, May 7, 1912, ASDMAE, Rappresentanza diplomatica Egitto—Il Cairo 1864–1940, B. 131, Fasc. 1.

35. Giolitti to Grimaldi, May 7, 1912, ASMAI II 137/1.

36. See the photographic insert in Del Boca, *La disfatta di Gasr bu Hàdi*. Precedents for the formal letters of submission appear in the Italian colonial archives from Eritrea as early as 1890. "Atto di sottomissione del Scek Mohammed Musa," August 25, 1890, ASMAI Archivio Eritrea, Pacco 10. French authorities in Chad also recorded acts of *soumission* to French authority from tribal leaders in the early twentieth century. Governor of Brazzaville to General Command, March 21, 1914, FR CAOM AEF GGAEF 5D/20.

37. French Vice-Counsel in Benghazi to the Minister of Foreign Affairs, "Les Italiens en Cyrénaïque," March 23, 1914, FR CAOM AEF GGAEF 5D/20.

38. "Interrogatorio dell'indigeno Abderabba ben Junes," November 26, 1914, ASMAI II 150/1/4.

39. Shukri makes reference to individuals handing over their weapons for "a handful of rice" during times of shortages. Shukri, *Al-Sanūsiyah*, 283.

40. For example, see "Interrogatorio di Ali Bu Sultan," October 14, 1914, ASMAI II 150/1/4; and "Interrogatorio di Sciab Ben Hamed el Keiresc," October 14, 1914, ASMAI II 150/1/4.

41. Political Military Office of the Occupying Forces of Benghazi, Report on population submissions in Cyrenaica, December 1913, AUSSME L8/233/8; and Ameglio, "Sottomissione dei capi," April 5, 1914, ASMAI II 148/1/3.

42. Governor Ameglio to Minister of Colonies, November 13, 1913, ASMAI II 136/1/4.

43. Governor Cigliana to the Ministry of Colonies, Telegram No. 97, November 16, 1914, AUSSME L8/232/15.

44. Baldinetti, *Orientalismo e colonialismo*, 45–46.

45. Aldobrandino Malvezzi De Medici, "La Tripolitania e i casi del Wadai," *Nuova antologia* 45, no. 921 (May 1910): 131.

46. Aldobrandino Malvezzi De Medici, *L'Italia e l'Islam in Libia* (Florence: Fratelli Treves, 1913), 231.

47. Ibid., 245.

48. Ibid.

49. French Vice Consul in Benghazi to the French Minister of Foreign Affairs, February 4, 1911, FR CAOM FM SG AFRIQUE/VI/191. See also Spaulding and Kapteijins, *An Islamic Alliance.*

50. French Minister of Foreign Affairs to the Minister of Colonies, January 31, 1911, FR CAOM FM SG AFRIQUE/VI/191; and French Vice-Consul in Benghazi to the French Minister of Foreign Affairs, "Situation actuelle des Senussis," March 6, 1911, FR CAOM AEF GGAEF 5D/20.

51. Aydin, *Politics of Anti-Westernism,* 97; Timothy Childs, *Italo-Turkish Diplomacy and the War Over Libya 1911–1912* (Leiden: Brill, 1990), 76. The Ottoman officers, some belonging to the Teskilat-i Mahsusa, who joined Enver Pasha and Mustafa Kemal in fighting the Italian invasion of Libya included Shakib Arslan, Nuri and Halil, Ali Fethi Okyar, Kuscubasi Esref and his brother Haci Selim Sami, Sulayman Askeri and Yakup Cemil, Ali Cetinkaya, Sadik Bey, Fuat Bulca, Nuri Conker, Rauf Orbay, and Mim Kemal Oke. They all went on to take important posts in the CUP government, but for ʿAziz ʿAli al-Misri, already in the Libyan territories as an Ottoman officer before the Italian invasion, involvement in the war against Italy shaped his development as a dominant force in Arab nationalism, pitting him against Enver Pasha and the CUP. See: Syed Tanvir Wasti, "Amir Shakib Arslan and the CUP Triumvirate," *Middle Eastern Studies* 44, no. 6 (2008): 934.

52. Childs, *Italo-Turkish Diplomacy,* 86. The redactors of a volume of the Oral History Project noted that many within the tribal *dor* (armed forces) who were associated with the Sanusiyya began to go to Istanbul or Egypt for military training in this period, leading to a long-term increase in efficacy among the anti-Italian forces. ʿAli Bashir al-Zawawa and Mohammad ʿAbd al-Nabi Daqali, introduction [1979] to *Mawsuʿat Riwāyāt al-Jihād,* Vol. 16 (Tripoli: Markaz al-Jihad, 1990), 105.

53. The sultan's representative retained the power to name qadi in civil courts and direct the management of waqf properties. Childs, *Italo-Turkish Diplomacy,* 160.

54. Anwar Bey had suggested calling the proposed administration "The Union of African states" to try to limit Sanusi influence, but Ahmad al-Sharif insisted that the theoretical state would be al-Hakuma al-Sanusiyya, or the Sanusi government. A. S. al-Horeir, "Social and Economic Transformations in the Libyan Hinterland during the Second Half of the Nineteenth Century: The Rule of the Sayyid Ahmad al-Sharif al-Sanusi" (PhD diss., University of California, Los Angeles, 1981), 174.

55. ʿAziz al-Misri left the Libyan territories in disgrace in July 1913. Defrance, French Minister in Cairo, to the French Minister of Foreign Affairs, "Conversation avec un notable Senoussiste," April 22, 1914, FR CAOM AEF GGAEF 5D/20.

Muhammad Fuʿad Shukri accused him of having taken large stockpiles of Ottoman weapons and funding with him when he left, paralyzing the Bedouin forces in the Sanusi *zawāyā*. ʿAziz al-Misri was later arrested in Istanbul, charged with treason, and sentenced to execution, but Kitchener persuaded the Ottoman government to release him. Kitchener feared that his trial would arouse Arab nationalist sentiment in Egypt. Elie Kedouri, *England and the Middle East: The Destruction of the Ottoman Empire, 1914–1921* (Boulder, CO: Westview Press, 1987), 47–48; Shukri, *Al-Sanūsiyah*, 155.

56. Fouchet, French Consulate in Cairo to the French Minister of Foreign Affairs, November 11, 1913, FR CAOM AEF GGAEF 5D/20.

57. Italian Occupying Forces, Command of the Second Division, "Tribù della Cirenaica," March 1914, ASMAI II 147/1/3. French intelligence reported the presence of five or six German officers near Kufra at the beginning of 1914 to train Sanusi troops, and there was some indication of a remaining force of around one thousand Ottoman troops. French Minister in Cairo to the French Minister of Foreign Affairs, "Conversation avec un notable Senoussiste," April 22, 1914, FR CAOM AEF GGAEF 5D/20; and Francesco Correale, "Weapons and 'Smugglers' throughout Western Sahara: From the Anti-Colonial Resistance to the First World War," in *Bridges Across the Sahara*, ed. Ali Abdullatif Ahmida (Newcastle, UK: Cambridge Scholars, 2009), 136.

58. Muhammad al-Tayyib ibn Idris al-Ashab, *Barqa al-'Arabiya: ams wa al-yawm* (Cairo: al-Tabah, 1947), 281; and el-Horeir, "Social and Economic Transformations," 247. When the Italians retreated from the Fezzan and the Sirte Desert, they lost the limited submission of Maghārba populations that they had acquired through the mediation of the Sayf al-Nasr family.

59. British Ambassador to Rome to the British War Office, May 3, 1915, WO 106/672.

60. Lisa Anderson, *State and Social Transformation in Tunisia and Libya, 1830–1980* (Princeton, NJ: Princeton University Press, 1986), 192–193.

61. Intelligence News, Cairo, April 4, 1915, BNA FO 141/653.

62. British Agent in Cairo to the Foreign Office, February 26, 1915, BNA FO 141/653. Muhammad Aisi blamed an Italian plot for the failure of agreements between the British and Ahmad al-Sharif. *Mawsuʿat Riwāyāt al-Jihād*, Vol. 22 (Tripoli: Markaz al-Jihad, 1990), 105.

63. Admiralty War Staff Intelligence Division, "The Senussi," May 26, 1915, ASMAI II 136/1/3. Found and translated by Italian intelligence.

64. British agent in Ramleh to Foreign Office, June 3, 1915, BNA FO 141/653; and Adviser of the Interior to the High Commissioner of Egypt, July 14, 1915, BNA FO 141/653.

65. Italian agent in Cairo to *Il Secolo* newspaper in Milan, July 24, 1915, BNA FO 141/653. On the references to *"al-hakuma al-Sanusiyya"* see Anderson, *State and Social Transformation*, 191; Evans-Pritchard, *Sanusi of Cyrenaica*, 122.

66. Kitchener to the Foreign Office, June 11, 1914, BNA PRO 30/57/45. The relationship between the khedive and Idris al-Sanusi developed after Idris performed the hajj in 1913, a journey that Salim Husayn Kabti recognized as the commencement of Idris al-Sanusi's political career. Kabti, *Idris al-Sanusi*, 14. Muhammad Fu'ad Shukri noted the warm reception Idris received as a guest of the khedive while on the hajj in 1913, and then as a guest of Sultan Husayn Kamil under the British protectorate upon his return in August 1914. Shukri, *Al-Sanūsiyah*, 280.

67. Governor of Cyrenaica to Minister of Colonies, April 12, 1915, ASMAI II 134/9/55.

68. Anderson, "Nineteenth-Century Reform," 337.

69. Ameglio to Minister of Colonies, August 14, 1915, ACS Carte Ameglio, b. 2.

70. Muhammad Aisi referred to Ahmad al-Sharif as temporarily fulfilling the duties of Idris al-Sanusi due to the latter's young age during his time as the recognized head of the *ṭarīqa*, thus contributing to a concept of Idris as the legitimate head of the Sanusiyya. *Mawsuʿat Riwāyāt al-Jihād*, Vol. 22, 105.

71. Governor of Cyrenaica, Political Military Office, "Zauie senussite della Cirenaica," February 1916, ASMAI II 147/1/4.

72. This time without the additional requirement of obtaining the approval of the Ottoman sultan as caliph because the Italians had renounced the Treaty of Lausanne. Historical Section of the Foreign Office, Committee of Imperial Defence, "Relations between Great Britain, Italy and the Senussi 1912–1924," 1927, BNA CAB 44/14.

73. Shukri, *Al-Sanūsiyah*, 282. Italian intelligence confirmed the dire conditions in Ajdabiya even in the summer of 1914. Conditions only worsened during the ensuing conflicts. Ameglio to Minister of Colonies, June 16, 1914, ASMAI II 134/6/33.

74. Matar, *The Return*, 127.

75. Shukri, *Al-Sanūsiyah*, 282–283.

76. Ameglio to Minister of Colonies, November 10, 1916, ASMAI II 134/14/94.

77. Ameglio to Minister of Colonies, October 10, 1917, ASMAI II 134/16/109.

78. Ameglio to Minister of Colonies, November 21, 1917, ASMAI II 134/16/110.

79. Talbot, "Report on the Negotiations of the Anglo-Italian Mission with Mohammed Idris el Mahdi el Senussi," July–September 1916, BNA FO 141/651.

80. When the negotiations began, Idris was less than thirty years of age.

81. Talbot, "Report on the Negotiations of the Anglo-Italian Mission with Mohammed Idris el Mahdi el Senussi," September 1916, BNA FO 141/651/1. As the Italian minister of colonies put it in a later memorandum, "The state of peace encourages the resurgence of atavistic jealousies among the tribes"; Colosimo to Tripoli, January 23, 1918, ASMAI II 134/17, Fasc. 113.

82. Cairo to the Foreign Office, December 3, 1917, BNA FO 141/652; and Talbot to the Residency in Cairo, March 22, 1917, BNA FO 141/651.

83. "Modus Vivendi No. 3," May 1, 1917, ASMAI II 139/1, Fasc. 3.

84. Cairo to the Foreign Office, November 23, 1917, BNA FO 141/652; and British Embassy in Rome to the Foreign Office, September 24, 1917, BNA FO 141/652.

85. Commander in Chief to the High Commissioner, August 25, 1916, BNA FO 141/651.

86. High Commissioner of Egypt to Talbot, April 4, 1917, BNA FO 141/651.

87. Ameglio to Minister of Colonies, June 5, 1917, ASMAI II 134/16, Fasc. 104. Minister of Colonies Gaspare Colosimo defended the modus vivendi against Ameglio's criticisms, denying that the agreement granted Idris al-Sanusi true sovereignty over the Cyrenaican interior. Colosimo to Ameglio, June 10, 1917, ASMAI II 134/16, Fasc. 104.

88. Mocagatta to Minister of Colonies, July 24, 1917, ASMAI II 134/16, Fasc. 105; and Political Military Report, August 25, 1917, ASMAI II 134/16, Fasc. 106.

89. High Commissioner in Egypt to Talbot in Tobruk, March 1, 1917, BNA FO 141/651; and E. A. V. De Candole, *The Life and Times of King Idris of Libya* (published privately by Mohamed Ben Ghalbon, 1988), 38.

90. De Vita and Pintor to Moccagatta, March 14, 1917, ACS Carte Luigi Pintor, Busta 1, Fasc. 1; and Wingate to Talbot, March 27, 1917, BNA FO 141/651.

91. Decree from Vittorio Emanuele III, April 1, 1918, ASMAI II 150/2/16; and Definition of the Gruppi Idrissi and the Campi Senussiti, May 27, 1920, ASMAI II 150/2/16.

92. Several of the maps can be found in ASMAI II 134/17, ASMAI II 134/18, and ASMAI II 134/19.

93. Colosimo to the Governor of Tripolitania, January 23, 1918, ASMAI II 137/17, Fasc. 113.

94. On Ahmad al-Sharif's life in exile, see Claudia Anna Gazzini, "Jihad in Exile: Ahmad al-Sharif al-Sanusi 1918–1933" (master's thesis, Princeton University, 2004).

95. Lisa Anderson, "Ramadan al-Suwayhli: Hero of the Libyan Resistance," in *Struggle and Survival in the Middle East*, ed. Edmund BurkeIII (Berkeley: University of California Press, 1993), 124; and Ahmida, *Making of Modern Libya*, 131.

96. Major M. S. MacDonnell and Captain L. V. A. Royle, August 1918, BNA FO 170/1147. The possible return of Ahmad al-Sharif to Cyrenaica was a constant source of anxiety among Italian colonial officials in the following years. See Juliette Bessis, *La Méditeranée fasciste: L'Italie mussolinienne et la Tunisie* (Paris: Editions Karthala, 1980), 85.

97. Minister of Colonies, "Progetto di decreto per la Libia," ASMAI II 173/2/3. The document does not have a date, but since it was focused on proposing a plan in the case of what he considered the probable declaration of war, it seems most likely to be from early 1915.

98. Ameglio, "Circolare sul tessere per funzionari e notabili indigeni," 1918, ASMAI II 126/1/14; Baldinetti, "Italian Colonial Rule and Muslim Elites," 101–102.

99. Anna Baldinetti, *David Santillana: L'Uomo e il giurista 1855–1931* (Rome: Istituto per C. A. Nallino, 1995), 68.

100. Nallino, *Notes sur la nature du "Califat" en géneral et sur le prétendu "Califat Ottoman"* (Rome: Minister of Foreign Affairs, 1919), 13–14, 21–22.

101. Enrico Insabato, *L'Islam et la politique des alliés* (Nancy-Paris-Strasbourg: Berger-Levrault, 1920), 60.

102. Minister of Colonies Colosimo to Minister of Foreign Affairs San Giuliano, August 1, 1913, ASMAI II 121/1/3.

103. See chapter 2.

104. P. Tarcisio Cav. Riccardi at the Franciscan Mission in Tripoli to Giovanni Giolitti, August 19, 1913, ASMAI II 121/1/3.

105. Minister of Colonies to Barone Carlo Monti, Direttore Generale del Fondo per il Culto, August 24, 1913, ASMAI II 121/1/3.

106. Antomelli to Barone Carlo Monti, Direttore Generale del Fondo per il Culto, September 8, 1913, ASMAI II 121/1/3.

107. Antomelli to Barone Carlo Monti, Direttore Generale del Fondo per il Culto, September 1913, ASMAI II 121/1/3. There is no clear date, but it is after September 13, when Carlo Monti wrote to Antomelli.

108. Gandolfi, Director of the Technical School in Tripoli, to the Superintendent of the Schools, March 5, 1917, and Ameglio to Minister of Colonies, February 27, 1917, ASMAI 121/1/3.

109. Ameglio to Minister of Colonies, February 27, 1917.

110. Ameglio to the Minister of Colonies, December 13, 1916, ASMAI 121/1/3.

111. Vittorio Ianari, *Chiesa, Coloni e Islam: Religione e politica nella Libia italiana* (Turin: Societa Editrice Internazionale, 1995), 104–105. For the article and Antomelli's response, see Antomelli to Ameglio, January 21, 1916, ASMAI 121/1/3.

112. Antomelli to Ameglio, January 21, 1916.

CHAPTER 4

1. Perhaps he took the stylish Torpedo with the specialized gold insignia Idris al-Sanusi ordered from Fiat in the spring of 1919. Governor of Cyrenaica, Political Military Office to Governor of Tripolitania, "Automobili del Saied," March 1, 1919, ASMAI II 140/4/25.

2. Interview with Mohammed Yusuf al-Tablaqi, in *Mawsuʿat Riwāyāt al-Jihād*, Vol. 22, 13.

3. Stefano Maggi, "The Railways of Italian Africa: Economic, Social and Strategic Features," *Journal of Transport History* 18, no. 1 (1997): 58.

4. By 1900 Italy had 16,429 km of railway in use compared to 38,109 km in France, 30,079 km in the United Kingdom, and 51,678 km in Germany. In Italy 40 percent of those tracks were found in the relatively urban regions of Piedmont

and Liguria. B. R. Mitchell, *International Historical Statistics, Europe 1750–1988* (New York: Stockton Press, 1992), repr. in Christopher Duggan, *A Concise History of Italy* (Cambridge, UK: Cambridge University Press, 1994), 127.

5. Minawi, *Ottoman Scramble for Africa*, 88–89.

6. Stefano Maggi, "The Railways of Italian Africa: Economic, Social and Strategic Features," *Journal of Transport History* 3, no. 18 (1997): 58.

7. Ministero delle Colonie, *La costruzione e l'esercizio delle ferrovie in Tripolitania ed in Cirenaica dalla occupazione al 30 giugno 1915* (Rome: Tipografia Nazionale Bertero, 1917), 33, 23.

8. Kitchener's despatch no. 101, June 19, 1914, BNA PRO 30/57/45.

9. Consulate General in Cairo to Minister of Foreign Affairs, December 13, 1906, ASDME, Rappresentanza diplomatica Egitto—Il Cairo 1864–1940, 108/12.

10. Saho Matsumoto-Best, "British and Italian Imperial Rivalry in the Mediterranean, 1912–14: The Case of Egypt," *Diplomacy and Statecraft* 18, no. 2 (2007): 302.

11. At the very least, an initial foundation for a possible agreement with Idris al-Sanusi that the khedive proposed to Italian representatives in 1914 established an Italian commitment to building hospitals in the region, thus introducing the principle of Italian investment in infrastructure in exchange for a Sanusi alliance. The British military attaché in Rome reported rumors that Idris had been a guest in the khedive's residence for some time in the summer of 1914 when Italian officials began discussing the possibility of negotiating with him instead of Ahmad al-Sharif. See C. G. Hobkirk to the Foreign Office, Rome, June 22, 1914, BNA PRO 30/56. On the British discovery of the arrangements between Italian representatives and the khedive, see "Memorandum on Relations with Italy from the Turco-Italian War to Date," Cairo, April 11, 1916, BNA FO 141/653.

12. Talbot, "Report on the Negotiations of the Anglo-Italian Mission with Mohammed Idris el Mahdi el Senussi," July–September 1916, BNA FO 141/651.

13. Luigi Pintor, "Seconda missione italiana presso il Said Mohammed Idris ben Mohammed el Mahdi es Senussi," May 5, 1917, ACS Carte Luigi Pintor, b.1, f.2.

14. Governor of Tripolitania to Minister of Colonies, November 4, 1918, ASMAI II 150/2/13.

15. Governor of Cyrenaica to Minister of Colonies, October 1, 1918, ASMAI II 150/2/13.

16. Arcari to Governor of Cyrenaica, October 13, 1918, ASMAI II 140/3/18.

17. "Situazione dei campi e posti avanzati senussiti della Cirenaica," September 1, 1919, ASMAI II 140/5/13.

18. Susan Pedersen, *The Guardians: The League of Nations and the Crisis of Empire* (Oxford: Oxford University Press, 2015); and Erez Manela, *The Wilsonian Moment* (Oxford: Oxford University Press, 2007).

19. Federico Cresti, "Il professore e il generale. La polemica tra Carlo Alfonso Nallino e Rodolfo Graziani sulla Senussia e su altre questioni libiche," *Studi Storici* 45, no. 4 (2004): 1121.

20. Ianari, *Chiesa, Coloni e Islam*, 110; and Cesare Marongiu Buonaiuti, *Politica e religioni nel colonialismo italiano* (Varese: Giuffrè Editore, 1982), 117.

21. Note that the promised Tripolitanian parliament was never convened. When a committee of local notables tried to force the application of the Libyan Statutes in 1921, the governor of Tripolitania at the time, Giuseppe Volpi, reacted by occupying the city of Misrata without the consent of the central government in Rome. Anna Baldinetti, *The Origins of the Libyan Nation* (London: Routledge, 2010), 41; Anderson, "Ramadan al-Suwayhli," 124; and Angelo Del Boca, *A un passo dalla forca: Atrocità e infamie dell'occupazione italiana della Libia nelle memorie del patriota Mohamed Fekini* (Milan: Baldini Castoldi Dalai, 2007), 154.

22. De Martino to Minister of Colonies, October 3, 1920, ASMAI II 141/1, Fasc. 1.

23. "Dichiarazione" to the Command of the X Battaglione Libico, June 9, 1920, ASMAI II 134/20/146.

24. Nicola Labanca, *La guerra italiana per la Libia 1911–1931* (Bologna: Il Mulino, 2012), 137.

25. De Martino to Minister of Colonies, October 3, 1920, ASMAI II 141/1/1.

26. There are numerous copies of the al-Rajma Accord in the Italian colonial archives. See, for example, Copy of the al-Rajma Accord with agreements on salaries for Sanusi notables, October 25, 1920, ACS FG 1/2/2; or "Testo concordato," ASMAI II 141/1/2.

27. Giacomo De Martino, *Cirene e Cartagine: note e impressioni della carovana De Martino-Baldari, giugno-luglio 1907* (Bologna: Nicola Zanichelli, 1908), 115.

28. Italian Consulate in Cairo, De Martino to Minister of Foreign Affairs, February 22, 1908, ASDMAE, Rappresentanza diplomatica Egitto—Il Cairo 1864–1940, 124/15; and Agreement for Establishment of Railway, May 1910.

29. See chapter 3.

30. Untitled report on economic development in Cyrenaica, ASMAI II 150/2/19. The report is not signed, but it is most likely by De Martino due to his references to similar developments he initiated as governor of Italian Somaliland in 1910–1916.

31. Federico Cresti, *Non desiderare la terra d'altri: La colonizzazione italiana in Libia* (Rome: Carocci, 2001), 62–69.

32. Frontier Districts Administration to the Residency at Ramleh, August 9, 1921, BNA FO 141/757. On the transformation to al-Marj, see Maggi, "Railways of Italian Africa," 63. The Italian administration changed the name of al-Marj to Barce, a reference to a name for the region in imperial Rome. By 1927 al-Marj became the center of activity of Italian colonials and industrialists due to the train services. According to Luigi Federzoni, the first fascist minister of colonies, the colonial population of the town grew from thirty Italians in 1922 to nine hundred by 1927. See Luigi Federzoni, *La politica coloniale del fascismo: Discorso pronunciato alla Camera dei Deputati nella tornata del 18 marzo 1927* (Rome: Tipografia della Camera dei Deputati, 1927), 27.

33. Governor of Cyrenaica, Political Military Office to Governor of Tripolitania, "Automobili del Saied," March 1, 1919, ASMAI II 140/4/25.

34. Director of Civil and Political Affairs to Governor of Cyrenaica, February, ASMAI II 134/20/ 142. There is no date on the report, but De Martino refers to its account in a memorandum to the minister of colonies on February 24, 1920. On the meeting of tribal notables, see Del Boca, *Gli italiani in Libia*, Vol. 1 (Rome: Laterza, 1988), 413–414.

35. De Martino to Minister of Colonies, February 24, 1920, ASMAI II 134/20/142.

36. Ibid.

37. Translation of a letter from Italian authorities to the Shaykhs of Barqa, Military Administrator of the Frontier Districts Administration to the British High Commissioner in Egypt, December 15, 1920, BNA FO 141/652. The letter was dated 23 Gamad I, 338 = 23 Jumada al-Awwal 1338 (February 14, 1920).

38. Reply from the shaykhs dated 29 Gamad Awal 1338 (February 20, 1920), BNA FO 141/652.

39. Triaud, *Légende noire*, 498. Triaud quoted a report from the French military commander in Chad, Col. Largeau, from a report noting that the French command needed to gain permission from the Maghārba to construct a well in Kufra for their own supply. Colonel Largeau, February 7, 1912, FR CAOM FM SG AFRIQUE IV 37bis.

40. "We accept in our country only the commercial purposes of the Italians (with the exception of railways)." Reply from the shaykhs dated 29 Gamad Awal 1338.

41. Commissary of Cirene to Pintor, June 6, 1922, ACS Carte Luigi Pintor, b. 5, f. 21. The Italians adopted the Roman name of Cirene for the city now known as Susa.

42. Frontier Districts Administration to the Chancery, the Residency in Cairo, October 29, 1921, BNA FO 141/652.

43. Military Administrator of the Frontier Districts Administration to the British Resident in Ramleh, July 6, 1921, BNA FO 141/757; Governor De Martino to Minister of Colonies, October 14, 1921, ACS Carte Luigi Pintor, b. 3, f. 14.

44. Captain De Angelis to Governor De Martino, October 18, 1921, ACS Carte Luigi Pintor, b. 3, f. 14.

45. "Appunti circa la conferenza tra Sua Eccellenza il Ministro delle Colonie e Sua Eccellenza il Governatore della Cirenaica," February 4, 1920, ASMAI II 134/20/ 142.

46. On the purpose of these armed camps known as "Gruppi Idrissiti" and "Campi Senussiti," see Definition of the Gruppi Idrissiti and the Campi Senussiti, no author, May 27, 1920, ASMAI II 150/2/16.

47. Minister of Colonies to Governor De Martino, October 16, 1921, ACS Carte Luigi Pintor, b. 3, f. 14.

48. Governor De Martino to Minister of Colonies, October 20, 1921, ACS Carte Luigi Pintor, b. 3, f. 14.

49. Idris to De Martino, October 28, 1921, ACS Carte Luigi Pintor, b. 3, f. 14; British Ambassador in Rome to Field Marshal Viscount Allenby, January 26, 1922, BNA FO 141/652.

50. Notes for the Minister of Colonies, July 1921, ASMAI II 136/1/11.

51. Erik J. Zürcher, *Storia della Turchia* (Rome: Donzelli, 2007), 185. A visit from Charles Richard Crane to the Libyan territories in 1922 underscored the popularity of Ahmad al-Sharif as a charismatic figure with a broad appeal. Crane reportedly requested a visit with the head of the Sanusi *zāwiya* in Benghazi to express his admiration of al-Sharif, whom he had previously met through a shared acquaintance in Ankara. Crane reportedly kept a photo of the Sanusi leader and a pistol, both gifts from al-Sharif. Pintor to Minister of Colonies, March 1922, ACS Carte Luigi Pintor, b. 4, f. 18.

52. Aydin, *Politics of Anti-Westernism*, 135; and Italian Delegate to the Ottoman Police to the Minister of Foreign Affairs, July 2, 1921, ASMAI II 136/1/11.

53. Aydin, *Politics of Anti-Westernism*, 146; Martin S. Kramer, *Islam Assembled: The Advent of the Muslim Congresses* (New York: Columbia University Press, 1986), 69; and Jacob M. Landau, *The Politics of Pan-Islam* (Oxford: Clarendon Press, 1990), 167–168.

54. Minister of Foreign Affairs to the Minister of Colonies, October 13, 1921, ASMAI II 136/1/9.

55. Minister of Colonies to Minister of Foreign Affairs, November 11, 1921, ASMAI II 136/1/9. There was some ambivalence within the Italian administration about how to respond to the possible return of Ahmad al-Sharif, which Claudia Gazzini has argued reflected divergent aims between the Ministry of Foreign Affairs and the Ministry of Colonies. However, after initial reluctance on the part of Minister of Colonies Giuseppe Giardini, the Ministry of Colonies and the Ministry of Foreign Affairs collaborated closely on the issue of his possible return. Rather than an interministerial conflict over objectives, the ambiguity reflected an attempt to balance among various forces as they tried to determine which posed a greater threat to Italy's claims to sovereignty and prestige: the return of al-Sharif to Cyrenaica or his possible involvement with competing imperial interests. Claudia Gazzini, "Jihad in Exile," 44.

56. Notes for the Minister of Colonies, July 1921, ASMAI II 136/1/11.

57. Minister of Colonies to Minister of Foreign Affairs, "Libia: Ex Senusso Saied Ahmad El Scerif," August 6, 1921, ASMAI II 136/1/11.

58. Pintor to the Minister of Colonies, November 22, 1921, ASMAI II 136/1/9.

59. Fabio Grassi, *L'Italia e la questione turca (1917–1923): Opinione pubblica e politica estera* (Turin: Silvio Zamorani, 1996), 212.

60. Malek Badrawi, *Political Violence in Egypt, 1910–1924: Secret Societies, Plots and Assassinations* (Richmond, Surrey, UK: Curzon Press, 2000), 185.

61. Ahmida, *Making of Modern Libya*, 129–132; Anderson, "Ramadan al-Suwayhli," 126. On Abd al-Rahman 'Azzam's involvement in Tripolitania, see Ralph M.

Coury, *The Making of an Egyptian Arab Nationalist: The Early Years of 'Azzam Pasha, 1893–1936* (Reading, UK: Garnet Publishing, 1998).

62. Notes for the Minister of Colonies, July 1921, ASMAI II 136/1/11.
63. Pintor to Minister of Colonies, January 3, 1922, ACS Carte Luigi Pintor, b. 4, f. 18. The Tripolitanian notables included Mohammad Mraied (the *kaymakam* of Tarhuna), Ahmad al-Suwayhli (the son of Ramadan al-Suwayhli), Abd al-Rahman 'Azzam, the *kaymakam* of Khoms, and a representative of the Warfalla tribes.
64. Pintor to Minister of Colonies, January 3, 1922; and Pintor to Minister of Colonies, March 13, 1922, ACS Carte Luigi Pintor, b. 4, f. 18.
65. Enrico De Leone, *Riformatori musulmani del XIX secolo nell'Africa e nell'Asia mediterranee* (Milan: Giuffrè Editore, 1973), 35.
66. See Volpi's introduction to a volume on colonial policies presented to Mussolini during his 1926 visit to the colonies: Angelo Piccioli, ed., *La rinascita della Tripolitania. Memorie e studi sui quattro anni di governo del Conte Giuseppe Volpi di Misurata* (Milan: Mondadori, 1926).
67. From a speech before the House of Deputies, June 22, 1922, on spending in the colonies. Giovanni Amendola, *Discorso Politici (1919–1925)*, ed. Sabato Visco (Rome: Carlo Colombo, 1968), 128.
68. Information from Senussi Gazzali, Benghazi July 1922, ACS Carte Luigi Pintor, b. 5, f. 21.
69. Pintor to Minister of Colonies, May 27, 1922, ACS Carte Luigi Pintor, b. 4, f. 18.
70. Pintor to Minister of Colonies, March 29, 1922; and Pintor to Volpi, 3 April 1922, ACS Carte Luigi Pintor, b. 5, f. 29.
71. Pintor to Governor of Tripolitania, June 25, 1922, ACS Carte Luigi Pintor, b. 4, f. 18.
72. Pintor to Amendola, May 9–10, 1922, ACS Carte Luigi Pintor, b. 4, f. 18. The only biographical study of Luigi Pintor I have seen ignored this moment in Pintor's career to focus on his involvement in pro-Sanusi accords. Despite his involvement in the negotiations with Idris al-Sanusi, Pintor transitioned into the fascist administration after a short vetting process as director general for the Colonies of North Africa until his death in 1925. See Giovanni Tosatti, "Le carte di un funzionario del Ministero delle Colonie: Luigi Pintor," in *Fonti e problemi della politica coloniale italiana*, ed. Carla Ghezzi (Taormina-Messina: Ministero per i Beni Culturali e Ambientali, 1989).
73. De Angelis to Pintor, April 26, 1922, ACS Carte Luigi Pintor, b. 5, f. 28.
74. Amendola to Pintor, May 13, 1922, ACS Carte Luigi Pintor, b. 4, f. 18.
75. Dr. Alaimo to Pintor, September 8, 1921, ACS Carte Luigi Pintor, b. 5, f. 26. However, Pintor suggested the Italian government only paid 'Umar al-Kikhiya 80,000 lire. Pintor to Governor of Cyreniaca, February 17, 1921, ACS Carte Luigi Pintor, b. 5, f. 20.
76. Orlando Pascalis, "Le responsibilità coloniali dell'on. Amendola" in *Il Popolo d'Italia*, January 28, 1925, ASMAI II 134/26/196.

77. "Relations between Great Britain, Italy and the Senussi 1912–1924," prepared by the Foreign Office for the Historical Section, Committee of Imperial Defence in 1927, BNA CAB 44/14; and British Secretary of State to British High Commissioner in Egypt, Lord Allenby, January 26, 1923, FO 141/585.

78. De Candole, *Life and Times of King Idris of Libya*, 42–44.

79. British High Commissioner in Egypt, November 29, 1921, BNA FO 141/585. Concern over Idris al-Sanusi's health complaints did induce the British High Commissioner to send a doctor.

80. Anna Baldinetti has pointed out that Idris was just one of a number of elites who left the Libyan territories in the wake of the Libyan Statutes. Disappointed with the unfulfilled promises of autonomy, Libyan notables found greater freedom to organize resources and gain international support for a burgeoning nationalist movement. Baldinetti, *Origins of the Libyan Nation*, 63.

81. Mujahidin in the Oral History Project recollect the difficulties they faced fighting against a growing fleet of Italian armored cars in the late 1920s. See, for example, Interview with Muhammad Bubakir al-Rifa al-ʿAwami, in *Mawsuʿat Riwāyāt al-Jihād*, Vol. 22, 52. Armored cars had the advantage over railway transportation of circumventing the costly process of laying tracks, but they limited the amount of supplies Italian troops could carry into the desert. It was also easier for mujahidin to acquire cars and trucks (rather than trains), either by getting them from abroad or by taking them from their Italian opponents.

CHAPTER 5

1. "La Cattedrale della Tripolitania," *L'Oltremare* III, no. 1 (January 1929): 32.

2. "Ceremonia di fede ed italianità a Tripoli, *L'Idea Nazionale*, January 20, 1923, ASMAI II 150/31.

3. Formerly the Istituto Coloniale Italiano, founded in 1906 under Giacomo De Martino. The institution changed names in 1928 and absorbed *L'Oltremare* at that point.

4. Federzoni wrote fondly of Cantalupo in his diary. Adriana Macchi, ed., *1927: Diario di un ministro del fascismo* (Florence: Passigli Editori, 1993), 44.

5. Giuseppe Volpi referred to a fascist approach to colonial rule as centered on a politics of prestige in *La politica coloniale del fascismo* (Padova: CEDAM, 1937). See also Luigi Goglia and Fabio Grassi, eds., *Il colonialismo italiano dal'Adua all'impero* (Rome: Laterza, 1993), 12–26.

6. Richard Bosworth has characterized Federzoni as one of the most influential and dangerous figures of his generation in Italy for his ability to bring the full weight of Italian nationalism into the Fascist Party. Richard Bosworth, *Mussolini's Italy: Life under the Dictatorship 1915–1945* (New York: Penguin, 2006), 49–50.

7. Silvia Casmirri, "Luigi Federzoni," in *Uomini e volti del fascismo*, ed. Ferdinando Cordova (Rome: Bulzoni editore, 1980), 268; and Sergio Romano, preface

to *Luigi Federzoni 1927: Diario di un ministro del fascismo*, ed. Adriana Macchi (Florence: Passigli editore, 1993), 8.

8. Federzoni, "Il Fascismo per le colonie," from the *Rassegna italiana*, Fascicolo LXV, 1923, ACS MAI 2072.

9. Orlando Pascalis, "La responsabilità coloniale dell'on. Amendola," *Il Popolo d'Italia*, January 28, 1925, ASMAI II 134/26/196. Al-Kikhiya represented an urban administrative class that developed along ethnic-national lines in Ottoman Libya among descendants of Turkish troops and North African women in the late nineteenth and early twentieth centuries. He was one of three such notables elected to the Ottoman parliament in 1908, and he continued his political career as an intermediary for Italian negotiations with Idris al-Sanusi during the Italian occupation. See Ahmida, *Making of Modern Libya*, 66.

10. Luigi Federzoni, *Venti mesi di azione coloniale* (Milan: Mondadori, 1926), 87.

11. Evans-Pritchard made a similar remark about Idris al-Sanusi's position during the initial Akrama negotiations. "The Sayyid's strength lay in his weakness." *Sanusi of Cyrenaica*, 141.

12. Luigi Pintor, Vice Director General in the Ministry of Colonies, internal report on Omar Mansur al-Kikhiya, March 22, 1923, ACS Carte Luigi Pintor, b. 6, f. 6. See also an undated document from Depositions of Pintor in 1921–1922, ACS Carte Luigi Pintor, b. 5, f. 20. In this document Pintor distinguishes between the Amendola in Rome placing faith in al-Kikhiya and Italian officials on the ground (like himself) being deeply distrustful of his intentions. Indeed, Pintor's communications with Amendola throughout 1921 indicate mounting frustration with having to deal with him as a mediator, primarily because Pintor seemed to feel that Omar Mansur considered himself to be of a higher status than the Italian functionary.

13. Request from Omar Mansur for reparations from the British Government, September 25, 1946, BNA FO 1015/2.

14. Pintor to Minister of Colonies, October 1923, ACS Carte Luigi Pintor, b. 6, f. 4.

15. Federzoni to Governor of Cyrenaica, December 12, 1922, ASMAI II 134/23/174.

16. "Ragione per tenere la Libia," ACS Carte Luigi Pintor, b. 2, f. 10 (there is no date, but it is likely from 1920); "Dichiarazioni alla commissione per gli esteri e per le colonie," September 1920, ACS Carte Luigi Pintor, b. 2, f. 10; and "Appunti schematici sopra alcuni questiti posti a S.E. il Ministro delle Colonie da membri della commissione parlamentare per gli affari esteri e per le colonie," February 3, 1921, Carte Luigi Pintor, b. 3, f. 15. See also Bessis, *Méditerranée fasciste*, 87.

17. Fabrizio Serra, *Italia e Senussia: Vent'anni di azione coloniale in Cirenaica* (Milan: Fratelli Treves, 1933), 131.

18. Del Boca, *Gli italiani in Libia*, Vol. 2, *Dal fascismo a Gheddafi* (Rome: Laterza, 1988), 73.

19. Cantalupo to Minister of Foreign Affairs, August 8, 1930, ACS FG 6/7/12.

20. "Riassunto informative sui compenenti la familgia Senussita e sugli "acuan" e capi più politicamente interessanti (compilato dal tenente Monacci)," ACS Carte Luigi Pintor, b. 5, f. 23 (there is no clear date, but it is most likely 1922). The report contrasted Al-Rida with Saf a-Din, "representing the rebel part of the Sanusi family."

21. Ali Abdullatif Ahmida referred to the rising influence of these Sanusi military commanders as a "social revolution" in Cyrenaica. "The ordinary tribal commanders rebelled against the compromising Sanusi elite." *Making of Modern Libya*, 137. In his interview, Muhammad Bubakir al-Rifa characterized as an open-ended question within the Sufi *ṭarīqa* who had the right to determine the direction of the Sanusiyya. "['Umar al-Mukhtar's] refusal to accept funding and al-Rida's acceptance of funding divided the Sanusi *ṭarīqa* with some shaykhs arguing that al-Rida as a member of the Sanusi family had more of a right to determine the terms of the relationship with the Italian government." *Mawsuʿat Riwāyāt al-Jihād*, 64.

22. Divisione Carabinieri Reali della Tripolitania to the Governor of Tripoli, September 27, 1923, ACS MAI 2046.

23. Federzoni to Governor of Tripoli, September 30, 1923, ACS MAI 2046.

24. Amendola to Pintor, March 25, 1922, ACS Carte Luigi Pintor, Busta 4, Fasc. 18.

25. Federico Cresti, *Oasi d'Italianitá: La Libia della colonizzazione agraria tra fascismo, guerra e indipendenza (1935–1956)* (Turin: Società Editrice Internazionale, 1996), xxiv.

26. Federzoni to the Chief of Staff, December 1922, ACS MAI 2072.

27. Adrian Lyttelton, *Seizure of Power: Fascism in Italy 1919–1929* (London: Weidenfeld, 1978), 105. See also Alberto Aquarone, "Violenza e consenso nel fascismo italiano," *Storia contemporanea* 10, no. 1 (1979): 145–155.

28. Governor of Cyrenaica, *Relazione di governo*, January 1923–May 1924, ASMAI II 134/25/190.

29. Division Command of Tripolitania to the Governor of Tripolitania, September 24, 1923, ACS MAI 2046.

30. Pintor to the Governor of Cyrenaica, January 11, 1924, ACS Carte Luigi Pintor, b. 6, f. 4.

31. Political Secretary of the PNF in Derna, "Relazione mensile 15 ottobre 15 novembre 1922," December 17, 1922, ACS MAI 2046.

32. Ibid. It is important to note that the *fascio* of Tripoli also took an active role in promoting a particular version of a fascist approach in colonial policy. The members of the *fascio* tried to block the nomination of a functionary known as a key player in negotiating peace treaties from the previous administration, peace treaties that the *fasci* complained had "reduced [Italian] dominion in Libya to a veiled form of protectorate." Vice Secretary of the Fasci Italiani all'estero e nelle Colonie to Mussolini, August 6, 1926, ACS MAI 2046. The involvement of the local *fasci* in Cyrenaica, however, reached a higher level as a source of irritation for the central party.

33. Secretary General of the Fasci Italiani all'Estero to the Minister of Colonies, March 13, 1925, ACS MAI 2046.

34. Mombelli to the Minister of Colonies, June 11, 1925, ACS MAI 2046. For an example of the complaints against Mombelli, see Delegate of the PNF to Cyrenaica, Gian Luigi Olmi, to Political Secretary of the PNF, November 8, 1924, ACS MAI 2046.

35. "Una più diretta presa di contatto, attraverso questa nuova dipendenza ger-archica, fra il Partito Fascista e le terre ridonate dal valore e dal sacrificio dell'Esercito grigio-verde e dalle Camicie Nere al dominio di Roma." PNF Foglio d'Ordini, n. 26, "Fasci delle Colonie," March 19, 1927, ACS MAI 2072.

36. Grandi to Diplomatic Agents, June 13, 1925, ACS MAI 2046.

37. Commissario Straordinario of the PNF to the Vice Secretary General of the PNF, April 18, 1927, ACS MAI 2046.

38. On the effort to make Libya Italian, see Roberta Pergher, "In Consent of Memory: Recovering Fascist-Settler Relations in Libya," in *In the Society of Fascists: Acclamation, Acquiescence, and Agency in Mussolini's Italy*, ed. Giulia Albanese and Roberta Pergher (New York: Palgrave, 2012), 171.

39. For an overview on the military campaigns of the Italian "reconquest," see the works of the imminent Italian military historian Nicola Labanca, especially his edited volume, *Un nodo: Immagini e documenti sulla repressione coloniale italiana in Libia* (Manduria: Piero Lacaita, 2002) and his more recent work, *La guerra italiana per la Libia 1911–1931* (Bologna: Il Mulino, 2012). On the mass internment of Libyan populations more specifically, see Labanca, "Italian Colonial Internment," in *Italian Colonialism*, ed. Ruth Ben-Ghiat and Mia Fuller (New York: Palgrave, 2005), 27–36. On the trial and execution of 'Umar al-Mukhtar, see Alessandro Volterra, "Morì, siccome 'n topo: Le fotografie dei processi a Omar al-Mukthar e ai resistenti libici," in *Quel che resta dell'impero: La cultura colonial degli italiani*, ed. Valeria Deplano and Alessandro Pes (Milan: Mimesis, 2014), 235–257.

40. On Federzoni at the end of his time as minister of colonies, see Michael R. Ebner, *Ordinary Violence in Mussolini's Italy* (Cambridge, UK: Cambridge University Press, 2011), 43; Frederick W. Deakin, "Il colonialismo fascista nel giudizio degli inglesi," in *Le guerre coloniale del fascismo,* ed. Angelo Del Boca (Rome: Laterza, 1991), 349; and Macchi, *Luigi Federzoni 1927,* 8.

41. Federzoni to Mussolini, November 24, 1926, ACS SPD CR 23/224R.

42. Minister of Colonies to Governor of Cyrenaica, December 1, 1926, ASMAI II 134/27/205.

43. Shukri, *Al-Sanūsiyah*, 161.

44. Governor of Cyrenaica, Monthly Report, July 1, 1925, ASMAI II 134/26/199.

45. Federzoni to the Minister of Finance, August 6, 1927, ACS SPD CR 23/224R.

46. Attilio Teruzzi, *Cirenaica verde* (Milan: Mondadori, 1931), 183.

47. "Operation Mogarba," January 18, 1928, ACS FG 4/6/7; Teruzzi to Governor of Tripolitania, January 28, 1928, ACS FG 4/6/8.

48. Enzo Santarelli, *Omar al-Mukhtar e la riconquista fascista della Libia* (Milan: Marzorati, 1981), 73.

49. Teruzzi, *Cirenaica verde*, 178.

50. C. A. Nallino, often cited as Italy's most famous orientalist, frequently criticized the fascist government for failing to consult with experts on Islamic issues. See Federico Cresti, "Il professore e il generale," 1123.

51. Bruno Ducati, "Lo Stato Senussita," *Rassegna italiana* 21 (1928): 178.

52. Fillippo Lo Bello, "La confraternita dei Senussi," *Rassegna italiana* 22 (1928): 656.

53. Giuseppe Macaluso Aleo, *Turchi, Senussi e Italiani in Libia* (Bengasi: Guido Vitale, 1930), 99–102. The book was originally published as a series of articles in *Cirenaica Nuova*.

54. C. A. Nallino, review of *Turchi, Senussi e Italiani in Libia* by Giuseppe Macaluso Aleo, *Oriente Moderno* 10 (October 1930): 520. The Royal Decree of October 25, 1920, no. 1755 conferred on Idris al-Sanusi the title of "head, as our delegate, of the autonomous administration of the oases of Awgila, Jallo, al-Jaghbub, and Kufra, with the ability to choose Ajdabiya as the center of the administration." Nallino further pointed out that the Arabic version of the agreement gave Idris the title "Emir of the Sanusi of Italy" (*al-amir al-sanusi al-italiyya*) to emphasize the concept of Idris's authority deriving directly from the Italian state.

55. Federzoni to Mussolini, April 22, 1927, ACS SPD CR 23/224R. See also Federzoni, *La politica coloniale del fascismo*, 21.

56. Cresti, *Non desiderare la terra d'altri*, 75.

57. On the settlement schemes of the 1930s, see Cresti, *Non desiderare la terra d'altri*; Choate, *Emigrant Nation*; and Claudio G. Segré, *The Fourth Shore: The Italian Colonization of Libya* (Chicago: Chicago University Press, 1974).

58. Barbara Spadaro, *Una colonia italiana: Incontri, memorie e rappresentazioni tra Italia e Libia* (Milan: Mondadori, 2013), 10.

59. Francesco Meriano, *La rinconquista della Tripolitania* (Milan: Imperia Casa Editrice del Partito Nazionale Fascista, 1923), 11–12.

60. Federzoni, "Il Fascismo per le colonie," *La Rassegna Italiana*, Fascicolo LXV, 1923, ACS MAI 2072.

61. Chiara Giorgi, *L'Africa come carriera: Funzioni e funzionari del colonialismo itlaiano* (Rome: Carocci Editore, 2012), 104–105.

62. Federzoni to the Governors of Colonies, June 9, 1928, ACS MAI 2061.

63. Casmirri, "Luigi Federzoni," 293.

64. Luigi Federzoni, New Guidelines for Promotion of Colonial Officials, February 25, 1928, ACS MAI 2061. Chiara Giorgi argues that Federzoni's reforms failed in his professionalization efforts due in large part to the dominance of military personnel in the colonial administration until the 1930s. Giorgi, *L'Africa come carriera*, 67.

65. Graziani, "Cultura professionale degli ufficiale," August 13, 1928, ACS FG 6/8/1.

66. Federzoni, *1927: Diario di un ministro*, 7; Lyttelton, *Seizure of Power*, 119.

67. Pintor to Minister of Colonies, October 1923, ACS Carte Luigi Pintor, b. 6, f. 6.

68. Anonymous soldier from the 2nd Libyan Legion to Minister of Colonies, July 3, 1926, ASMAI II 134/27/204.

69. Cordova, *Agli ordini del serpente verde*, 56.

70. Filberto Sabbadin, *I frati minori lombardi in Libia: La missione di Tripoli (1908–1991)* (Milan: Edizioni Biblioteca Francescana, 1991), 38.

71. Peter C. Kent, *The Pope and the Duce* (New York: St. Martin's Press, 1981), 38; and Alba Rosa Leone, "La politica missionaria del Vaticano tra le due guerre," *Studi Storici* 21, no. 1 (1980): 124.

72. Marongiu Buonaiuti, *Politica e religioni*, 157.

73. Federzoni to Mussolini, February 6, 1928, ACS SPD CR 23/224R. On the extraordinary allotment for public funds in 1928, see Federzoni to Volpi, February 4, 1928, ACS SPD CR 23/224R.

74. Ianari, *Chiesa, Coloni e Islam*, 116. Mussolini to De Bono, 1929, ASMAI 150/31/140.

75. Federzoni to Mussolini, January 1928, ACS SPD CR 23/224R.

76. The Franciscan mission complained of obstacles to maintaining a church in Barce based on the Freemasonry of local officials and their support of the Sanusi *zawāyā* in the region. Padre Napareno Sorriva of the Fransicscan mission to Sig. Barone, Segretario Particolare del Duce, January 2, 1929, ASMAI II 150/31.

77. In 1924 the mission finished construction on the church in Homs with money from the colonial government (200,000 lire). The church in Misrata was constructed entirely with state funding in 1925 and cost 270,000 lire. The building plans also included a project to create a new entrance for the original Maltese church in Tripoli, Santa Maria degli Angeli, which was built in compliance with Ottoman laws prohibiting a Christian church from constructing open entrances along the street. Sabbadin, *I frati minori lombardi in Libia*, 41.

78. Sabbadin, *I frati minori lombardi in Libia*, 40.

79. Kent, *Pope and the Duce*, 37.

80. Danilo Veneruso, "Il pontificato di Pio XI," in *Storia della chiesa*, Vol. 23, *I Catolici nel mondo contemporaneo (1922–1958)* (Milan: Edizioni Paoline, 1991), 34. On Mussolini's adoption of Catholicism as a symbol of the nation at home and abroad, see Emilio Gentile, *The Sacralization of Politics in Fascist Italy*, trans. Keith Botsford (Cambridge, MA: Harvard University Press, 1996), 111.

81. Military Command of Tripoli, "L'occupazione del Fezzan," June 1930, AUSSME L8/158/13.

82. Graziani, "Le Popolazioni," 1931, ACS FG 9/13/5; David Atkinson, "Nomadic Strategies and Colonial Governance," in *Entanglements of Power: Geographies of Domination/Resistance*, ed. Joanne P. Sharp, Paul Routledge, Chris Philo, and Ronan Paddison (London: Routledge, 2000), 112.

83. Del Boca, *Gli italiani in Libia*, Vol. 2, 182. Conditions in the internment camps were notoriously desperate. There are no exact figures on how many people died

during the internment, but most historians estimate that at least 40,000 died from a variety of causes. Some put the number higher, at 50,000–70,000. Ali Abdullatif Ahmida, *Forgotten Voices: Power and Agency in Colonial and Postcolonial Libya* (New York: Routledge, 2005), 44.

84. Abubakir Mawsa al-Madaʿi recounted stories of people returning after independence to find relatives on their land, who had been granted ownership from the Italian government with no compensation for the original inhabitants. *Mawsuʿat Riwāyāt al-Jihād*, Vol. 22, 125.

85. Del Boca, *Gli italiani in Libia*, Vol. 2, 175.

86. Minister of Foreign Affairs to Italian Legate in Cairo, July 29, 1930, ACS FG 11/16/2.

87. Graziani to the Minister of Colonies and Governor Badoglio, April 18, 1934, ACS FG 11/14/9.

88. Graziani to Minister of Colonies, April 18, 1934, ACS FG 11/14/9.

89. Renzo De Felice, *Il fascismo e l'Oriente: Arabi, ebrei e indiani nella politica di Mussolini* (Bologna: Il Mulino, 1988), 33.

90. For accounts of Italy's planned settlement programs, see Federico Cresti, *Oasi di italianità*; Martin Moore, *Fourth Shore: Italy's Mass Colonization of Libya* (London: Routledge, 1940); Segré, *Fourth Shore*; and Choate, *Emigrant Nation*.

91. Vice Governor of Cyrenaica to the Governor of Libya, April 18, 1934, ACS FG 11/14/9.

CONCLUSIONS

1. René Albrecht-Carrié, "Peace with Italy—An Appraisal," *Political Science Quarterly* 62, no. 4 (1947): 493–494.

2. Enrico Insabato, *La collaborazione italo-araba e il Sudan* (Rome: Danesi, 1950), 10.

3. Some Italian settlers maintained a presence in the former colonies for decades. Pamela Ballinger refers to the period between 1943 and 1961 as the "long colonial twilight" in Libya due to the continued presence of Italian settlers and "parastatal" organizations managing agricultural projects. "Colonial Twilight: Italian Settlers and the Long Decolonization of Libya," *Journal of Contemporary History* 51, no. 4 (2016): 813–838.

4. Raymond F. Betts, *Decolonization*, 2nd ed. (New York: Routledge, 1998), 32.

5. "Relazione della 3° commissione permanente (Affari Esteri e Colonie), Stato di provisione del Ministero dell'Africa Italiana per l'esercizio finanziario dal 1° luglio 1948 al 30 giugno 1949," ACS MAI 2064.

6. Francesco Saverio Caroselli, "Gli accordi anglo-libici," *Rivista di studi politici internazionali* 20, no. 3 (1953): 345–358.

7. Baldinetti, *Origins of the Libyan Nation*, 107–108; John Wright, *Libya: A Modern History* (Baltimore, MD: Johns Hopkins University Press, 1982), 47; and Saverio Caroselli, "Gli Accordi Anglo-Libici."

8. Ministero dell'Africa Italiana, "La Senussia," 1949, 52–53, ASMAI II 181/70/362.

9. Evans-Pritchard, *Sanusi of Cyrenaica*, 155.

10. F. E. Stafford, "The Ex-Italian Colonies," *International Affairs* 25, no. 1 (1949): 54.

11. Quoted in Scott Bills, *The Libyan Arena: The United States, Britain, and the Council of Foreign Ministers* (Kent, OH: Kent State University Press, 1995), 21.

12. Ismail R. Khalidi, "The Constitution of the United Kingdom of Libya: Background and Summary," *Middle East Journal* 6, no. 2 (1952): 221.

13. Wright, *Libya*, 54. Wright explains that the decision pushed aside an alternative plan coauthored by the British foreign secretary, Ernest Bevin, and the Italian minister of foreign affairs, Carlo Sforza, in May 1949. The Bevin-Sforza plan called for a gradual process of state formation in which Cyrenaica would remain under British protection, Italy would maintain control over Tripolitania, and Fezzan would go to France in continuation with the temporary administration established immediately at the war's end. Bevin and Sforza planned for the regions to unify and gain independence after ten years, subject to UN approval. The Bevin-Sforza plan gained wide support in the United Nations, but facing disapproval among Arab leaders (established primarily through the reports of the Pelt Commission), the plan quickly fell to the wayside.

14. Lisa Anderson, "'A Last Resort, an Expedient and an Experiment': Statehood and Sovereignty in Libya," *Journal of Libyan Studies* 2, no. 2 (2001): 17. Anderson has argued that the inconclusive results of the Pelt Commission were just as much a product of the international nature of the commission's delegations, "as each delegation pursued lines of inquiry that coincided with the positions of their governments rather than eliciting Libyan views."

15. As Dirk Vandewalle has pointed out, Idris confirmed the suspicion that he felt little interest in the fate of Tripolitania when he admitted to the American ambassador that he preferred an emirate in Cyrenaica alone rather than a monarchy that united the entire country. Dirk Vandewalle, "Libya's Revolution Revisited," *MERIP Middle East Report* 143 (1986): 31.

16. Baldinetti, *Origins of the Libyan Nation*, 130.

17. Adrian Pelt, *Libyan Independence and the United Nations: A Case of Planned Decolonization* (New Haven, CT: Yale University Press, 1970), 560. This decision meant that the next in line to the throne would be his younger brother, Muhammad al-Rida. Idris took his division between the Sanusi *ṭarīqa* and the Libyan state a step further by inserting a clause in the Libyan Constitution establishing that except for those individuals in the direct line of descent for the throne (i.e., Muhammad al-Rida), no members of the Sanusi family could serve in a ministerial position. Adrian Pelt applauded Idris's decision as "one more indication of [King Idris's] policy of not claiming more power than a correctly conceived and functioning constitutional monarchy should allow."

18. John Davis notes that the Zuwaya grew substantially in number during the fascist "reconquest." As the last part of Cyrenaica the Italians occupied, Kufra remained

a place of refuge for various Cyrenaican tribes driven out of their homes by the colonial troops, and the Zuwaya "proved flexible in matters of genealogy, and acquired large numbers of "members by writing" (*mukatibin* as contrasted with members by birth), granting land to them and to others who sought freedom from Christian colonial control." Davis, *Libyan Politics*, 63.

19. George Joffe, "Qadhafi's Islam in Local Historical Perspective," in *Qadhafi's Libya, 1969–1994*, ed. Dirk Vandewalle (London: Macmillan, 1995), 145. Writing in the mid-1990s, François Burgat also credited Qadhafi with having bridged the nationalism of Nasser with the rise of political Islam in the 1980s. "Qadhafi has been more religious than Nasser and closer to the traditional values of Islam. Even if he foundered in the end, Qadhafi from the beginning attempted to make Libya the first Arab state to embark upon at least a partial re-Islamization of positive law." François Burget, "Qadhafi's Ideological Framework," in *Qadhafi's Libya, 1969–1994*, ed. Dirk Vandewalle (London: Macmillan, 1995), 49. Despite his rejection of those in the Sanusiyya as religious and political leaders after his political coup, some aspects of Qadhafi's interpretation of Islam echoed Sanusi teachings. In particular, Qadhafi, like the Sanusiyya, focused on *ijtihād* or the idea that the meanings of Islamic law were open to continuous revelation, as a parallel to his ideology of continuous revolution. According to Hanspeter Mattes, this approach allowed for a more open application of Islamic law as justification for revolutionary principles of the Qadhafi regime. Hanspeter Mattes, "The Political Role of Islam in the Present: Libya," in *Islam in the World Today*, ed. Werner Ende and Udo Steinback (Ithaca, NY: Cornell University, 2010), 455. For an argument against the idea that Qadhafi's interpretations of Islam demonstrated any interest in the teachings of the Sanusiyya, see Edward Mitchell, "Islam in Colonel Qadhafi's Thought," *World Today* 38, nos. 7/8, (1982): 319–326.

20. Lisa Anderson, "Qadhafi and His Opposition," *Middle East Journal* 40, no. 2 (1986): 229–230.

21. Lisa Anderson, "Obligation and Accountability: Islamic Politics in North Africa," *Daedalus* 120, no. 3 (1991): 101, 106.

ESSAY ON SOURCES

1. Interview with Muhammad Bubakir al-Rifa al-ʿAwami, in *Mawsuʿat Riwāyāt al-Jihād*, Vol. 22, 52.

2. In 2009 the name of the center changed to the Markaz al-Lībī lil Maḥfuẓāt wa al-Dirāsāt al-Tarīkhiyya, or the National Centre for Archives and Historical Study. The change in title accompanied an expansion of the center's facilities and its growing importance as a depository for primary and secondary sources on Libyan history beyond the colonial period, but its primary concern remained the documentation of the history of the colonial era and narratives of anti-Italian resistance in Libya.

3. In the section of his autobiography recounting his involvement in the project, Jan Vansina noted the difficulty in interviewing women by what was presumably an all-male team of researchers conducting the oral interviews. Jan Vansina, *Living with Africa* (Madison: University of Wisconsin Press, 2005), 180.

4. "Taqrīr ʿām wa mawjuz ʿan āʿmāl al-shaʿba" [General and public report of the division], Qisim al-riwāyat al-shifawiya," last modified June 4, 2012, http://www.libsc.org.ly/mrkaz/index.php/2015-10-29-06-55-55/2015-10-29-06-58-15/37-2012-06-04-09-32-16.

5. Vansina, *Living with Africa*, 179–180.

6. Ibid., 182.

7. The editors of volume 30 of the series, for example, chose to retain the original dialects of the mujahidin. They provided only summaries of the interviews in standard Arabic. Naʿima al-Hada Mashinah, introduction to *Mawsuʿat Riwāyāt al-Jihād*, Vol. 30 (Tripoli: Markaz al-Jihad, 1991), 10.

8. K. O. Dike, *Trade and Politics in the Niger Delta, 1830–1885: An Introduction to the Economic and Political History of Nigeria* (Oxford: Clarendon Press, 1956); Lydon, *On Trans-Saharan Trails*, 15.

9. Lynn Abrams, *Oral History Theory* (New York: Routledge, 2010).

10. George Ewart Evans, *Where Beards Wag All: The Relevance of the Oral Tradition* (London: Faber, 1970).

11. Luisa Passerini, "Work Ideology and Consensus under Italian Fascism," *History Workshop* 8 (1979): 84.

12. Alistair Thomson, "Four Paradigm Transformations in Oral History," *Oral History Review* 34, no. 1 (2007): 54–55.

13. Ibid., 56.

14. Interview by author with Jan Vansina, April 2007. See also Vansina, *Living with Africa*. Somewhat ironically, the account Vansina gave me in my interview with him mimicked the account in the printed book. Perhaps more experience with Vansina's own methods would have helped me escape this repetition.

15. A couple of those interviewed noted that Egyptians provided them with wire cutters to maintain access to supplies. For example, interview with Muhammad Bubakir al-Rifa, in *Mawsuʿat Riwāyāt al-Jihād*, Vol. 22, 50.

16. Interview with Muhammad Bubakir al-Rifa, in *Mawsuʿat Riwāyāt al-Jihād*, Vol. 22, 38.

17. Baldinetti, *Origins of the Libyan Nation*, 7.

18. Interview with Muhammad Bubakir al-Rifa, *Mawsuʿat Riwāyāt al-Jihād*, Vol. 22, 51.

19. *Mawsuʿat Riwāyāt al-Jihād*, Vol. 12 (Tripoli: Markaz al-Jihad, 1991), 31.

20. Interview with Hasan al-ʿAjili Amhamad, in *Mawsuʿat Riwāyāt al-Jihād*, Vol. 12 (Tripoli: Markaz al-Jihad, 1991), 16.

21. *Mawsuʿat Riwāyāt al-Jihād*, Vol. 15 (Tripoli: Markaz al-Jihad, 1990), 5.

22. Interview with Muhammad Bubakir al-Rifa, in *Mawsuʿat Riwāyāt al-Jihād*, Vol. 22, 67.

23. Interview with Abubakir Mawsa al-Madaʾi, in *Mawsuʿat Riwāyāt al-Jihād*, Vol. 22, 136.

24. Interview with Mohammed Yusuf al-Tablaqi, in *Mawsuʿat Riwāyāt al-Jihād*, Vol. 22, 22.

25. Interview with Muhammad Bubakir al-Rifa, *Mawsuʿat Riwāyāt al-Jihād*, Vol. 22, 87.

26. Kobi Peled, "Palestinian Oral History as a Source for Understanding the Past: Insights and Lessons from an Oral History Project among Palestinians in Israel," *Middle Eastern Studies* 50, no. 3 (2014): 413–414.

Bibliography

ARCHIVES

ACS: Archivio Centrale dello Stato
    Carte Luigi Pintor
    CPC: Casellario politico centrale
    FG: Foglie Graziani
    SPD: Segretario particolare dello Duce
AEF GGAEF: Afrique Equatoriale Française, Government General AEF
Archivio Storico De Propaganda Fide
ASDMAE: Archivio Storico Diplomatico del Ministero degli Affari Esteri
    ASMAI: Archivio Storico del Ministero di Africa Italiana
    Rappresentanza diplomatica Egitto—Il Cairo 1864–1940
AUSSME: Archivio dell'Ufficio Storico dello Stato Maggiore dell'Esercito Italiano
BNA: British National Archives
    CAB: Cabinet Papers
    FO: Foreign Office
    WO: War Office
FR AOM: Archives d'Outremer
    FM SG AFRIQUE VI: Fond Ministérials Serie geografique Afrique VI
Frati Minori: Papers of the Frati Minori of Lombardia

NEWSPAPERS

Corriere d'Italia
La Civiltá Cattolica
La Tribuna
L'Idea Nazionale
L'Oltremare
L'Osservatore Cattolico

New York Times
Rassegna italiana

LIBYAN ORAL HISTORIES

Aisi, Muhammad. *Mawsuʿat Riwāyāt al-Jihād*. Vol. 22. Tripoli: Markaz al-Jihad, 1990.

al-ʿAjili Amhamad, Hasan. *Mawsuʿat Riwāyāt al-Jihād*. Vol. 12. Tripoli: Markaz al-Jihad, 1991.

Bashir, ʿAli al-Zawawa, and Mohammad ʿAbd al-Nabi Daqali. Introduction to *Mawsuʿat Riwāyāt al-Jihād*. Vol. 16. Tripoli: Markaz al-Jihad, 1990.

al-Madaʿi, Abubakir Mawsa. *Mawsuʿat Riwāyāt al-Jihād*. Vol. 22. Tripoli: Markaz al-Jihad, 1990.

Mashinah, Naʿima al-Hada. Introduction to *Mawsuʿat Riwāyāt al-Jihād*. Vol. 30. Tripoli: Markaz al-Jihad, 1991.

al-Rifa al-ʿAwami, Muhammad Bubakir. *Mawsuʿat Riwāyāt al-Jihād*. Vol. 22. Tripoli: Markaz al-Jihad, 1990.

al-Tablaqi, Mohammed Yusuf. *Mawsuʿat Riwāyāt al-Jihād*. Vol. 22. Tripoli: Markaz al-Jihad, 1990.

PUBLISHED AND SECONDARY SOURCES

Abbink, Jon, Mirjam De Bruijn, and Klaas Van Walraven, eds. *Rethinking Resistance: Revolt and Violence in African History*. Leiden: Brill, 2003.

Abrams, Lynn. *Oral History Theory*. New York: Routledge, 2010.

Abun-Nasr, Jamil M. *Muslim Communities of Grace: The Sufi Brotherhoods in Islamic Religious Life*. London: Hurst, 1988.

Agnesa, Giacomo. Preface to *I Corpi consultivi dell'amministrazione colonial negli stati d'Europa*, by Angiolo Mori. Rome: Tipografia della Camera dei Deputati, 1912.

Ahmida, Ali Abdullatif. *Forgotten Voices: Power and Agency in Colonial and Postcolonial Libya*. New York: Routledge, 2005.

Ahmida, Ali Abdullatif. *The Making of Modern Libya: State Formation, Colonization, and Resistance, 1830–1932*. Albany: State University of New York Press, 1994.

Albrecht-Carrié, René "Peace with Italy—An Appraisal." *Political Science Quarterly* 62, no. 4 (1947): 481–503.

Amendola, Giovanni. *Discorso Politici (1919–1925)*. Edited by Sabato Visco. Rome: Carlo Colombo, 1968.

Anderson, Lisa. "'A Last Resort, an Expedient and an Experiment': Statehood and Sovereignty in Libya." *Journal of Libyan Studies* 2, no. 2 (2001): 14–25.

Anderson, Lisa. "Legitimacy, Identity, and the Writing of History in Libya." In *Statecraft in the Middle East: Oil, Historical Memory, and Popular Culture*, edited by Eric Davis and Nicolas Gavrielides, 71–91. Miami: Florida International University, 1991.

Anderson, Lisa. "Nineteenth-Century Reform in Ottoman Libya." *International Journal of Middle East Studies* 16 (1984): 325–348.

Anderson, Lisa. "Obligation and Accountability: Islamic Politics in North Africa." *Daedalus* 120, no. 3 (1991): 93–112.

Anderson, Lisa. "Qadhafi and His Opposition." *Middle East Journal* 40, no. 2 (1986): 225–237.

Anderson, Lisa. "Ramadan al-Suwayhli: Hero of the Libyan Resistance." In *Struggle and Survival in the Modern Middle East*, edited by Edmund BurkeIII, 119–136. Berkeley: University of California Press, 1993.

Anderson, Lisa. *State and Social Transformation in Tunisia and Libya, 1830–1980*. Princeton, NJ: Princeton University Press, 1986.

Aquarone, Alberto. "Violenza e consenso nel fascismo italiano." *Storia contemporanea* 10, no. 1 (1979): 145–155.

al-Ashhab, Muhammad al-Tayyib ibn Idris. *Barqa al-ʿArabiya, ams wa al-yawm*. Cairo: al-Tabah, 1947.

Atieno Odhiambo, E. S. "Matunda y Uhuru, Fruits of Independence." In *Mau Mau and Nationhood: Arms, Authority, and Narration*, edited by E. S. Atieno Odhiambo and John Landsdale, 37–45. London, James Currey, 2003.

Atkinson, David. "Nomadic Strategies and Colonial Governance." In *Entanglements of Power: Geographies of Domination/Resistance*, edited by Joanne P. Sharp, Paul Routledge, Chris Philo, and Ronan Paddison, 93–121. London: Routledge, 2002.

Aydin, Cemil. *The Politics of Anti-Westernism in Asia: Visions of World Order in Pan-Islamic and Pan-Asian Thought*. New York: Columbia University, 2007.

Badrawi, Malek. *Political Violence in Egypt, 1910–1924: Secret Societies, Plots and Assassinations*. Richmond, Surrey, UK: Curzon Press, 2000.

Baldinetti, Anna. *David Santillana: L'Uomo e il giruista 1855–1931*. Rome: Istituto per C.A. Nallino, 1995.

Baldinetti, Anna. "Italian Colonial Rule and Muslim Elites in Libya: A Relationship of Antagonism and Collaboration." In *Guardians of the Faith in Modern Times*, edited by Meir Hatina, 91–108. Leiden: Brill, 2009.

Baldinetti, Anna. *Orientalismo e colonialismo: La ricerca di consenso in Egitto per l'impresa di Libia*. Rome: Istituto per l'Oriente C. A. Nallino, 1997.

Baldinetti, Anna. *The Origins of the Libyan Nation*. London: Routledge, 2010.

Ballinger, Pamela. "Colonial Twilight: Italian Settlers and the Long Decolonization of Libya." *Journal of Contemporary History* 51, no. 4 (2016): 813–838.

Baratieri, Daniela. *Memories and Silences Haunted by Fascism: Italian Colonialism MCMXXX–MCMLX*. Bern: Peter Lang, 2011.

Barrera, Giulia. "The Construction of Racial Hierarchies in Colonial Eritrea: The Liberal and Early Fascist Period (1897–1934)." In *A Place in the Sun: Africa in Italian Colonial Culture from Post-Unification to the Present*, edited by Patrizia Palumbo, 81–115. Berkeley: University of California Press, 2003.

Battaglia, Roberto. *La prima guerra d'Africa*. Turin: Einaudi, 1958.

Bergna, P. Costanzo. *La missione francescana in Libia*. Tripoli: Nuove arti grafiche, 1924.

Bessis, Juliette. *La Méditeranée fasciste: L'Italie mussolinienne et la Tunisie*. Paris: Editions Karthala, 1980.

Betti, Claudio M. *Missioni e colonie in Africa Orientale*. Rome: Edizioni Studium, 1999.

Betts, Raymond F. *Decolonization*. 2nd ed. New York: Routledge, 1998.

Bills, Scott. *The Libyan Arena: The United States, Britain, and the Council of Foreign Ministers*. Kent, OH: Kent State University Press, 1995.

Bollettini, Fabrizio. "Leone Caetani e la questione libica." *Studi Romani* 41, no. 1 (1993): 30–40.

Bosworth, Richard. *Mussolini's Italy: Life under the Dictatorship 1915–1945*. New York: Penguin, 2006.

Bourbon del Monte Santa Maria, Giuseppe. *L'Islamismo e la Confraternita dei Senussi: Notizie Raccolte*. Città di Castello: Tipografia dell'Unione Arti Grafiche, 1912.

Bruner, Stephen. "Leopoldo Franchetti and Italian Settlement in Eritrea: Emigration, Welfare Colonialism and the Southern Question." *European History Quarterly* 39, no. 1 (2009): 71–94.

Bruzzi, Silvia. "Saints' Bodies, Islamic and Colonial Medicine in Eritrea (1887–1940)." In *Themes in Modern African History and Culture*, edited by Lars Berge and Irma Taddia, 69–84. Padova: Biblioteca Universitaria, 2013.

Buccianti, Cinzia. "Le scuole cattoliche a Tripoli nel XIX secolo." *Oriente Moderno* 13, no. 7/12 (Luglio–Dicembre 1994): 181–202.

Burget, François. "Qadhafi's Ideological Framework." In *Qadhafi's Libya, 1969–1994*, edited by Dirk Vandewalle, 47–66. London: Macmillan, 1995.

Caetani, Leone. Preface to *Annali dell'Islam*. Vol. 5. Milan: Ulrico Hoepli, 1912.

Caetani, Leone. *Studi di storia orientale*. Vol. 1, *L'Arabia dalla preistoria all'Islam*. Rome: Edizioni di Storia e Letteratura, 2012. First published by Ulrico Hoepli in 1911.

Canavero, Alfredo. "I cattolici di fronte al colonialism." In *Adua: Le ragioni di una sconfitta*, edited by Angelo Del Boca, 91–114. Rome: Laterza, 1997.

Candeloro, Giorgio. *Il movimento cattolico in Italia*. Rome: Riuniti, 1974.

Caroselli, Francesco Saverio. "Gli Accordi Anglo-Libici." *Rivista di Studi Politici Internazionali* 20, no. 3 (1953): 345–358.

Casajus, Dominique. "Henri Duveyrier face à Prosper Enfantin: ribelle ou rival?" *Ethnologies comparées* 8 (2005): 1–8.

Casajus, Dominique. "Le destin saharien d'un saint-simonien rebelle: Henri Duveyrier chez les Touaregs." *Gradhiva* [Musée du quai Branly] 33 (2003): 11–31.

Casmirri, Silvia. "Luigi Federzoni." In *Uomini e volti del fascismo*, edited by Ferdinando Cordova, 243–301. Rome: Bulzoni editore, 1980.

Ceci, Lucia. *Il vessillo e la croce: colonialismo, missioni cattoliche e Islam in Somalia (1903–1924)*. Rome: Carocci, 2006.

Ceci, Lucia. "Missioni e colonialismo italiano in Somalia (1903–1906)." *Studi Storici* 43, no. 1 (2002): 41–105.

Childs, Timothy. *Italo-Turkish Diplomacy and the War Over Libya 1911–1912.* Leiden: Brill, 1990.

Choate, Mark. *Emigrant Nation: The Making of Italy Abroad.* Cambridge, MA: Harvard University Press, 2008.

Ciammaichella, Glauco. *Libyens et Français au Tchad (1897–1914): La Confrérie senoussie et le commerce transsaharien.* Paris: Editions du Centre National de la Recherche Scientifique, 1987.

Clancy-Smith, Julia. *Mediterraneans: North Africa and Europe in the Age of Migration, c. 1800–1900.* Berkeley: University of California Press, 2011.

Cordell, Dennis D. "The Awlad Sulayman of Libya and Chad: Power and Adaptation in the Sahara and the Sahel." *Canadian Journal of African Studies* 19, no. 2 (1985): 319–343.

Cordova, Ferdinando. *Agli ordini del serpente verde: La massoneria nella crisi del sistema giolittiano.* Rome: Bulzoni, 1990.

Corradini, Enrico. *L'ora di Tripoli.* Milan: Fratelli Treves, 1911.

Correale, Francesco. "Weapons and 'Smugglers' throughout Western Sahara: From the Anti-Colonial Resistance to the First World War." In *Bridges Across the Sahara*, edited by Ali Abdullatif Ahmida, 129–153. Newcastle, UK: Cambridge Scholars, 2009.

Coury, Ralph M. *The Making of an Egyptian Arab Nationalist: The Early Years of 'Azzam Pasha, 1893–1936.* Reading, UK: Garnet Publishing, 1998.

Cresti, Federico. "Il professore e il generale. La polemica tra Carlo Alfonso Nallino e Rodolfo Graziani sulla Senussia e su altre questioni libiche." *Studi Storici* 45, no. 4 (2004): 1113–1149.

Cresti, Federico. *Non desiderare la terra d'altri: La colonizzazione italiana in Libia.* Rome: Carocci, 2001.

Cresti, Federico. *Oasi d'Italianitá: La Libia della colonizzazione agraria tra fascismo, guerra e indipendenza (1935–1956).* Turin: Società Editrice Internazionale, 1996.

Da Nembro, Metodio. *La missione dei Minori Cappuccini in Eritrea (1894–1952).* Rome: Istitutum Historicum Ordinis Fratrum Minorum Capuccinorum, 1953.

al-Dajani, Ahmad Sidqi. *Al-Haraka al-Sanusiyya: Nash'atuha wa Numuwwuha fi al-Qarn al-Tasi 'Ashar.* Beirut: Dar Lubnan, 1967.

Daughton, J. P. *An Empire Divided: Religion, Republicanism, and the Making of French Colonialism, 1880–1914.* Oxford: Oxford University Press, 2006.

Davis, John. *Libyan Politics: Tribe and Revolution.* Berkeley: University of California Press, 1987.

De Candole, E. A. V. *The Life and Times of King Idris of Libya.* Published privately by Mohamed Ben Ghalbon, 1988.

De Felice, Renzo. *Il fascismo e l'Oriente: Arabi, ebrei e indiani nella politica di Mussolini.* Bologna: Il Mulino, 1988.

De Grand, Alexander. *Hunchback's Tailor: Giovanni Giolitti and Liberal Italy from the Challenge of Mass Politics to the Rise of Fascism, 1882–1922*. Westport, CT: Praeger, 2001.

De Leone, Enrico. *Riformatori musulmani del XIX secolo nell'Africa e nell'Asia mediterranee*. Milan: Giuffrè Editore, 1973.

De Martino, Giacomo. *Cirene e Cartagine: note e impressioni della carovana De Martino-Baldari, giugno-luglio 1907*. Bologna: Nicola Zanichelli, 1908.

Deakin, Frederick W. "Il colonialismo fascista nel giudizio degli inglesi." In *Le guerre coloniale del fascismo*, edited by Angelo Del Boca, 340–360. Rome: Laterza, 1991.

Del Boca, Angelo. *A un passo dalla forca: Atrocità e infamie dell'occupazione italiana della Libia nelle memorie del patriota Mohamed Fekini*. Milan: Baldini Castoldi Dalai, 2007.

Del Boca, Angelo. *Gli italiani in Africa Orientale*. 2 vols. Milan: Mondadori, 2001. First published by Laterza in 1976.

Del Boca, Angelo. *Gli italiani in Libia*. 2 vols. Rome: Laterza, 1988.

Del Boca, Angelo. *Italiani, Brava Gente? Un mito duro a morire*. Vicenza: Neri Pozza Editore, 2005.

Del Boca, Angelo. *La disfatta di Gasr bu Hàdi, 1915: Il colonnello Miani e il più grande disastro dell'Italia colonial*. Milan: Mondadori, 2004.

Del Boca, Angelo. "The Myths, Suppressions, Denials, and Defaults of Italian Colonialism." In *A Place in the Sun: Africa in Italian Colonial Culture from Post-Unification to the Present*, edited by Patrizia Palumbo, 17–36. Berkeley: University of California Press, 2003.

Deringil, Selim. "'They Live in a State of Nomadism and Savagery': The Late Ottoman Empire and the Post-Colonial Debate." *Comparative Studies in Society and History* 45, no. 2 (2003): 311–342.

Deringil, Selim. *The Well-Protected Domains: Ideology and the Legitimation of Power in the Ottoman Empire 1876–1909*. London: I. B. Tauris, 1998.

Di Paola, Pietro. "The Spies Who Came in from the Heat: The International Surveillance of the Anarchists in London." *European History Quarterly* 37, no. 2 (2007): 189–215.

Dike, K. O. *Trade and Politics in the Niger Delta, 1830–1885: An Introduction to the Economic and Political History of Nigeria*. Oxford: Clarendon Press, 1956.

Dirar, Uoldelul Chilati. "Church-State Relations in Colonial Eritrea: Missionaries and the Development of Colonial Strategies, (1869–1911)." *Journal of Modern Italian Studies* 8, no. 3 (2001): 391–410.

Duggan, Christopher. *A Concise History of Italy*. Cambridge, UK: Cambridge University Press, 1994.

Duveyrier, Henri. *Exploration du Sahara: Les Touâreg du nord*. Paris: Challamel Ainé, 1864.

Duveyrier, Henri. *Le Confrérie musulmane de Sidi Mohammed Ben 'Ali Es-Senousi et son domaine géographique, en l'année 1300 de l'hégire (1883 de notre ère)*. Paris: Société de Géographie, 1884.

Ebner, Michael R. *Ordinary Violence in Mussolini's Italy*. Cambridge, UK: Cambridge University Press, 2011.

Evans, George Ewart. *Where Beards Wag All: The Relevance of the Oral Tradition*. London: Faber, 1970.

Evans-Pritchard, E. E. *The Sanusi of Cyrenaica*. Oxford: Clarendon, 1949.

Federzoni, Luigi. *1927: Diario di un ministro del fascismo*. Edited by Adriana Macchi. Preface by Sergio Romano. Florence: Passigli Editori, 1993.

Federzoni, Luigi. *La politica coloniale del fascismo: Discorso pronunciato alla Camera dei Deputati nella tornata del 18 marzo 1927*. Rome: Tipografia della Camera dei Deputati, 1927.

Federzoni, Luigi. *Venti mesi di azione coloniale*. Milan: Mondadori, 1926.

Felici, Osea. *L'Egitto e la guerra europea*. Quaderni della guerra 55. Milan: Fratelli Treves, 1916.

Finaldi, Giuseppe. "Culture and Imperialism in a 'Backward' Nation? The Prima Guerra d'Africa (1895–96) in Italian Primary Schools." *Journal of Modern Italian Studies* 8, no. 3 (2003): 347–390.

Finaldi, Giuseppe. *Italian National Identity in the Scramble for Africa*. Bern: Peter Lang, 2009.

Forgacs, David. *Italy's Margins: Social Exclusion and Nation Formation since 1861*. Cambridge, UK: Cambridge University Press, 2014.

Forsyth, Douglas J. *The Crisis of Liberal Italy: Monetary and Financial Policy, 1914–1922*. Cambridge, UK: Cambridge University Press, 1993.

Gabrielli, Francesco. *Orientalisti del Novecento*. Rome: Istituto per l'oriente C.A. Nallino, 1993.

Gazzini, Claudia Anna. "Jihad in Exile: Ahmad al-Sharif al-Sanusi 1918–1933." Master's thesis, Princeton University, 2004.

Giorgi, Chiara. *L'Africa come carriera: Funzioni e funzionari del colonialismo itlaiano*. Rome: Carocci Editore, 2012.

Goglia, Luigi, and Fabio Grassi, eds. *Il colonialismo italiano dal'Adua all'impero*. Rome: Laterza, 1993.

Gotti Porcinari, Carlo. *Rapporti Italo-Arabi (1902–1930): Dai documenti di Enrico Insabato*. Rome: E. S. P., 1965.

Grange, Daniel J. *L'Italia et la Méditerranée (1896–1911)*. Rome: École Française de Rome, 1994.

Grassi, Fabio. *L'Italia e la questione turca (1917–1923): Opinione pubblica e politica estera*. Turin: Silvio Zamorani, 1996.

Gründer, Horst. "Christian Missionary Activities in Africa in the Age of Imperialism and the Berlin Conference of 1884–1885." In *Bismarck, Europe, and Africa: The Berlin Africa Conference 1884–1885 and the Onset of Partition*, edited by Stig Förster, Wolfgang J. Mommsen, and Ronald Robinson, 85–103. Oxford: Oxford University Press, 1988.

Gutelius, David P. V. "The Path Is Easy and the Benefits Large: The Nasiriyya, Social Networks, and Economic Change in Morocco, 1640–1830." *Journal of African History* 43, no. 1 (2002): 27–49.

Haimann, Giuseppe. *Cirenaica (Tripolitania)*. 2nd ed. Milan: Ulrico Hoepli, 1886.

Hastings, Adrian. *The Church in Africa 1450–1950*. Oxford: Clarendon Press, 1994.

Hatina, Meir. "Where East Meets West: Sufism, Cultural Rapprochement, and Politics." *International Journal of Middle East Studies* 39 (2007): 389–409.

Heffernan, Michael. "The Limits of Utopia: Henri Duveyrier and the Exploration of the Sahara in the Nineteenth Century." *Geographical Journal* 155, no. 3 (1989): 342–352.

Heiss, Andrew. "Manufacturing Consent: Italy, the *Mutamassirun*, Egypt, and the Invasion of Libya." Master's thesis, The American University in Cairo, 2010, http://dar.aucegypt.edu/bitstream/handle/10526/689/2010mestandrewheiss.pdf?sequence=1.

Hendrickson, Jocelyn N. "The Islamic Obligation to Emigrate: Al-Wansharīsī's *Asnā al-matājir* Reconsidered." PhD diss., Emory University, 2009.

al-Hesnawi, Habib. "Italian Imperial Policy towards Libya, 1870–1911." In *Modern and Contemporary Libya: Sources and Historiographies*, edited by Anna Baldinetti, 49–62. Rome: Istituto italiano per l'Africa e l'Oriente, 2003.

al-Hesnawi, Habib. "Note sulla politica coloniale italiana verso gli arabi libici (1911–1943)." In *Le guerre coloniale del fascismo*, edited by Angelo Del Boca, 31–48. Roma: Laterza, 1991.

Hoffman, Valerie J. "Annihilation in the Messenger of God: The Development of Sufi Practice." *International Journal of Middle East Studies* 31, no. 3 (1999): 351–369.

al-Horeir, A. S. "Social and Economic Transformations in the Libyan Hinterland during the Second Half of the Nineteenth Century: The Rule of the Sayyid Ahmad al-Sharif al-Sanusi." PhD diss., University of California, Los Angeles, 1981.

Ianari, Vittorio. *Chiesa, coloni e Islam: Religione e politica nella Libia italiana*. Turin: Società Editrice Internazionale, 1995.

Insabato, Enrico. *L'Islam et la politique des alliés*. Nancy-Paris-Strasbourg: Berger-Levrault, 1920.

Joffe, George. "Qadhafi's Islam in Local Historical Perspective." In *Qadhafi's Libya, 1969–1994*, edited by Dirk Vandewalle, 139–156. London: MacMillan, 1995.

Jonas, Raymond. *The Battle of Adwa: African Victory in the Age of Empire*. Cambridge, MA: Belknap Press of Harvard University Press, 2011.

Kabti, Salim Husayn. *Idris al-Sanusi: al-amir wa-al-malik*. 3 vols. Benghazi: Dar al-Kutub al-Wataniya, 2013.

Kapelj, Sara. "'L'Italia d'Oltremare': Razzismo e costruzione dell'alterità africana negli articoli etnografici e nel romanzo 'I prigionieri del sole'." PhD diss., Università degli Studi di Trieste, 2011, https://www.openstarts.units.it/dspace/bitstream/10077/7407/1/Kapelj_phd.pdf.

Karpat, Kemal. *The Politicization of Islam: Reconstructing Identity, State, Faith, and Community in the Late Ottoman State*. New York: Oxford University Press, 2001.

Kayali, Hasan. *Arabs and Young Turks: Ottomanism, Arabism, and Islamism in the Ottoman Empire, 1908–1918*. Berkeley: University of California Press, 1997.

Kedouri, Elie. *England and the Middle East: The Destruction of the Ottoman Empire, 1914–1921*. Boulder, CO: Westview Press, 1987.

Kelikian, Alice A. "The Church and Catholicism." In *Liberal and Fascist Italy 1900–1945*, edited by Adrian Lyttelton, 44–61. Oxford: Oxford University Press, 2002.

Kent, Peter C. *The Pope and the Duce*. New York: St. Martin's Press, 1981.

Khalidi, Ismail R. "The Constitution of the United Kingdom of Libya: Background and Summary." *Middle East Journal* 6, no. 2 (1952): 221–228.

Knysh, Alexander. "Sufism as an Explanatory Paradigm: The Issue of Motivations of Sufi Resistance Movements in Western and Russian Scholarship." *Die Welt des Islams* 42, no. 2 (2002): 139–173.

Kramer, Martin S. *Islam Assembled: The Advent of the Muslim Congresses*. New York: Columbia University Press, 1986.

Labanca, Nicola. *In marcia verso Adua*. Turin: Einaudi, 1993.

Labanca, Nicola. *La guerra italiana per la Libia 1911–1931*. Bologna: Il Mulino, 2012.

Labanca, Nicola. *Oltremare: Storia dell'espansione coloniale italiana*. Bologna: Il Mulino, 2002.

Labanca, Nicola, ed. *Un nodo: Immagini e documenti sulla repressione coloniale italiana in Libia*. Manduria: Piero Lacaita, 2002.

Landau, Jacob M. *The Politics of Pan-Islam*. Oxford: Clarendon Press, 1990.

Le Gall, Michel. "The Ottoman Government and the Sanusiya: A Reappraisal." *International Journal of Middle Eastern Studies* 21 (1989): 90–106.

Leone, Alba Rosa. "La politica missionaria del Vaticano tra le due guerre." *Studi Storici* 21, no. 1 (1980): 123–156.

Lydon, Ghislaine. *On Trans-Saharan Trails: Islamic Law, Trade Networks, and Cross-Cultural Exchanges in Nineteenth-Century West Africa*. Cambridge, UK: Cambridge University Press, 2009.

Lyttelton, Adrian. *Seizure of Power: Fascism in Italy 1919–1929*. London: Weidenfeld, 1978.

Macaluso Aleo, Giuseppe. *Turchi, Senussi e Italiani in Libia*. Bengasi: Guido Vitale, 1930.

Maggi, Stefano. "The Railways of Italian Africa: Economic, Social and Strategic Features." *Journal of Transport History* 18, no. 1 (1997): 54–71.

Malvezzi De Medici, Aldobrandino. "La Tripolitania e i casi del Wadai." *La Nuova Antologia* 45, no. 921 (May 1910): 122–132.

Malvezzi De Medici, Aldobrandino. *L'Italia e l'Islam in Libia*. Florence: Fratelli Treves, 1913.

Manela, Erez. *The Wilsonian Moment*. Oxford: Oxford University Press, 2007.

Marongiu Buonaiuti, Cesare. *Politica e religioni nel colonialismo italiano*. Varese: Giuffrè Editore, 1982.

Matar, Hisham. *The Return: Fathers, Sons and the Land in Between*. New York: Random House, 2016.

Matsumoto-Best, Saho. "British and Italian Imperial Rivalry in the Mediterranean, 1912–14: The Case of Egypt." *Diplomacy and Statecraft* 18, no. 2 (2007): 297–314.

Mattes, Hanspeter. "Libya." In *Islam in the World Today*, edited by Werner Ende and Udo Steinback, 451–458. Ithaca, NY: Cornell University, 2010.

Meriano, Francesco. *La riconquista della Tripolitania*. Milan: Imperia Casa Editrice del Partito Nazionale Fascista, 1923.

Minawi, Mostafa. *The Ottoman Scramble for Africa: Empire and Diplomacy in the Sahara and the Hijaz*. Stanford, CA: Stanford University Press, 2016.

Ministero degli Affari Esteri. *I documenti diplomatici italiani*. Quarta serie, 1908–1914, Vols. 5–6. Rome: Istituto Poligrafico e Zecca dello Stato, 2001.

Ministero delle Colonie. *La costruzione e l'esercizio delle ferrovie in Tripolitania ed in Cirenaica dalla occupazione al 30 giugno 1915*. Rome: Tipografia Nazionale Bertero, 1917.

Ministero della Guerra. Stato Maggiore del Regio Esercito, Ufficio Storico. *Campagna di Libia*. Vol. 1. Rome: Poligrafico per l'Amministrazione della Guerra, 1922.

Miran, Jonathan. "A Historical Overview of Islam in Eritrea." *Die Welt des Islams* 45, no. 2 (2005): 177–215.

Mitchell, Edward. "Islam in Colonel Qaddafi's Thought." *The World Today* 38, nos. 7/8 (1982): 319–326.

Moore, Martin. *Fourth Shore: Italy's Mass Colonization of Libya*. London: Routledge, 1940.

Nagesh, Tekeste. *Italian Colonialism in Eritrea, 1882–1941: Policies, Praxis and Impact*. Uppsala: Uppsala University Press, 1987.

Nallino, C. A. Review of *Turchi, Senussi e Italiani in Libia* by Giuseppe Macaluso Aleo. *Oriente Moderno* 10 (October 1930): 515–520.

Nallino, Carlo Alfonso. *Le odierne tendenze dell'islamismo*. Florence: Biblioteca Scientifico-Religiosa, 1902.

Nassar, Hala Khamis, and Marco Boggero. "Omar al-Mukhtar: The Formation of Cultural Memory and the Case of the Militant Group That Bears His Name." *Journal of North African Studies* 13, no. 2 (2008): 201–217.

O'Fahey, R. S. *Enigmatic Saint: Ahmad Ibn Idris and the Idrisi Tradition*. Evanston, IL: Northwestern University, 1990.

Özcan, Azmi. *Pan-Islamism: Indian Muslims, the Ottomans and Britain (1877–1924)*. Leiden: Brill, 1997.

Passerini, Luisa. "Work Ideology and Consensus under Italian Fascism." *History Workshop* 8 (1979): 82–108.

Pedersen, Susan. *The Guardians: The League of Nations and the Crisis of Empire*. Oxford: Oxford University Press, 2015.

Peled, Kobi. "Palestinian Oral History as a Source for Understanding the Past: Insights and Lessons from an Oral History Project among Palestinians in Israel." *Middle Eastern Studies* 50, no. 3 (2014): 412–425.

Pelt, Adrian. *Libyan Independence and the United Nations: A Case of Planed Decolonization*. New Haven, CT: Yale University Press, 1970.

Peters, Emyrs L. *The Bedouin of Cyrenaica*. Edited by Jack Goody and Emanuel Marx. Cambridge, UK: Cambridge University Press, 1991.

Pergher, Roberta. "The Consent of Memory: Recovering Fascist-Settler Relations in Libya." In *In the Society of Fascists: Acclamation, Acquiescence, and Agency in Mussolini's Italy*, edited by Giulia Albanese and Roberta Pergher, 169–188. New York: Palgrave, 2012.

Perlato, Giuseppe. "The War in Libya and the Italian Nationalism." In *The Libyan War 1911–1912*, edited by Luca Micheletta and Andrea Ungari, 39–58. Cambridge, UK: Cambridge Scholars Publishing, 2013.

Piazza, Giuseppe. *La Nostra Terra Promessa: Lettera dalla Tripolitania, Marzo-Maggio 1911*. 2nd ed. Rome: Bernardo Lux, 1911.

Pollard, John. *Catholicism in Modern Italy: Religion, Society, and Politics since 1861*. London: Routledge, 2008.

Pollard, John. *Money and the Rise of the Modern Papacy: Financing the Vatican, 1850–1950*. Cambridge, UK: Cambridge University Press, 2005.

Rainero, Romain. *L'anticolonialismo italiano da Assab ad Adua (1869–1896)*. Milan: Edizione di Comunità, 1971.

Reynolds, Michael A. *Shattering Empires: The Clash and Collapse of the Ottoman and Russian Empires 1908–1919*. Cambridge, UK: Cambridge University Press, 2011.

Robecchi Bricchetti, Luigi. *Il commercio di Tripoli*. Rome: Società Geografica Italiana, 1896.

Rochat, Giorgio. "L'Impiego dei gas nella guerra d'Etiopia, 1935–36." *Rivista di storia contemporanea* 17, no. 1 (1988): 74–109.

Sabbadin, Filberto. *I frati minori lombardi in Libia: la missione di Tripoli (1908–1991)*. Milan: Edizioni Biblioteca Francescana, 1991.

Said, Edward. *Orientalism*. New York: Vintage Books, 1979.

Santarelli, Enzo. *Omar al-Mukhtar e la riconquista fascista della Libia*. Milan: Marzorati, 1981.

Scarabel, Angelo. "Una rivista Italo-Araba d'inizio secolo: An-Nadi (Il Convito)." *Oriente Moderno* 58, nos. 1/3 (1978): 51–67.

Sedgwick, Mark. *Against the Modern World*. Oxford: Oxford University Press, 2004.

Segré, Claudio G. *The Fourth Shore: The Italian Colonization of Libya*. Chicago: University of Chicago Press, 1974.

Seri-Hersch, Iris. "Confronting a Christian Neighbor: Sudanese Representations of Ethiopia in the Early Mahdist Period." *International Journal of Middle East Studies* 41, no. 2 (2009): 247–267.

Serra, Fabrizio. *Italia e Senussia: Vent'anni di azione coloniale in Cirenaica*. Milan: Fratelli Treves, 1933.

Shukri, Muhammad Fuʿad. *Al-Sanūsiyah, din wa dawla*. Oxford: Centre for Libyan Studies, 2005. First published by Dar al-Fikr al-ʿArabi, Cairo, in 1948.

Shukri, Muhammad Fuʿad. *Milad dawlat Libya al-Haditha: Wathaʿiq tahrikhiya wa-istiqlaliya*. Cairo: Matabʿat al-lʿtimad, 1957.

Simon, Rachel. *Libya between Ottomanism and Nationalism: The Ottoman Involvement in Libya during the War with Italy (1911–1919)*. Berlin: Klaus Schwartz Verlag, 1987.

Soave, Paolo. *Fezzan: Il deserto contesto (1842–1921)*. Milan: Giuffrè Editore, 2001.

Sòrgoni, Barbara. "Italian Anthropology and the Africans: The Early Colonial Period." In *A Place in the Sun: Africa in Italian Colonial Culture from Post-Unification to the Present*, edited by Patrizia Palumbo, 62–80. Berkeley: University of California Press, 2003.

Spadaro, Barbara. *Una colonia italiana: Incontri, memorie e rappresentazioni tra Italia e Libia*. Milan: Mondadori, 2013.

Spaulding, Jay, and Lidwien Kapteijns. *An Islamic Alliance: ʿAli Dinar and the Sanusiyya, 1906–1916*. Evanston, IL: Northwestern University Press, 1994.

Stafford, F. E. "The Ex-Italian Colonies." *International Affairs* 25, no. 1 (1949): 47–55.

Teruzzi, Attilio. *Cirenaica verde*. Preface by Benito Mussolini. Milan: Mondadori, 1931.

Thomson, Alistair. "Four Paradigm Transformations in Oral History." *Oral History Review* 34, no. 1 (2007): 49–70.

Triaud, Jean-Louis. *La légende noire de la Sanûsiyya: Un conférie musulmane saharienne sous le regard français (1840–1930)*. Paris: Éditions de la Maison des sciences de l'homme, 1995.

Triaud, Jean-Louis. *Tchad 1900–1902: Une Guerre Franco-Libyenne oubliée?* Paris: Editions l'Hartmattan, 1987.

Trimingham, J. Spencer. *The Sufi Orders in Islam*. Oxford: Oxford University Press, 1971.

Triulzi, Alessandro. "Adwa: From Monument to Document." *Modern Italy* 8, no. 1 (2003): 95–108.

Vandewalle, Dirk. *A History of Modern Libya*. Cambridge, UK: Cambridge University Press, 2006.

Vandewalle, Dirk. "Libya's Revolution Revisited." *MERIP Middle East Report* 143 (1986): 30–35.

Vansina, Jan. *Living with Africa*. Madison: University of Wisconsin Press, 2005.

Veneruso, Danilo. "Il pontificato di Pio XI." In *Storia della chiesa*. Vol. 23, *I Catolici nel mondo contemporaneo (1922–1958)*, 29–63. Milan: Edizioni Paoline, 1991.

Venosa, Joseph. "Adapting to the New Path: Khatmiyya Sufi Authority, the al-Mirghani Family, and Eritrean Nationalism during the British Occupation, 1941–1949." *Journal of East African Studies* 7, no. 3 (2013): 413–431.

Verdicchio, Pasquale. "The Preclusion of Postcolonial Discourse in Southern Italy." In *Revisioning Italy: National Identity and Global Culture*, edited by Beverly Allen and Mary Russo, 191–212. Minneapolis: University of Minneapolis Press, 1997.

Vestal, Theodore M. "Reflections on the Battle of Adwa and Its Significance for Today." In *The Battle of Adwa: Reflections on Ethiopia's Historic Victory Against European Colonialism*, edited by Paulos Milkias and Getachew Metaferia, 21–36. New York: Algora Publishing, 2005.

Vikør, Knut. *Sufi and Scholar on the Desert Edge: Muhammad b. Ali al-Sanūsi and his Brotherhood*. Evanston, IL: Northwestern University, 1995.

Volpi, Giuseppe. Introduction to *La rinascita della Tripolitania. Memorie e studi sui quattro anni di governo del Conte Giuseppe Volpi di Misurata*. Edited by Angelo Piccioli. Milan: Mondadori, 1926.

Volpi, Giuseppe. *La politica coloniale del fascismo*. Padova: CEDAM, 1937.

Volterra, Alessandro. "Morì, siccome 'n topo: Le fotografie dei processi a Omar al-Mukthar e ai resistenti libici." In *Quel che resta dell'impero: La cultura colonial degli italiani*, edited by Valeria Deplano and Alessandro Pes, 235–257. Milan: Mimesis, 2014.

Volterra, Alessandro, ed. *Progetto Ascari*. Rome: Edizioni Efesto, 2014.

Wasti, Syed Tanvir. "Amir Shakib Arslan and the CUP Triumvirate." *Middle Eastern Studies* 44, no. 6 (2008): 925–936.

Webster, R. A. *Industrial Imperialism in Italy 1908–1915*. Berkeley: University of California Press, 1975.

Wright, John. *Libya: A Modern History*. Baltimore, MD: Johns Hopkins University Press, 1982.

Ziadah, Nicola A. *Sanusiyah: A Study of a Revivalist Movement in Islam*. Leiden: Brill, 1983.

Zürcher, Erik J. *Storia della Turchia*. Rome: Donzelli, 2007.

SCRAP MAP BIBLIOGRAPHY

Reference 1: Ruth Ben-Ghiat and Mia Fuller, eds. *Italian Colonialism*, xx. New York: Palgrave, 2005.

Reference 2: Alison Pargeter, *Libya: The Rise and Fall of Qaddafi*, xvii. New Haven, CT: Yale University Press, 2012.

Reference 3A: Emyrs Peters, *The Bedouin of Cyrenaica: Studies in Personal and Corporate Power*, edited by Jack Goody and Emanuel Marx, 12. Cambridge, UK: Cambridge University Press, 1990.

Reference 3B: "Situazione dei campi e posti avanzati senussiti della Cirenaica." September 1, 1919. ASMAI II 140/5/13.

Index

CPSIA information can be obtained
at www.ICGtesting.com
Printed in the USA
BVHW031940180520
579766BV00004BA/11